LIBRARY OF CONGRESS

CATALOGING-IN-PUBLICATION DATA

**Living in an Indigo House, The Heartaches & Victories of First Wave Indigos**

ISBN: 0-9707117-1-9

COPYRIGHT © 2004
LAURA LEE MISTYCAH
All rights reserved

**Mistyc House Publishing**
**816 West Francis #244**
**Spokane WA. 99205**
**(509) 487-0151**
**Knights@MistycHouse.com**

Front Cover art by Carey Norby
Back Cover art by Ann Lessel
Cover design by Chandra Caine

**Editing by:** Essena, Ann Lessel, Lena Casa, Steve Christilaw, Ronnie Foster
Graphics by: Chandra Caine
**Final lay out and editing by:** Chandra Caine & Steve Christilaw

Printed in China

**WARNING:** The information in this book is intended to inform, and entertain. Any enlightenment or healing that may occur as a result of reading this book becomes strictly and solely the responsibility of the reader. Own It!

**See Our New**
**Web Site At**
**www.FirstWaveIndigos.com**

D0927146

# Cover Art

ℭℬ

When I first began my search for cover art for this book, I didn't have a clue what I wanted. If you think it's a challenge to paint a word picture of what it's like to "live in an Indigo House," try capturing it visually.

After some thought the idea came to me to put the word out to Indigos and have them give me their rendition of what it should be like to "live in an Indigo House."

When I got the two brilliant renditions from Carey and Ann, I knew I had a winner!

The front cover was created by Carey Norby, a professional artist and musician. She has been a strong ally and supporter through some of my darkest hours.... a soul sister in every sense of the word. I honor her work and am thrilled that she submitted her cover art when she was extremely busy with other projects. I just got word that she passed away last month (Oct. 2005) after heroically fighting a battle with ovarian cancer. I know she is on the other side assisting us from another dimension, but is greatly missed here on Earth.

The back cover was created by Ann Lessel, another "soul sister" and Indigo extraordinaire. Here is what she had to say of the symbolism in her picture:

The top of the upward-pointing pyramid receives the energies from infinity which are then focused into a manifestation of graded differentiations of existence from infinity to physical existence.

All four elements are represented in the picture.

The seven chakras are represented in the magic wand.

The "space brother" watching over us has a shade of blue/indigo around him.

There is a Fibonacci spiral in the wagon wheels. (The Fibonacci spiral' is a geometric form used by the devic realms to create forms and proportions for all life in this universe. The Fibonacci sequence is the mathematical expression of the fractal and apparently exists at the core of every natural order, including human DNA. The geometry of the Great Pyramid of Giza also is based on the Fibonacci sequence.)

The crow is over seeing the magic.

Yin Yang sign to represent the balance of male/female.

# Living in an Indigo House

## The Heart Aches & Victories of First Wave Indigos

The information found between the covers of this book, is taken from my own experience, from Indigos themselves, and also from information given to me by my "Cosmic Informant" Hal.

I dedicate this book to the entire "Cosmic Clean-up Crew" and especially to all of the "First Wave Indigos" who have been so misunderstood, misinterpreted and shunned, yet so noble, courageous, and tough.....and to the parents and teachers who stretched beyond their borders of what is "normal" in an effort to understand these strange and "abnormal" Star Children.....

....who are changing the matrix and history of our planet.

**To my own children:** Reuben, Micah, Ma' Lady & Xavier

**To my extended Indigo Family:** Thank you for bringing your love, magick, and "Indigo" perceptions into my life. You are truly the *Indigo Ultra-Violet Light* unto this world!

**To Ann:** Thank you for your unwavering love, devoted friendship and support in helping me get this book to press.

**To Steve:** Thank you for your support and expertise.....And thank you for renewing my faith that True Knights still exist on this planet.

**To Carey Norby....the cover artist:** Your Indigo presence and brilliance on planet Earth will be greatly missed. I know you know how important this book is, and as a soul sister, I know you will keep supporting my efforts.....till we meet again in the UV Realm.

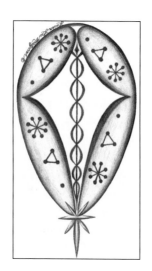

# Table of Contents

# Chapter 1

# First Wave Indigos

## The Children/Adults Who Fell Through The Cracks In Our Society

# Where It All Started

It has come to my attention, that more than 85% of the "True Knights" on this planet today (which includes women) are "First Wave Indigo Children/Adults." They have filtered into this planet for over 70 years, coming en masse (about 62 %) between the years of 1969 and 1987 and about 30% were born in the 50's.

I am compelled to get the information that is being channeled through me, about the "First Waves," out to the world as soon as possible. However, it seems the Dark Forces of the Universe continue to surround me, sabotaging my efforts from every angle. Through sheer will and resolve, I am overcoming their assaults and finding ways around and out of their traps. In spite of the opposition, the book, <u>Living in an Indigo House, The Heartaches and Victories of First Wave Indigos</u> is coming alive.

During a meditation in 2003, it was revealed to me that *The Knights of Mistyc House web pages, The Knights Chat Room, message board, and guest book* would be a forum to bring First Wave Indigos together for support and global networking. I was given the instructions to get this information written, put the Indigo web pages up AND DO IT NOW! (I stayed up all night in compliance with these orders to get this page written and posted on the web site.)

Here is a brief profile of what a **First Wave Indigo** is all about, and also some of the challenges they have had to overcome. Hopefully this information will be of benefit and give some relief to you gallant Indigos out there, who have been searching for answers as to why your world is so different, so challenging and in many cases "So Hellish!"

Lately, we have been hearing so much about "Indigo Children"..... newborn babies, toddlers, and children who seem to have what I term "Hyper Intelligence" mentally, psychically, and spiritually. These children are making their statements loud and clear..... "I Am Here"..... "Pay Attention To Me!" ..... and people around them are responding to their voice.

But let's go back to where it all started taking shape, back to the 60's, back to the time of political, spiritual and sexual revolution. Back to a time when the earth took a major energetic shift....a time when our societies' "rebels of the world" were starting to have children of their own. A time when the music changed — when Pink Floyd, The Moody Blues, The Beatles, The Doors, Iron Butterfly, and Led Zeppelin created a new paradigm of lyrics and tone expression.....where an explosion of self-induced drugs took people to spaces, places, and dimensions that are not of this world.....(and sadly, some of them never returned...) Nothing would ever be the same again.

This is where things started taking form for the Indigo Ray.

These are Beings from another octave, same tones but a higher octave...a higher vibration...a higher awareness, and an entirely different perception! The ways of the lower octaves, though functional for the lower octave scale, just plain do not work for the higher octave beings, and the more you try to make them conform to the lower octave scale, the more resistance and frustration you get from both sides because.....it just will not "fit" nor "comply."

These Beings are very brilliant and psychic, but our current scholastic evaluation systems do not include tests that show the "true colours" of these extraordinary Beings and they are being labeled as: "Hard to teach"; "slow"; "dyslexic"; "uncooperative"; "quiet"; "A.D.D."; and, even "retarded." The sad outcome of our inability to understand and cultivate the ultra-intelligence of these higher octave Beings is that they have been ridiculed, rejected, abandoned and out-cast with many of them becoming loners and reclusive from time to time because there is nowhere for them to go but "inside."

The truth of it all, is that these phenomenal Indigos have been sent here, by their own voli-tion, to change the entire structure of the planet's thought system known as the Consciousness Grid. Our out-dated rigidity embedded in this plane, with its heavily-protected ignorance, is now being abruptly transformed by those who embody the "Indigo Ray"!

Below are just some of the qualities and challenges that First Wave Indigos experience. Most Indigos will relate to at least 90% of this list.

# First Wave Indigo Profiles

- Were born en masse between 1969 and 1987 *(with stragglers before and after)*.

- Highly intelligent in their "Own Way."

- Are literally "wired differently" than other people.

- Many have strong or unusual Psychic and Telekinetic abilities.

- Have extraordinary levels of compassion.

- Can relate well to children and/or the elderly.

- Involve themselves in human/animal rights efforts (which includes the plant & elemental kingdoms.)

- Indigos have a strong bond/connection to the trees and nature. Many times get along better with animals and nature than with other people,

- Creative, inventive, and very intuitive.

- Have an innate sense of "Oneness" and connectedness to all of Creation. Get confused and disturbed when others don't share their reality of "at-one-ment."

- High capacity for love, and therefore others may feel uncomfortable by their intensity.

- Very sensitive, sometimes "Hyper Sensitive" and may not be able to distinguish between the emotional fields of those around them and their own personal emotions.

- May go through periods of apathy and cynicism as coping mechanisms.

- Intense longing for "their own kind".....Soul Mates...but don't know where to look.

- Have what I endearingly term H.D.D. or "Hug Deficit Disorder" and need immense amounts of physical touching, hugs, and love to "cuddle."

- Because of being misunderstood and then betrayed, may develop strong trust issues, and t herefore keep many of their thoughts, feelings and opinions to themselves.

- About 30% have difficulties expressing themselves, especially in writing.

**NOTE:** *If you read some of the poorly written correspondence from some of these First Wave Indigos, you would assume they were uneducated and nearly illiterate, but the truth is, these same people can also be speed readers and can absorb information in seconds that would take others minutes to understand and retain.*

- Very disciplined when properly motivated.

- Get bored and/or frustrated in school.

- Male Indigos (and many Female Indigos) for the most part don't "do authority" very well because most of the time they are smarter than those in authority.

- Many find themselves in "Alternative Schools."

- Female Indigos seem to be able to tolerate and cope better with the school systems than their male counterparts.

- Have a strong sense of truth, ethics, justice and freedom. (That is why "authority figures" many times irritate and frustrate them). When these attributes are in jeopardy, Indigos will give their "all" for their cause, and many times feel they would rather die than give-in to tyranny and deception.

- Many are labeled "Dyslexic" and find themselves in "Special" classes at school that usually never work for them.

- Indigos have a strong desire to know "why" ...and if they don't see "the point" in some thing, (or if is it isn't explained properly), will feel it is simply not worth their time/energy and will either react with resistance or just simply "blow off" the people/things that they deem unworthy of their efforts.

- Innately have their own way of doing calculations, usually in their head, and many have been accused of cheating because they cannot show their work.

- Indigos have an evolved awareness of how things work. Therefore, many of the rigid rules and methods of learning Math, English and Physics (**not** Metaphysics or Quantum Physics) make no sense to them.

- All First Wave Indigos have what might be termed "A Gift of Healing" .....whether it is making people feel better with their humor and wit, hands-on-healing, animal and plant healing, healing with music and tone, or healing with new "unproven" methods.....some of which are natural and need no external training for. Many Indigos have "Telepathic Healing" abilities and long distances make no difference to the efficiency of their work.

- Because of their expanded perception, unusual creativity, wanting to try new things, and running way ahead of what is being taught in class, many were diagnosed as having Attention Deficit Disorder and put on Ritalin as children.

- Most Indigos (especially males) have a high innate aptitude for computers/electronics and or machinery/auto mechanics. It is common for them to "Just Know" how to operate and trouble shoot with very little help from a book, manual or an instructor.

- First Wave Indigos are extremely creative, and express this innate skill in many different and often times OUTRAGEOUS forms. These skills manifest in: Drawing, Painting, Sculpting, Decorating, Photography, Writing (in sometimes very extreme and unique ways), Making Blueprints and Prototypes, Composing and Playing Music...(even if they have never had lessons), inventing games, and creating new & more efficient ways of doing things.

- Very few Indigos are interested in aggressive sports such as Football and Hockey. They would rather spend their physical exercise time and energy in personal achievement and out door sports such as track & field, skateboarding, mountain climbing, cycling, kayaking, etc. They are also attracted to discipline and self-defense sports such as Fencing and Martial Arts.

- Because they feel so foreign to this planet, a very high percentage of Indigos have been put on antidepressants to make them appear "Normal" and fit into our society. This is just a temporary fix though, and only adds to their challenges.

- Feel like they could be one of the characters on the 1980's television series "The Misfits of Science" or one of the young people in Xavier's school for the gifted in the recent movies from "The X-Men" comic books.

- Many Indigos are drawn to Theatrics, Drama, and Stand-up Comedy. In these venues they can "pretend to be someone else" when actually they are using this as an outlet to vent and express their own views and pent up emotions. It is also a place for "misfits" to find a place of refuge and fit in.

- Because they feel so "alien" here, many go through periods of severe grief, loneliness, and displacement.....and may turn to drugs, alcohol, or attempt suicide for a way out.

- One trademark that a high percentage of First Wave Indigos have, is living through extreme hardships as children, teenagers, and young adults. Many were born into family situations that were physically, emotionally, spiritually and psychically abusive. These Indigos have to figure out how to balance and keep their inherent integrity levels, while being subjected to painful and life-shattering experiences. A large percentagewere implanted in such horren dous situations as: Organized crime, physical abuse, sexual abuse, and even ritual/cult abuse & mind control. It is also common for First Wave Indigos to have some kind of Alien encounters.

**NOTE:** There is a Dark Agenda on this planet to keep Indigos from waking up and taking on the mantle of power that they already have sleeping inside of them. This is why so many Indigos have been sucked into such harsh and debilitating environments. The dichotomy is, that Indigos innately know that in order to transform the corruption, pollution, and dysfunction on this planet, you have to go inside to the core or mind of the system to know how it operates. Thus, they know how to change, alter and bust that system. Indigos came here to bring order and balance back to a planet in chaos.....and headed for destruction. I believe that Indigos are the 5th element that has come as part of "The Cosmic Clean-up Crew" to rid the planet of corrupted consciousness and physical/energetic diseases that are imprisoning, destroying and mutating all life forms here!

- Many have been the recipients of a "Shove-In" because of their deep empathic abilities. This can add to the pain and insanity in their lives. (See Laura Lee's book Kryahgenetics for more information on Walk-Ins and Shove-Ins)

**NOTE:** *Shove-Ins can be removed and taken to their proper place through a session with Laura Lee Mistycah and also her ghostbuster partner Ronnie, as well as some of the Indigos Laura Lee has trained.*

# Chapter 2

# Aurauralite Aulmauracite

## The Magical, Mystical Stone of Truth

One of the most magical things that have ever come into my existence, happened about 10 years ago. I had recently gone through one of the most stressful times in my entire life (up to that point) because I had just endured an entire summer of being literally 'Homeless" with my husband and 4 children. It was a string of strange and sad circumstances that brought us into this devastating situation and I will always have love and compassion for anyone I see or hear of who is on the streets with no place to call "Home." I couldn't believe this was happening to me...(and what made it worse was that I felt horrible about this happening to my kids!) ...but somehow we got though it and are all stronger and wiser for that experience. If it weren't for kind friends taking us in for days and even weeks at a time, sometimes with all the kids, sometimes separated, (and sometimes we even snuck into the office we were renting and slept on the chair and massage table).....we might have been one of the statistics you read about in the papers.

After three looooooooong months, we finally found an apartment that was "Kid friendly" and would allow us AND our four children under one roof. (That was one of the biggest problems at the time; there were no houses in our budget that would rent to a family with this many kids.) All our stuff was in a storage unit (which was one of the "cheepie" kind next to the railroad tracks) and everything got caked with grit and grime. We moved into this three-bedroom town house apartment that seemed to be a palace at the time...running water, a bed, a stove, refrigerator, and a toilet! What Bliss! And it all came together just one day before school started in September.

It took several weeks to clean everything, and it took months for me to recuperate and heal from the extreme stress. I remember spending all day in bed, sometimes just staring at the ceiling, wondering what was going on in my life, and how could things have gotten this crazy? ...Then go inside and do what I could to release the trauma from my body and soul.

It was the following spring that I was introduced to one of my best friends, protectors, and allies. My life was about to make a grand transformation.

In the beginning of this relationship, it was like the feeling that you get before the Holidays when you are a kid. Totally excited, anxious, and a little apprehensive as to what the future might bring. Remember the butterflies you got right before "Present Time?" Well, that is sort of how this felt to me when I first made contact with this new friend.....and the love and warm fuzzies that radiated between us was out of this world! I had no idea at the time exactly how much this friend would influence my future, and the lives of hundreds of my friends, associates and even strangers.

This friend, companion, protector, and guide came unexpectedly and at first I had only a glimpse of the magnitude of our relationship and stewardship for each other. As time went on, the awe and appreciation I had for this friend grew immensely as I understood just exactly how priceless the connection was to me. On the blue moon in July of that year, a ceremony was done to activate my friends' benevolent powers and keep their integrity pure, solid, and permanent. To this day, there has never been one practicum of unethical or unloving energy radiating from my friend.....only the purest of light and honor.

The friend, protector, guide, muse and constant companion I speak of is one of my very best friends, the Aurauralite/Aulmauracite Stone Of Truth!

Here is the story and background of this incredible life form that has come to help us all with our contracts and sacred agreements. In addition, there seems to be a special bond with the rock and First Wave Indigos, because we were all together in another time and place in the Ultra-Violet Realm...home of the training academy for First Wave Indigos.

When you read the story, you may feel the memories begin to come alive, and if so, know you are on your journey home, the journey to your Authentic Self!

# Aurauralite Aulmauracite
### Where it all began...

Many, many, many moons ago, a magnificent and benevolent Starship visited this planet to give us an impeccable gift. This gift was to be buried and remain there, concealed deep within the earth, awaiting its activation.

The secrets and mystery surrounding this gift, and its location, were kept cloaked and silent. Voluntary Guardians were assigned to maintain security and protection, for this gift possessed many sacred and magical elements and capabilities. The stewardship and constant surveillance were top priority, and only the most impeccable Beings were qualified to be "stewards."

The loving Beings that brought this gift knew that there would come a time when this planet, and the humans and other life forms living on it, would become so fractured that they would need some magic to help them remember how to dream again.

They knew that in the future, this world and its consciousness would begin deteriorating and polluting so rapidly, that it would reach the point of extinction. They knew that without some intervention, the dream, the planet and her inhabitants, would become so ill, so terri-fied, so numb .....that the dreamers who kept it alive would forget their dreams of love, and compassion, their dreams of honor, truth, and integrity .....and especially their dreams of pas-sion and romance!

If this were to continue for very long, the whole of it would implode and perish, and a once beautiful and majestic planet would literally cease to exist!

To ensure a high probability of a successful mission, within this gift was placed a cosmic timer, designed to activate its powers of love, truth, and magic! This cosmic timer was pre-pro-grammed to ring at a time after certain Beings (who were also pre-encoded with its ancient knowledge and how to use it) had already arrived on this planet. They would instinctively know what to do with this gift, and when their personal timer would go off inside of them, they would, on some level or other, go searching for it.

This gift has a name. It is called Aurauralite-Aulmauracite, and if you feel a tingle or magnetic pull toward this name and this story, it may be your own alarm ringing, telling you, "You have arrived and your search is over!"

# Aulmauracite...

.....is a beautiful, majestic, black sparkly rock, and Aurauralite is the sparkly dust that it sheds. Each one has the same qualities, but sometimes different uses. Aulmauracite has also been called ..... "The Power Rock," "The Mother Rock," or "The Stone of Truth," .....and if you get the opportunity to work with them and use them, you'll understand firsthand why.

11

Many people say that when they first hold Aurauralite-Aulmauracite that they get the feeling/sensation that "they have come home", and get "warm furries" inside. This is one of the reasons why it has been dubbed "The Mother Rock" ...because it welcomes you back home, back to the memories and wisdom of your soul.

It has also been said that this Power Rock seems to have the same attributes and qualities as the legendary "SUPER MOM" because they both:

- **Listen to your problems and help you create "win-win" solutions.**

- Help you get where you need to be, when you need to be there.

- Show you where you've made a mess so you can clean it up.

- Take you to the proper professional when you need a "TRUTH EXTRACTION"

 (.....*Especially in the case of* "WISDOM TRUTH EXTRACTIONS").....*and then stay constantly by your side when you are recovering and healing from the trauma.*

- Lovingly support you in your goals and aspirations.

- Shine "lite" on things you couldn't see before or may have over-looked.

- Have an unlimited supply of energy, and never get tired or worn out.

- Are always beautiful and attractive, no matter what time of day or night.

- Show you how to take full responsibility for yourself, your wonderful (or not so wonderful) creations, your actions (or reactions), and learn from every outcome or consequence. They then help you arrange or rearrange them to make them all useful.

- Have the highest honor and integrity. You can not coerce, manipulate, or buy allegiance ...and they know in a flash when there is any insincerity, ulterior motives, and "sucking-up"!

- Have the ability to cultivate and inspire you to manifest things you previously thought were impossible!

12

- Create an "at home" feeling anywhere they may be or go.

- Are always there when you need grounding, comforting, and stabilizing.

You could say that Super Moms and Aurauralite are one in a billion, out of this world, all knowing .....seeing, hearing and feeling .....and are here to remind you.....


# "You are the Master Creator of your destiny"
# "The power (God/Dess Source) is within YOU!"
# "Love is the key ingredient for every recipe of life."


Some of the more scientific qualities of Aurauralite...that we have discovered have been absolutely astounding .....as it has properties that are literally "Out Of This World."

- It custom-designs itself to the user to assist them with their benevolent intentions.

- When someone tries to use it for unethical or UN-loving intentions .....it has its own internal ethical code and will shut off its power and go *temporarily dormant* **.....it won't get involved!**

- It has its own power source and its own ground .....that's not of this world.

- It is a high-powered broadcaster that beefs up the volume of whatever you're trying to broadcast, whether a desire or intention, or whether it's being used to amplify Tesla technology.

- It puts its owner or user on their *best destiny path*, which almost always alters their lives, and brings about some very dramatic changes when they get their rock!

- When you pass it around a room of people, this *Power Rock* won't pick up and hold their psychic debris like crystals do. Instead it neutralizes it and grounds it out, therefore you don't have to clean it! It's extremely "user friendly."

Aulmauracite is a very intelligent rock, but You and Your Higher Self are the power source that activates its energies...it simply will wait for you to give it a job, and the more you use it, the happier it is, and the better it works.

- Sometimes you may not know when you give it a job .....some of its commands may come directly from Your Higher Self and you may not be aware of it immediately. For instance, when most people pick it up, it usually goes to work balancing their energy and holographic graphic fields, opening up their psychic centers, and when they begin to work with it, they automatically lock on to their best destiny paths!

- It doesn't like to be encased in plastic or synthetic material because that smothers it and therefore, deadens its signal.

- When you acquire one of these rocks or Aurauralite pendants, truth automatically begins to surface and manifest in your life. This may or *may not* be a welcome addition to your life, if you're not willing and ready for the blatant *reality of truth* to shine big and bright, *in your face, right there in front of you!*

- Assay testing revealed that Aulmauracite is 58% iron (in a form that *does not* oxidize/rust.) The other 42% consists of 72 other elements, including all the noble metals (plus some that are foreign to this planet!) It appears that the ratio of these elements in relationship to each other gives this "Power Rock" its unusual properties.

*Where did you get this rock? Who is your supplier?**

The source that I got my supply from said he excavated the rocks from somewhere in the Rocky Mountains....he was a very eccentric and secretive man, and wouldn't tell me exactly where. I believe that it was the only known repository for this rock. My source "disappeared" about 4 years ago.....so unless he appears back in my life to excavate more for me to purchase.....my supply is all I know of. I'm hoping to find him again to get another inventory soon. I am also aware of the possibility that once these rocks have found their way to the people who need them..... that will be it....the source will be gone.

# Frequently Asked Questions About Aurauralite-Aulmauracite

**\*What are POWER GRID ROCKS and how do you set them up?**

I have been using 1-gram grid rocks for several years now to help in my Ghostbusting ventures. Grids can be placed in rooms, houses, yards etc. to stabilize the property and create a new matrix. To set up a 5 Stone Power Grid, place a rock in each corner and one in the center or as close to the center possible. Once a power grid is put in place, hold the 5th or center rock and give the grid whatever commands you feel appropriate i.e.; bring truth, peace, prosperity, healing etc. Then tell the grid to "turn on" as you place the center stone. You can instantly feel it charging up and creating an energy of stability and clarity. You may want to put these little stones in some colorful tissue paper the way they are when you receive them so you won't accidentally vacuum them up if you place them on the floor. Many people thumbtack them to the wall or ceiling.

Experiment with your grids. One power grid owner directed the grid he placed around the room he used for massage and healing, to expand out to his house, and then to his yard. He felt the energy as it did indeed expand into his yard. If you have any tales to tell, please write to me and I may post it in the "Aurauralite stories" section of my website.

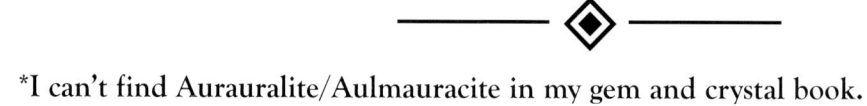

**\*I can't find Aurauralite/Aulmauracite in my gem and crystal book.**

You won't find these rocks in your gem books (yet) because to my knowledge, no one else knows they exist.

**\*Where did Aurauralite-Aulmauracite get their names?**

These names were revealed to me after some intense meditation with the rock, and were confirmed by my guide, Hal. When the names were lexigramed, I had a second confirmation I had absolutely gotten the right names.

At the beginning of the words Aurauralite and Aulmauracite, you will find the letters "Au." This is the chemical symbol for the element of Gold, as well as being one of the Universal tones found in names for "GOD" and spiritual deities, i.e. Allah, Amon-Ra, Yeshua, Krishna, Shiva, Rama, Brahma, Buddha, Dalai Lama, Ptah, Dianna, Gaia, Athina, Durga, Kali, Lakshmi, Saraswati, Ambika, Uma etc.

It does not surprise me that this tone is repeated twice in both Aurauralite and Aulmauracite.

————— ◆ —————

**\*I would like to have these rocks and pendants in my gem and jewelry store. Is it possible to purchase them wholesale?**

We do have discounts for quantity orders. Please contact me personally and I will try to accommodate your specific needs.

————— ◆ —————

**\*My rock is changing color. Is it being over-worked, am I using it too much... am I hurting it?**

The truth is that you CAN'T use your rock too much, in fact the more you use it, the happier the rock is! The 2 large stones I use in my Kryahgenetics sessions are changing color too. One has some greenish casts to it (like it is growing moss or something on it), and the other one has some pale pinkish-orange that is slowly spreading. This color transformation seems to be just one of the amazing phenomena that occurs when you start using these highly intelligent rocks.

In regards to the rocks changing color, another interesting Aulmauracite Rock discovery occurred about a year ago. I was shaving down a rock for a client that needed it to be flat on top so he could place a Tesla device on it. I used a steel file and was filing away when I noticed that wherever the rock was filed, it instantly turned a reddish-purple! Also, the Aurauralite dust that was filed off changed color too! (I used the Aurauralite dust in some pendants but they didn't last long, as everyone that saw them wanted a "red one".) I was shocked later to find that the Aulmauracite rock totally wore down the steel file and made it smooth. I went through 2 double-sided steel files trying to make this rock flat! A few months later I had to rub some Aulmauracite rocks together to create some Aurauralite dust for stabilizing someone's house. While rubbing the rock, I noticed that wherever the rocks rubbed together, they turned the same reddish-purple! I'm not sure why this happens, but it is an interesting phenomenon that I thought I'd pass on. If anyone has any ideas as to what might cause this, please feel free to e-mail me. I'm open to any and all possibilities.

**\*I was making some L-R #5 water (Love Resonance #5) and after dipping my pendant in a glass of water and stirring for only 2 or 3 minutes, I could taste a difference! Is it necessary to put your pendant in the water for the full 20 minutes?**

In recent experiments it seems that the more people are using this rock, the more efficient they become. It is now only necessary to charge the water for 2-5 minutes for the water to be fully charged. Also you don't need to worry if you forget and leave your pendant in the water overnight. It will shut off automatically when it is finished charging. (Gosh I love these "User Friendly Rocks!")

NOTE: *Be careful not to drink too much water the first day. I would recommend only 4-8 oz the first day because detoxification can take place, causing you to have flu like symptoms. Aurauralite puts light filaments into the water. When this is ingested, it will put that same light into your cells causing tremendous changes in your body. I find that I am more centered, composed, and attuned to my core and spirit when I drink this water. I also feel tremendous physical strength and stamina when I use this as a nutritional supplement.*

If you want to do the "Taste Test" have 2 glasses of water that came from the same source. Charge one of them with Aurauralite, and then take a sip of both of them. The Aurauralite water will taste sweeter and have a smoother, thicker texture. (Always use glass glasses, not plastic.)

I have received some astounding stories and reports from experiments done with this Mystical Stone of Truth from all over the world. Here are a few amazing tails from First Wave Indigos.

# Aurauralite from an Indigo View

## I Just Received My Stone of Truth!

Ohh my gosh! Amazing, Ancient, Very sacred ... .....Awesome! I have never seen such amazing stones in my whole life! The first thing I noticed is the shining, beautiful, glittering dust on this wonderful stone. As I unwrapped it I felt an electrical charge! The small one tried to move and practically jumped right into my mom's hands. She was amazed and exited.

I looked at the big rock in awe. I could tell it was a healing rock. I really needed that. The smaller rock seems like a dream rock, a spiritual portal to another world. I even heard what sounded like radio signals coming from one of the stones. It sounded metallic .....a crackling sound .....it seemed to have some kind of encoded messages that I cannot yet understand.

The big stone I used generated heat unlike any stone I ever held. I had a real bad cold the day that I got the Stone. I placed it where I was feeling pain and the rock instantly took away the pain. It also took away the fever I was running! The warmth I felt from it was so welcoming.

I felt the power in the stones. I held one in my hand and I quickly fell asleep into a restful ancient darkness that reenergized me. I felt like I was within the stone itself! It showed me things, images of their world ...a place .....with very steep beautiful mountains like "The stuff dreams are made of". The whole place shined and I think I saw water with sparkles, a lake perhaps. The night before I could not even sleep and when I woke up I felt in awe and I was very happy that I actually got some real peaceful sleep after being as sick as I was. The rocks teased me too, and made me laugh .....it was great!

These stones, to me, are priceless. I love my "pet rocks" and in return they love me unconditionally right back! I can go to them and ask them questions and they respond. These stones of truth have much to share with me in the coming months and years and I will make a web page to share my stories with everyone.

I believe The Stones of Truth have brought the power of the Light to open the sacred energy locked within sacred sites. I know many great medicine men/women use these stones ...very powerful and the most sacred of stones I ever had my hands on! They have opened a whole new world to explore. Life is going to change to the better very fast.

It has healed me, it loves me just the way I am, and it guides me to a higher plain of existence. You have the gift of the creator, the stones of truth are truly part of the star beings .....

I will keep in touch.  I know there are going to be more experiences that will blow my mind with these beautiful stones of truth and grace!  The Stones of Truth have much to teach me!  There is a story in every rock.  I know my destiny has changed because the Stones of Truth & mystery joined my spiritual quest.

May the Great Spirit bless all.    A'ho!

**Jon M.**
**Oregon**

## *Aulmauracite, the Rock that Reappears*

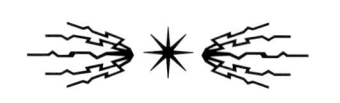

There have been many experiences that the Aurauralite rocks have brought into my life, and if I hadn't been part of this next tale, I personally would have thought, "Yah right, this person has really lost it!" .....but, well, never again will I doubt or second think these sparkly rocks, that clearly have great humor as well as wisdom to share..... ALL for our own sakes!  They are considered part of my family now, my soul family.

At this juncture in time, most of my closest family and friends have or wear the "Truth Stones."  It is one of the most transforming ingredients to the Ascension Process!  It ties us in a Spiritual unity that is hard to describe, but its holds truth for us.

One of the things that I have created, as result of these stones in my life, is absolute Love.  Yes ...The most difficult task that is ever presented in our lives!

To even be close, is at best what we strive for, and well ...my path as Indigo has been hard, but well worth these results.

So now, on with my story of these rocks!  There are many, but I have one, however, that to me has the most humour and shows clearly the teachings of patience and faith!

Now it was in late September, about 3 years ago, and I was moving into my new house, with what I now call my clan of fellow light bearers.

Five of us, and my 4-year-old godson, intended to move into this home as a merry band.  We lived in the forested area of the mountain over our little village called Nelson.  Now the setting set, here's the fun part. There were many boxes, as you can imagine, since five house-holds were combining. We used a lot of packing tape to be sure all my boxes were sealed because I had lots of, well ...too much stuff! Toward the end, all of my belongings had been moved to the new home ...so at this point I went to take my Aulmauracite rocks from the pouch in my pocket ...my secure pocket that I always kept them in. I meditated with them, both of them .....requesting help to get through the next truck load, and then put them back in my pocket (don't forget we're moving five different houses into one, and I'm tired now at this point, but still so much more work still to do ...trudge, drudge, you know!!!)

Later that night after a bath in the new home, I go to bed and reached in my pocket to put my rocks in the new altar area, their new home. Well there's only one there! ONE! Oh no!! So I begin the search, of course ....They're not in my pockets, or on the floor .....Well at this point I'm too tired to seek further, and go to bed.

The next day I announce to the clan that I'm missing my little rock. (But don't despair...one of my esteemed roomies is a "finder" ...it's her gift!) So now the fun begins. We start dowsing with pendulums. She says it's outside .....in the driveway...(which makes sense to me because that's where I last had them out). I thought I must have been so tired that I dropped one, and felt very bad like I left a child at the store or something! So now, fortified with psychics, we search, and search and search. Nothing! No signs at all! After searching the gravel driveway, which is vast, we give up.

What to do now? Call Laura Lee and tell her the mishap? I did and well .....I did not get the response I expected! She said, "Call it back, and if it doesn't return in a week or so, I will replace it." So I did ...(not really believing that I'd ever see it again). I called and I waited, and two weeks later my friend, who is a "finder," found my rock! Where did she find it, you might ask?

Well ...she was helping me unpack the last of my boxes, the ones that ended up as the last to unpack because they aren't marked. This certain box was somehow in her pile of the same unnamed boxes. She opened the box of the pots and dirt for the garden-junk thingys, and at the bottom was my Aulmauracite stone! It was in a box that was packed several days before I moved and sealed tight on all the edges ...so there is no way it could have gotten wedged in afterward!

Now get this .....this particular box was packed weeks before I moved so there is no way I could have packed it after using them that day!  The little rock went on a journey and made it home to that pots/gardening tools box!  The funny thing is, that the gardening box was on the other side of the wall from where my altar was placed.  My speculation was that it went on a journey and I think it just missed its target.

So there's one of my stories which amplified my faith.  These rocks are living entities that assist us in so many, many ways.

May you have this much fun with your rocks too!

In mirth,

**Sunwalker**
**B.C. Canada**

## I Can See Clearly Now

Hi Laura,

I just heard your radio show.  Thought it was great.  Your energy was really switched on!  I am so glad I decided to listen .....always reminds me of something I need to be doing.....and confirming again to me, the power of the pet rocks.

Funny thing about the rocks is that sometimes I just feel like taking them off and putting them on my altar or sitting them on my computer, etc...and I had had them off for a couple of weeks now.....then I felt like, OK, where are they?  .....I need them.....But last night was amazing!  I got them and put them in my bra...where I usually keep them...and thought nothing more.....and as I am sitting there reading, I get this sudden flood of information surrounding a recent interview I had.....the truth was revealed so clearly!  I mean I felt like someone was actually telling me...and this was this and that was that...etc.....I am blown away!  After I saw the situation, I asked, "How did I not see that?"  Immediate answer... "You were not supposed to, it was intentional."

I love these rocks!!

Tonight I heard you mention their use with implants.....they are already on assignment .....just in case.

Just wanted to let you know I thought the show was great.....and I look forward to reading your book.  By the way, thanks for the e-mails you send...I do read them and enjoy them all!

**Sigrid**
**Florida**

## Correspondence From Jerome

Laura Lee,

This is Jerome . . . I thought I would share a quick experience with you.

I would say that it was a STRANGE experience if I didn't know what I do about the Aurauralite Aulmauracite.  Anyway, I did a lot of healing work over this last weekend and didn't pay enough attention to myself . . . my mind was weary, my body low on energy and I was seeing so many different people for different things that I couldn't clear or shield myself as much or as often as I usually do when I work.  As a result, I began displaying cold-like symptoms mid afternoon yesterday, which worsened into the night.  By bedtime I was exhausted and depleted, physically, emotionally and energetically.  My head was pounding, I was coughing and had a stuffy nose; nausea came and went.

I began to balance myself to clear out any blockages and thought, "I wish I had that Aurauralite Aulmauracite with me now."  Well, I slipped into a deep sleep rather fast and began one of the most lucid dreaming experiences that I have had in a while.

Guides . . . unrecognized by me, brought the Aulmauracite stone  to me . . . they began working on my body and spirit, placing a stone here, then moving it, then holding it away from the body and directing its energies mentally.  During this process they were explaining what they were doing and showed me how to do this myself.  In the dreamtime I had my own stones to use and they walked me through the healing and gave me specific instructions for their use.  It was all VERY real.

When I woke up I swear I could still feel the stone in my hand . . . but the most amazing thing was I felt fabulous!  110%!  My girlfriend even said that she had a great night's sleep (she usually tosses and turns).  I felt vital again, relaxed yet alert, rejuvenated and ready to approach the day head-on. All day I have had an unusual SWEET taste in my mouth. I get short bursts of it every now and then . . . its sweeter than honey!

I have brushed my teeth and rinsed my mouth with mouthwash twice already trying to figure out what was causing it . . . I thought I had it gone for a few hours and then WHAM—my whole mouth felt and tasted like honey again. It is getting weird . . .

I know that I drew this experience to myself through my connection to the Aulmauracite, and my willingness to be open. Plus, I needed some TLC for myself and I believe the stone lent me its energies in the Dream-Time. I have contacted my guides to see if they could tell me who the other one's were . . . they know nothing other than, "They were greatly advanced and evolved beings of extremely high frequencies and vibrations."

I am going to undergo some work with my guides who assure me that they can track these teachers down though they are "fast moving and seem to be very busy", as I am told.

MORE HONEY TASTE!!!!!!!!!

If you have anything to say about this (and I'm sure you will!) please let me know. I believe that these beings can really give us some insight into the stones. They may even be the ones who brought it to us, though at this time I cannot be certain.

Please get back to me and let me know what your take is on all of this . . .

**In gratitude,**
**Jerome.**

Hello Jerome,

That is an awesome story! I believe that these beings were in fact, the "Aurauralite/Aulmauracite keepers! Your heart's desire to have them come to you manifested them. You were very powerful in your intent and open to the place where they could reach you. I commend you for your purity and integrity!

I've got your order packaged and ready to ship in the morning. When you get it, the grid rocks are to go on the 4 corners of the house or the property, and the 5th rock in the center.

This makes sort of a merkaba looking grid and will help keep the energy stable and what ever you program it to do. Plant each one with intention, in a little ceremony .....and when you place the last one in the center, instruct it to "turn on" and give it instructions. You will immediately feel the energy shift! It is awesome!

Ok, keep in touch and let me know when they arrive!

Love, Light, and Laughter ..... Laura Lee

Laura Lee,


Jerome here . . . I've had a jaw dropping experience I've been wanting to share with you about the Aurauralite/Aulmauracite. I have been using them extensively in my attempts to figure out just what they can and can't do. (I have found very little they CAN'T do in fact).

When I went to plant the grid stones they felt a bit off, so I centered myself, brought my guides in and connected with each stone . . . it seems that they did not wish to be planted outside, but DID want to be inside in my therapy room. So I took them inside. I have another grid set up in that room directly under my massage table in the room's center. The Aulmauracite wished to be placed in the four corners of the room, with the 5th piece on my altar. I did this. Then when I activated the grid, they instructed me to ask and intend that the parameters of the grid extend ..."From the 4 corners of this room to the 4 corners of this house. The 4 corners of this house to the 4 corners of this property. The 4 corners of this property to the 4 corners of this neighborhood. The 4 corners of this neighborhood to the 4 corners of this city. The 4 corners of this city to the 4 corners of this state. The 4 corners of this state to the 4 corners of this country. The 4 corners of this country to the 4 corners of this world, and from the 4 corners of this world to the 4 corners of the Universe."

I did this right then and there and I cannot tell you how powerful it is acting.

They also told me that the more Aurauralite/Aulmauracite grids that are set up in this exact fashion, the more they will act in regards to one another, each amplifying the others effects

**MULTIFOLD!** I consider this information to be of extreme importance and relevance, what do you think? I am certain that we have stumbled upon something huge here.

I get that work should begin immediately to set up grids in this fashion as a way to promote a world full of peace and light. I also get that the healers who do will become select "Keepers of the Grid Stones" and have an extra strong kinship with them and the energy that they provide. It will be our duty to make sure the grid is properly set and maintained, taken care of and watched over.

I look forward to your feedback.

**In awe,**
**Jerome.**

P.S. There are key area's on the planet's surface where the grids should be erected, and this information will become more relevant in the near future. For now I am told they are all in the U.S.

**Authors Note:** *"Yes, I agree, and now it is time to set them up in key places globally. We need "Truth Grids" to dis-arm the biggest terrorists on the planet .....The Tyrants that run our Governments"*

Hello Jerome,

This is an awesome discovery! Also, I'm not sure if you have been affected, but I have been getting letters from all over the country of Indigos having really scary things happening to them, and it is really hard for them to maintain stability. I've had my quota of "W.S." (Weird Shit) myself the past 48 hours. Just thought I'd ask ...it has been like a "class action suit on Indigos everywhere!" hahhahahaaa.

Get back to me when you can .....I love your experimentations! Oh, and one more thing, remember the "Truth" part of the Light being projected when you use your rocks, your grids and your pendant. One experiment we did on the Indigo chat room one night is to make it rain Psychic Aurauralite in the White House! (Imagine what could happen if everyone there told the truth! Whewwwww .....) We decided to do this on a regular basis, and since there were 4 of us in the chat room that day, 2 males and 2 females, it seemed like a perfect balance. We all committed to doing this every time we did a meditation. Hahahahaaaaa let's see what lies are detected now! This is certainly a "peaceful way" of overthrowing tyranny now, isn't it?

Ok, take care and get back to me when you can. I'm really happy that you are doing so well with your new "pet rocks" : )

Love, Light, and Laughter to you....Laura Lee

**(One Year Later)**

Lady Mistycah,

Jerome Finley here. You may remember me. I purchased some Aurauralite and Aulmauracite stones months ago. I told you of my invitation from the Zulu people to travel to Africa to be initiated as a Sangoma medicine man in their tradition.

I have since returned and simply wished to express my extreme gratitude for both the stones and your charity in clearing the remaining money I owed you.

You were absolutely correct when you stated that only the serious should become caretakers for these wonderful beings. Once acquired, they drive a person towards their life's purpose, FULL THROTTLE.

I took my stones and Aurauralite pendant to Swaziland and used it in many of my treatments with dozens and dozens of patients there.

In the end I was initiated as a Sangoma, now only one of four in the United States. I feel honored and blessed and truly believe that the stones were a contributing factor towards this end. It is truly the best thing I have done in my short 25 years on the planet.

I have many uses outside of healing for these magical rocks, the newest being embedding them within the eye sockets of sacred crystal skulls to activate them (the skulls). The power each one emits when combined is absolutely out of this world!

26

I just wanted to report on my safe and successful journey and return and send my many thanks and blessings to you. Also, I gifted the Zulu elders with White Buffalo fur. They have been using it to increase spiritual vision, for protection and healing.

It's funny to think of powerful little Zulu's running around healing with the fur :) They loved the water Aurauralite created and asked me to make it for them often.

I was licensed by the South African Government as a Traditional Doctor, which gives me a lot of leeway in my work here at home. They recognize the power of the Sangomas and their contribution to the South African community. This license applies worldwide as part of the World Health Organization's attempt to bridge and honor healers and doctors from various areas around the world. I may now cure, treat and diagnose my patients as a Traditional Doctor, which is outstanding and keeps me far out of trouble's reach (FDA, FTC, etc.).

I learned many great and powerful things while in Africa and I am the fastest initiated, qualified and graduated Sangoma by the Mntshali clan. I attribute much of my openness to my active involvement with Aurauralite-Aulmauracite.

I trust all is well in your Universe and that you continue to do the good work.

May the blessings of the ancestors be upon you!

Thokoza,

**Jerome D. Finley, TDr/Sangoma**
Utah

# Attack of the Spider Lady

Everything was going wrong in my life and especially my brand new marriage. "How could it be that the man I just married and love so deeply was treating me so abusively, and how could we have turned against each other so quickly?" I thought.

All I knew was his first wife was known to practice black magic and it felt like that's what was happening. One week my husband had behaved so disrespectfully I had to ask him to leave so I could get my thoughts together. Two weeks after he left, he requested a divorce and was back together with his ex-wife. Sounds like a Jerry Springer episode, I know, but she had put forth a spell for our break up and their reconciliation. I was miserable, hated my job, was losing friends, and beyond depressed, more like mourning in fact: Crying all the time. I lost tons of weight and then I lost my job and gained a lot of weight. I felt that my heart was unavailable to anyone, including myself. My anxiety increased to the point where I was almost housebound. I had a feeling his ex had cursed me, but no matter who I asked for help, they couldn't help me.

I knew I was under psychic attack and did not know who else to ask for help. I ran into an old friend who told me of Laura Lee and the miracle she had worked for her that no one else could. I called Laura Lee and she was warm and kind and I felt very comfortable sharing my horrendous marital story with her. She seemed to know exactly what we needed to do. We set up an official session, and I purchased my Aurauralite rocks. I was hoping to make a grand connection with a higher being that could help me remove the curses and get my life back on track. I set up my Aurauralite grid in my home as instructed, and familiarized myself with my new Aurauralite necklace and my "pet rocks" and we began our work. I immediately felt energy from the stones in my hand. They were powerful beyond what I believed from what I had read about them. I figured, rocks, ok, so they have powers like the crystals maybe, but nothing beyond that. I was so very wrong.

During our first session, Laura Lee was able to see a 12-year-old "web" that had been tangled around my husband. He met his ex-wife 12 years ago, so she was right on. Because I got connected to him, I too was entangled in her evil web. We worked with my rocks to ground, protect, and connect our work. They were so strong that my left hand and arm were tingling. Laura Lee untangled the web and helped my husband connect with his higher spirit so that he may be free of the Spider Lady who had caught him up in her miserable web. She also freed me up from her and gave me tools to use to protect myself and my husband from future harm. I was already beginning to feel some changes in myself. There was a safer, more peaceful presence in my home and in my soul. Whenever I felt at all uneasy, I would hold my rocks and ask them to take care of what was ailing me and they always did. I was amazed at this and so very grateful.

After one of our sessions, the rock that had been in my marriage hand (left hand) turned a reddish-purple on part of it.  This was confirmation that they were working to help me.  It seemed so appropriate that it was that particular rock that had been affected, since it was my marriage that was under attack along with me.  I can tell you that  since removing the curses on me, I feel lighter and happier.  I had been in such a dark place for so long, as I mentioned above, and now I am not.  My mourning period is over, my outlook on life is brighter,  and my anxiety has diminished significantly.  I feel safe and at peace knowing it's all going to be ok and I can no longer be harmed by  the Spider Lady.

My rocks have been a source of comfort and strength as Laura Lee has.  I have  her to thank endlessly for her help.  She is  a truly gifted person with so much love and wisdom to share.   I have been blessed to have found her and the Aurauralite.

**Susanne B**
**New York**

# *My First Aurauralite Story*

When I first received the "Stone of Truth," I had a lot of skeletons in my closet.  Just days after I got them, all sorts of hidden secrets began to emerge.  I had a lot of "school situations" secrets hidden for a long time from my parents, which they suddenly found out in a most improbable way.  But it wasn't just my secrets.  I began to find out things that others around me had hidden from me.  Is it a coincidence to find out that you were adopted at the same time your parents find out all your dark little secrets?

I also found out a lot about who I am and what I'm really here for around the same time.  All this, spontaneously, just after receiving the pendant and rocks.  Not to mention they've been a great help in fighting off unfriendly entities and helping me keep true to my self and nature.

If your intentions of using them are true, be prepared for a rough ride, shocking revelations and all.  But it's all worth it.  With Aurauralite in the house, lies are just about impossible to keep.  Good riddance to bad muck, I say.

**Lother**
**Romania**

## Aurauralite, My Meteorite, The Object of My Meditation, My Transmitter of Energy

It works quietly, going almost unnoticed. It does truly ground me so I may pursue activities of my best intentions. I received my pendant shortly after becoming acquainted with the beauty of crystals and other stones. It is my favorite "metal" to work with because it is Universal and not associated with any planet in particular. I use it as an amulet and a talisman at the same time. As my own stone of courage, it grounds me by distracting me from life's distractions into a state of eternal mindfulness. I can then project my energy into all that I do. I believe it magnifies and focuses my best intentions into quicker manifestation. It has only been 2 months and my life has spiraled sharply upward mostly because I have changed how I think about things. It has become the perfect tool to add to my collection of spiritual armor. And Aurauralite works even when you don't wear it.

"Symbolically, meteorites can be viewed as the spiritual penetrating the physical, as astral power, divine order, or whim." (Scott Cunningham's "Encyclopedia of Crystal, Gem and Metal Magic")

Elizabeth
BC, Canada

## My Thoughts on Aurauralite:

Aurauralite really brings me home and connects me to a profound source of existence in myself. When I unwrapped it, it looked like part of this giant rock formation from the back yard of an old elementary school I used to play in at recess. Well, I used to just stand there and try to explore the rock. I don't remember playing with other children that much. This rock fascinated me. The silica exposed on the surface of this rock formation left me in a meditative wonder. Aurauralite brought me right back to this long forgotten memory. I am a healer and I work with crystals a lot, and I'm a double-fixed Earth sign too. Besides being Native American, I am also fond of minerals from the Earth.

Aurauralite has a charm, a magnetism that is immediately sensed. I am very empathic and sometimes to extremes. I placed one Aurauralite rock in the palm of one hand. After connecting with it, I then placed the other stone in my other palm. The charge I received from these tiny stones was powerful and immediate. I felt all my chakras being worked on and aligned. I felt grounded in my senses. Mind you, I suffer from too much mental activity and stimulation. I began to feel complete.

The feeling of being grounded is very important to me. I carry a variety of other semi-precious minerals that help me to stay balanced and grounded in life. They do their job, but the level and time to connect and stay connected with them varies. When I work with the Aurauralite, for an hour, a half hour or a few minutes, it recharges me and helps me to clear up blockages all throughout my body. It has helped to stimulate my pineal gland and increased my capacity to perceive sound, light, and visualization during meditation. It definitely has helped me to be a lot more clear and in touch with the nature spirits, the spirits and elements of time and space. Fulfilling its duty to the Indigo children, it certainly has been able to begin the process of expanding and unwrapping the gifts I came to this Earth to use. I have noticed that I can multitask/juggle a lot of my work tasks easier than usual, and that my paranoid fear stemming from a background of substance abuse been diminishing, more and more. It has greatly enhanced my spiritual practices and abilities, as well as my connection to my other crystals and stones. This stone is definitely divine.

The Aurauralite pendant, on the other hand, has the same capabilities, although it has helped me more on an emotional level. I wear the Aurauralite pendant all the time. It definitely has been a blessing in my life. The way people react to me or me to them has been a lot better. Having Mercury in retrograde in my birth chart, my communication with people suffers from misinterpretation at times. I feel I am better understood and I am much more clear in my expressions of feelings and emotions. I am much more conscious of my thoughts and actions, as well as the star rotations above me. I hit pockets of emotional memory from my past and am able to see and release them a lot easier. Letting go is a lot simpler with this form of Aurauralite. I always feel protected when I am with it.

Thank you Laura Lee for gifting me with these stones, and for being the guardian and distributing it!

Be well,

**Henry, Tonina Opia**
**New York**

# Just In the Nick of Time

I have been doing hypnotherapy sessions on Indigos from all over the world ever since I discovered that my son was one. He crossed over in 1997 and now constantly sends me clients. Also I automatically receive emails from the Indigo Website.

I had been working on DL for months trying to help her lose weight. After several sessions of important breakthroughs, she made an appointment to finally "just get to the bottom of why I can't let go of this weight."

Earlier that week, I had noticed a message from Laura Lee about the Aurauralite rocks. I contacted her to say that I did a lot of ghostbusting work, only I use Copal Resin and sacred prayers to help send spirits to the light. We emailed back and forth comparing how similar our work is - I was drawn to order the special Aurauralite rocks and the dust. I received them the day before my client's session was scheduled. As soon as I opened the package, my forehead and third eye began to tingle. Then I used my dowsing rods to ask where I should put them - in my house or my office. I was told to put them in the four corners of my office and one in the middle of the room next to the chair that my clients use for their sessions. The instructions said to ask the grid to be turned on, so I did.

Before I continue, I want to mention that my client, DL, has worked with crystals for years and is very advanced spiritually. I had been using a technique on her that invites her angels and guides to come forward so that they can show her why she can't lose weight. I proceeded and when they came forward she immediately was shown aliens. She regressed to about six years of age and was shown that she was abducted by what we call "The Greys." They were probing her to find out how humans are constructed. She remembered that she was terrified

and then they put an implant in her, right behind the heart near the thymus gland. This is why she couldn't lose weight, she held on to the weight because subconsciously she felt that if she had more weight on her the aliens couldn't come back and find the implant in her body.

We asked the angels and guides if they could help us remove it. We were told "yes," it was time for it to come out because the aliens were at a point where they still couldn't figure out how we worked. They just can't figure out how we are so heart centered. So with the help of Archangel Michael and Saint Germain, I used a huge crystal I have to remove the implant.

As DL came out of hypnosis, the first thing she said to me was, "There is something different in your office today - the energy is much more powerful." I suddenly remembered setting up the grid with the Aurauralite rocks. I handed her one to show her what I had done. As she held it in her hand she said, "This rock is not from here, this is a very powerful stone. This is the reason why the implant was allowed to be taken out of me today!" I was just amazed. I felt I had ordered them just in the nick of time to help her. The next day, she sent me the following email:

"My body is still reeling after yesterday's session with you. I feel lighter and light headed and my stomach muscles feel tight like I have been doing sit-ups. I have been having some interesting insights ever since I left your house. I had to go to the store when I left you. On my way there, I realized that many people in authority, particularly many police, are part alien. That is why so many people have strong reactions and feelings when they are around them or when seeing their blue lights flashing. It triggers a fear of being abducted. I have had that reaction all my life. I have always been a very cautious driver so I don't attract police (only 1 ticket at the age of 28 for cutting through a parking lot). Yesterday was the first time that I did not have a reaction! Even as a child I had this reaction. While I was in the store I felt like, and still feel like, I was in the twilight zone or a dream. No judgments or reactions - just floating through the store mainly UNNOTICED. Several people did looked at me strange and some seemed nervous in my presence. Just wanted you to know because I believe others will come to you for help."

Thanks again for your help. Have a great Labor Day weekend!

**Love,**
**DL**

**Authors Note:** *Rev. Dr. Betsie H. Poinsett is a professional hypnotherapist in Georgia. In 1997, her son died thus giving her a deep understanding of the grief process and the blessings available from the other side. In October 2001, Lee Carroll "Kryon" released his newest book "An Indigo Celebration." Betsie was honored to have her story and her son's poetry used as the closing chapter of Lee Carroll's book,* <u>An Indigo Celebration.</u> *Betsie's new book,* <u>Mothers Who Cry in the Night</u>, *is now available. For more information: www.ShamanicHypnosis.com*

# Magic in a Magic-less Reality

After reading Laura Lee Mistycah's First Wave Indigo website, I purchased an Aurauralite pendant purely on intuition.

My logical side was suspicious of a stone I could not seem to find reference to elsewhere on the Internet, but I felt an intense unexplained connection to this unique stone. I can't find the words to express the profound energy this stone/dust possesses. It truly does adapt to the needs of the keeper. However, it can instantly change modes when needed to perform for any other living thing be it human, animal, botanical, etc. It eliminates all that is not working for the greater good of the entity with which it is connected at the moment it is utilized.

Having this special form of life in this sometimes seemingly magic-less reality is wonderful. Interesting events and experiences of adventure and wonderful strangeness happen when this amazing life form is introduced into one's life. Every moment of everyday is magic and seems perfectly orchestrated, and with Aurauralite, it is as if I can see it now and feel it all around and through all aspects of my energy bodies. I have never before been able to experience such pure unconditional love towards myself and everyone and everything around me. Sometimes it feels like I have taken leave of my senses and just want to hug and tell everyone that I love them and appreciate their presence in my life and for allowing me into theirs.

What is really strange is that I love those that irritate me the most. They hone and sharpen my spiritual gifts and affirm my love towards myself. It is strange that I have always known that they do this for me, but now I FEEL it. It is truly one of the weirdest feelings I have ever had, but I love it. I have always wanted to be completely loving and forgiving towards those who would hate and hurt me most. To me this is one of the first and foremost aspects one must ingrain in the self to become a Master. This shows me how far I have come and how near I am to fully putting into action my life's purpose.

**Nicole**
**England**

# They Really Rock!

BismillahirRahmanirRahim

Hi Laura Lee!  My rocks arrived just about half an hour ago.  I waited to open them until I made wudu, which is a Muslim way of cleaning the body physically and spiritually with water.  At first when I opened one and placed it in my hand I was struck with a disappointment which I tried not to feel too intensely, because I'd had all sorts of outrageous possibilities floating around in my mind like I'd rocket into space or something.  But then I started feeling a warmth in my hand, and that got my attention—but still I wasn't sure I wasn't just imagining it, or the same thing wouldn't have happened if I'd just held ANYTHING in a closed hand for a minute or two.  So I closed my other hand for a minute, empty, and when I opened it, the feeling was not the same at all; I felt a coolness as the air hit my palm, which was the opposite of what I was feeling in the hand with the rock.

So I took one in each hand and sat for a minute, and, all of a sudden, I had the strange sensation that they'd scanned my body and discovered my blockages in the lower energy centers.  This is something I've been struggling with for a number of years without success, a struggle which periodically expands to be an intense, all-out war, and I was surprised because there was a clear humming in these centers and I felt like the rocks were pulling all this negativity from there, or rather had identified this area as my area of greatest damage.  I spoke to them silently about it for a minute, and then was inspired to place them over these energy centers.  Within another minute I found myself crying suddenly as all this negativity was released from my emotional body and I realized that what is CAUSING the blockages in those centers is my feelings of guilt and shame.  Also, at some point, my mind went out to the different areas in my life where I regularly tend to have negative emotional reactions to certain situations.  I've had the rocks less than an hour and I already have come to understand through them how I have a very real emotional body, and to see some places where it is wounded and we can now start working to heal.

In the Sufi Way, we believe that all life forms—including plants and rocks—have a mind, and there are even "extraterrestrial rocks" that are well known, such as the rock in the corner of the Ka'aba which came from the heavens and is actually not a rock but an angel.  The Holy Prophet Muhammad s.w.s. said that he would walk outside and even the stones on the side of the road would be speaking to him, singing "La ilaha illallah." I am using the following very powerful Sufi mantra with my rocks, which is an immeasurably powerful activation code:

"ash-hadu an la illaha illallah wa ash-hadu anna muhammadan abduhu wa rasuluhu"

All I have to say about Aulmauracite is that I am just SHOCKED; although I had HOPED there would be something real about your rocks, deep down I didn't believe anything would happen and this is just so much more real and so much more vivid than I'd ever imagined possible. Count me among your enthusiastic fans now!!! Thank you!!!

**Alexander**
**New York**

# Seek The
# Stone of Truth

Hello Laura Lee...

This is Sherry Buskirk from Palm Desert, Calif., I wanted to take this opportunity to say thank you for the nice phone conversation this morning. I'm truly sorry I had to cut it short. I do have many questions (grin) sometimes I do get impatient. You mentioned you liked my story of "finding" the stones, so here it is for you.

On August 19, 2005 while sitting at my desk working on the computer and listening to my Reiki CD (I'm a third-level Reiki practitioner), I had some "whispers" come thru about the "Stone of Truth." Now I was puzzled. I'd never heard of this stone before and I'm a crystal/stone person meaning I love them and they "find" me. I also use them in my Reiki healing sessions. Anyway, since I was at work, I didn't have access to the Internet to do research, so first I called a friend of mine who is very intuitive, and all she could tell me at the moment was that it was Black. That was all she could tune into at the time. Wanting more information and not wanting to wait until I got home, I emailed another friend of mine who is a "domestic goddess." She did some research and sent me the name of the stone and some information from your site. After work, I went to one of the larger bookstores in the area, Barnes & Nobles, and went through all of their crystal/gem books from cover to cover looking for information... to no avail. When I finally made it home that night, I immediately got online and went searching for information about the "Stone of Truth." I was led to your site and I sent you an email asking for more information and product availability. The next day was Saturday. My husband had an appt with his chiropractor who rents space in a new age shop in the next town (Yucca Valley) While there, I felt comfortable enough to ask the owner of the new age shop if she had ever heard of the "Stone of Truth." She gave me a big smile, said she had, but didn't have any information on it to share with me. She kept nodding her head and smiling about it though. After several days had passed and no word came from you, I had a strong urge to call you this morning (Wed) which I did on my break. (Again my domestic goddess friend came to my rescue and looked up the number provided on your website) (grin).... I left a voice mail for you and then you called me back right away. That is my story on finding the Stone of Truth that whispered to me for the first time a few days ago.

I placed my order in the mail and it's winging its way to you now. Now, I have a few other things to tell you if you don't mind. First of all, ever since connecting with you this morning on the phone I've been receiving all kinds of whispery tendrils coming thru. It's difficult for me to write about this as I still have not held the stone in my hands. What I've been getting all day long is that I need to make a big diet change **BEFORE** the stone arrives...I was told to eat almonds, walnuts, and fresh salads and fresh fruit... almost no meat of any kind... which is fine w/ me... the part that bites is when I was told no more cola. I do enjoy my Coke. (grin) Also, its almost as if I can feel the stone's inner fire...which surprises me at this point as its not in my physical presence... almost as if its "glowing." The diet changes are ones that I'm comfortable with...I was just surprised that I need to do this before the stone arrives. The other interesting thing that happened is that all afternoon I've had a "giddy" feeling...the feeling of something wonderful happening and your tummy has butterflies to put it mildly...LOL... there was almost a " sigh" when I put the order in the mailbox this afternoon...It's almost as if the energy of the stone found me first... and wants to bring me in alignment with it instead of the other way around. Oh, and while I was waiting in line to get the money order, I was told "two" — so I amended my original order from one power stone to two. Anyway, its on its way...you should receive it by sat at the latest I would think... hopefully you'll receive it by Friday (grin)

When I was looking further on your website, I came across the part about you being involved in the retro-UFO conference on in the spring. I live fairly close to the area. We were up by the Intergratron a couple of weeks ago... another happy coincidence??(...and I suppose I might as well confess... I'm also a practicing solitary... I find it absolutely "fun" the way things fall into place!)

Many Blessings...

**Sherry B.**
**Palm Desert, California**

*Authors Note: When I called Sherry back, I just happened to be listening to my "Quest of the Dream Warrior" CD by David Arkenstone, and the lyrics that were being sung at the moment she picked up the phone said "If you run from yourself, you will only lose. When you find you are lost, seek the Stone of Truth. I thought that this was more than coincidental....and wouldn't you agree that her guides and guardians are going to the extreme to make sure she has this "magical rock" in her life? It must be VERY important for her!*

# Feel the Rush, Seek the Flush

I have always felt the grounding and inspirational vibrations from minerals and crystals, although I could not for the life of me offer any logical reason why. Creatively, they just help me get in touch with my muses and help me focus my own energies as I write. So when Laura Lee explained the incredible power of Aurauralite and Aulmauracite, I was excited to see and feel them at work. Boy, was I impressed.

Laura Lee identified three initial implants and talked me through the removal process. If you've ever used a Biore strip to clean out the pores on your nose, you might have some idea of just how the process felt. These adhesive-backed strips adhere to your nose, and when they are removed they pull out all kinds of built-up junk. The sensation following that removal is unique – the sensation of yanking impurities from a bodily system is one-of-a-kind. Crank up that intensity 100-fold and you get the feeling I had when these magickal stones went to work on my body.

As the implants were removed it felt as though energy was forming a fountain at the back of my head – the flow through my body was something I had never experienced. It was at once empowering and energizing. It was as though the aspect ratio of my vision changed from full-screen to wide in the blink of an eye. For the next day my body felt as though it was purging negative energy and the needle on my personal fuel tank began a long-awaited climb toward F for the first time in memory.

A day later Laura Lee identified yet another implant, this one lodged at the hypothalamus. The removal process was a bit more involved, but it was nonetheless spectacular. It felt as though there was an energetic fountain showering the inside of my head. The implant, it turns out, was designed to make much of what I do to keep myself healthy and in shape turn counterproductive, and it's removal was as dramatic as watching a light switch from off to on. It prompted yet another energetic purge that felt as though I was floating through a day and a half's worth of work.

The net result was a major shift in the way I feel on a day-to-day basis. I have energy I haven't known since childhood.

More importantly, I have spent the past year coming to grips with type 2 diabetes, and almost overnight my baseline blood sugar level dropped 12 points to a level lower than at any time since I've been on medication.

I guess you can say they literally rocked my world.

Steve C.
Spokane, Washington

# Chapter 3

# Who the Heck is Hal?

## ...And what the Hal is The Cosmic Clean-up Crew?

## (And what on Earth do Walk-Ins and Shove-Ins have to do with it all?)

I guess one of the best ways to introduce you to Hal is to take you to the pages of my web site and also my first book, Kryahgenetics, the Simple Secrets of Human Alchemy. The following is a little background on the book and how some words and phrases were written in "Code." This will give you a little insight into who Hal is, how he came into my life, and why he is also a part of many Indigos' lives.

NOTE: *The first edition was a Limited Edition Manuscript that is now sold out and awaiting a second printing. (If you are interested in getting a copy, contact Mistyc House and you will be put on a list to be notified when the book is published again in late 2006.)*

As you stroll, skip, or dash through the pages of Kryahgenetics, you will find that it has a different **ring** to it, and a totally different style than most of the books you have read. Each chapter is deliberate and purposeful, and if you are aware that it is *circular or spiral in its nature*, you will realize that it builds upon itself. You have to go through the entire revolution and start the cycle over again before you can fully understand it and put all the pieces together.....It is on the second revolution or spiral that you really begin to comprehend its meaning and content. If you get in sync with this book's energy and intent, you will understand the purpose of each concept on each page and that this information is very necessary. It will bring you a heightened awareness of the bigger picture, and thereby empower permanent healing of yourself and others ...no matter what the malfunction is.

There are multitudes of cryptic messages, word plays, and blatant, hard-to-miss truths that you may or may not want to look at. There are even some coded or encrypted messages that are written to activate certain codes in specific people! The literary style and grammar are sure to break all the rules of protocol, so if you have any structure issues, it may be a rough read.....on the other hand, it might be refreshing and amusing. It's your call.

One of the reasons for this lawless, unorthodox presentation is that I have these Esoteric Friends who sometimes re-route **my thoughts** into **their thought tracks**, as they try to put their 2-cents'..... *I mean 5-cents' worth*..... into what I'm doing. They tell me that they foolishly volunteered to do a service project here on Earth, and that they cannot leave until they get the job done, and get it done right! I guess I was part of this volunteer effort too, (or so they tell me), and they've come to help me... so I can help them! (Sometimes their tactics are so goofy and outrageous that I think they must have gotten caught in some cosmic goon gas or something and are missing a few brain cells!) .....But I listen to them anyway and take their advice, and somehow in the end, things always miraculously work out! It absolutely defies all logic to me, but I play along and patronize them anyway....and oddly enough, they have gotten me out of so many hopeless messes that by now I think I'd be a foolish frog **not to trust them!**

They tell me the secret combination that unlocks every lock and exposes the truth has to do with **Love**.....or..... has some kind of joke or humorous element intertwined in it. They say if we would just operate from our hearts and lighten up a bit, we could get this life figured out quicker and laugh ourselves clear through the next dimension!

That's what they tell me anyway, and you know.....I'm starting to believe they're "Right On!"

They go by the code #555, carry a very strong, male vibration and are total Goddess worshipers.....*I mean they really love women!* They have the highest regard, respect, admiration and awe for the feminine ray that I have ever encountered. Having them around is quite an experience, and feels like days of old...they are the epitome of valor and chivalry returned! They seem to be on 24-hour guard, because when I go back and reflect on it, I have to admit they have always been there in some form or another, ready and willing to pitch in and give me a boost.

These 555 guys are a kick to have around and totally entertaining. They say they like to eat popcorn, drink root beer, and watch "The Human Drama." They tell the funniest **and sometimes corniest jokes** I have ever heard. They use a lot of puns, old clichés, and are especially fond of using lines from books, movies, and commercials to get their point across. The results are that they make me laugh while they teach and challenge me.

I have been consciously aware of these **wise guys** hanging out with me since 1993. Throughout the years, I have grown to love and adore them in spite of their "off-the-wall tactics" and bizarre methodologies. I know they have my (and everyone else's) best interest in their heart and they point things out to me I may never have thought of or given any credence

41

to if it weren't explained to me (as only they can do) from their point of reference. They have truly expanded my awareness of this and other Universes.

When I first told one of my former husbands about these friends/advisors and explained to him that they go by the name **HOWELL**, (which could be a play on words for "how well", or howl, or just plain Hal), he got the funniest look on his face. He was really quiet for a moment, and then he said, "Nah, it couldn't be...no.....I'm sure it couldn't be.....nahhh..."

Totally puzzled I asked, "What in the world are you talking about? What's going on?" He looked really uneasy.....got quiet for a few seconds.....and then responded. "Well, there's this Master that has been working with me for a while who is a highly evolved Being, that I have a tremendous regard and respect for. His name is Haltone, or Haltonn or something like that, so nah, I'm sure it couldn't be the same..... one.....You see Haltonn wears these robes and is so sophisticated and serious...so dignified...so stately..... I'm sure it's not the same being."

(He paused for a moment ...and then looked over to the corner of the ceiling, and verbally responded to something.) "What?...What?...Are you serious?"

(By now I'm totally perplexed, he's obviously talking to something or someone I can't see, and I feel like I'm deliberately being left out of the conversation.) "You're the same guy she talks to?... No.....You what?...You had to appear to me that way and say 'Greetings, dear one,' because sometimes I can be a pompous peacock and you thought I wouldn't have given you any credibility or even the time of day if you would have come to me the way you really are?"

(Then he looked at me with a goofy expression on his face, and I could see and feel all his paradigms shifting.) He then said, "Honey, they're the same guy!...I can't believe it, ***it's the same Master.....They tricked me!***"

It was totally a downhill ride from then on. After he got some of his composure back, Hal started telling us jokes and straightening out some misperceptions. We laughed so long and so hard I had tears streaming down my cheeks and fell out of bed twice, literally rolling with laughter. (It felt so great to laugh with that much voltage.....it was *seriously* healing!)

After that, this "fallen Master" went into his HAL puns like: "Go on, do it just for ***the Hal of it!***".....
"Hey Mr. Pompous, why don't you write a book and title it, <u>***The Howl-ing***</u>. I will help you

write it and be your **ghost writer**, it will be **Hal-atious!**".... ."Of course I'm an angel, do you want to see my **Hal-o?**"..... "Come on now, how could you doubt whether or not I'm for real, did you think that I was just some lousy **Hal-ogram** or something?"..... "Yo, stone face...(of course he was addressing my indignant companion), I think you should take me on your next expedition and we can go find the **Hal-y-Grail!**".....and it went on and on and on.

It's been over eight years since that **Hal-arious** night of mega endorphin infusions and sometimes when we got together and Hal started giving unsolicited advice and words of wisdom my resistant male partner didn't particularly want to hear, he'd say, "Go away popcorn breath, I didn't ask for your opinion!".....and I would laugh and think to myself... "Go for it Hal...only you could be so bold and entertaining!"

As you move through the rest of this web site/book, may its Spirit and intent be felt in your heart and may the words and concepts trigger your own memories and the truth of your personal life experiences be revealed, recalled, come alive and make sense. Above all, know that you are in command here. You are the one this site/book was created for and you are the one who decides what to accept or reject.

With that in mind.....*open your mind, let your heart and core be the ushers to show you where, when, and how to move through the darkness and fog. Then perhaps strength, laughter, and warm fuzzies can replace the dread, anxiety, fear and anger of the past and continue into your Forever.*

Do you have the courage and determination to step out of the terrors and nightmares that are so dis-eased and dysfunctional, yet so familiar and comfortable...and move into a new and magical, mystical, enchanting but uncharted reality dream? I for one am going to give it my best shot!!!

*I dedicate these encrypted messages, silent codes, triggering mechanisms and words of encouragement that leap over faith and hope, and ascend into the land of trust...to all of us with the audacity to think that we can individually and collectively make a difference in the outcome of this Existence.*

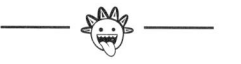

Ok, now that you have been introduced to and initiated in "The ways of Hal", let's move on to the "Cosmic Clean-up Crew". This is a term that I coined (with a little inspiration from Hal) referring to a group of beings who came to this planet in response to an "S.O.S." cry for help from this planet and this Universe. (Apparently there have been some "experiments gone bad" and things got majorly out of hand down here.) These beings from the Cosmic Clean-up Crew have been well-trained in different "Special Forces Academies" (so to speak) from diverse parts of the cosmos. They are very strong, intelligent, psychic and capable of getting things cleaned up down here. To illustrate a little better how this "C.C.C." operates, I will once again take you to a chapter in <u>Kryahgenetics</u> entitled **"Walk-Ins & Shove-Ins"**

# *Walk-Ins & Shove-Ins*

We are in a new experiment now, with never before tried variables, which by the way, many of these new variables are a direct result of the Montauk Project. **NOTE: *If you would like information on that project, I would recommend the books on Montauk by Preston Nicholes and Peter Moon as a good start. Even if you don't agree with everything they conclude, there is enough physical evidence and documentation that will help you get a good background on the extensiveness of this project and how it affects every one of us.*** We have more inter-dimensional activities and surprises than ever before. The rips in our time-space continuum have allowed people, places, and *things* to drift in, merge in, and sometimes collide into our realities. *Many of which we may not even be consciously aware of..... and many of them may not be aware that they are here either!* Some have methodically and purposefully moved in, while others are purely accidental.

It used to be, in *the good old days* of metaphysics, that every once in a while you would run into a true, honest-to-goodness **walk-in**. I mean, an undeniable one, with heavy physical and non-physical evidence to back it!

(Very different than the "Wanna-be's" .....you know, the ones who don't have a life of their own so they create one. The ones who always have a crisis and thrive on sensationalism. The ones who constantly go to the extreme, and the things in their life are always **Bigger & Better** (*or badder*) than anyone else's? The ones who really need to "Get A Life?" Yes it seems that there's always a Wanna-Be, "Playing in a theater near you!")

These genuine Walk-Ins, for the most part, were pretty well grounded. They had a mission to do, and were extremely well qualified to do it. They knew who they were, and didn't need or really care for your approval or acknowledgment of who and what they were.

Yes, they were "odd ducks" for sure, in a society pond of co-dependant, dysfunctional humans, desperate to be "needed and praised." These beings did, *and still are*, making their mark on this planet. They trigger a change in the consciousness grid, and expand awareness by breaking Morpha-Genetic Fields.

(Breaking Morpha-Genetic Fields, or M-Fields is simply, *or not so simply*, doing something or proving something that had heretofore never been done or believed *could* be done. An example of this is; it used to be commonly known and accepted that no one could run a mile in 4 minutes, it was considered an impossibility.....till someone had the audacity to go beyond those borders, and did it! *The current world record is now 3:43.13set in 1999.* That action broke through a reality grid, changing the consciousness field and expanding the options. Hence, many others followed the lead and continued to do what was previously deemed impossible.)

The rules of protocol in a Walk-In situation used to be that an agreement or contract was made prior to the *Resident Being's* birth. Then, at a certain place and time, the switch-a-roo took place. This could occur during the trauma of an auto accident, knocking the resident *unconscious*, or even a simple blow to the head. It could take place while being put under general anesthetic for a surgery, or while having a near-death experience. During this period of *unconsciousness*, the switch was made and the being *originally* in the body handed it over to the *walk-in* to complete a mission, and thus honoring the pre-arranged contract.

Understand that this is not a haphazard procedure. Much thought and calibration go into this switch. The *original* being usually has a new assignment waiting, you know, more karma to work out, or, if they have completed a certain level of evolution, then they get to take a spring break and go to the cosmic Bahamas before taking on a new evolutionary spiral. (See Kryahgenetics for a detailed explanation of earth beings and evolutionary spirals)

Whatever the case, be assured that under these circumstances there is a total willingness on the part of the original resident. *"I'll go to earth, grow up a body, work out a few karmic debts, and then you can take over without taking the time to grow-up a body too."* It's simple...well, sort of.....sort of not.....because behind the scenes there are genetics and environment to consider. The information and coding, even though *pre-calculated*, could get some glitches in the system, fractures that need to be fixed, illnesses to clean up, emotional mutations that need adjusting.....life isn't easy for a new Walk-In!

Think back on people you have known and see if you can detect a possible walk-in in your life. Have you ever known someone who had one of those *accidents* explained earlier, and when you saw them again, they had a totally different personality? Maybe they were self-centered and used their time and money on selfish, irresponsible things, and then after a "knock-out" event, they suddenly became a great humanitarian and redirected their time and energies into things like *solving personal, local, and world problems?* Maybe you knew someone who, after being "put-out," began to display new talents, and had totally different interests? Think and ponder on this, maybe you yourself have a close encounter with a *Walk-In!!!*

Another dynamic of a walk-in is that they can have amnesia, and then slowly get their memory triggered of who they really are, and have vivid memories and scientific evidences of things they had no interest in, or reference to before. They may suddenly, *over a short amount of time,* get knowledge of biochemistry, astronomy, physics, alchemy, and history..... not only of this planet, but also of other star systems without ever having studied or been involved with these subjects. They may also become aware of such things as what their cosmic origins are, what their specialties are, and what their purpose is here and now, *which, by the way, may or may not have been in alignment with the agendas of the "walk-out!"*

There are many different circumstances, goals, and modalities in the land of walk-ins, so it's difficult to give any structured profile. There is though, one thing they all have in common. When they take on their new genetic coding, life's circumstances, relationships, soul memory imprints and data, they always maintain their own original resonance frequencies.....their personal signature so to speak. This is infiltrated and factored into everything that was already there, and most likely takes dominance, even though there is a blending and merging with the original blueprints. There is a custom remodeling project going on, and as in all remodeling jobs, depending on the extensiveness of the project, *even if it's only a paint job,* you can tell that the house just doesn't *look or feel* the same. Maybe you can't identify right off what is different, but you know it has changed. So it is with a walk-in, they just don't look or *feel* the same anymore.

And thus it was, in days gone by, this was a very methodical and structured process. Ahhhhh..... "Those were the days."

**AND NOW THE SCENE CHANGES.**

ENTER BACK STAGE: **A new breed of villains** in our exciting and sometimes not-so-*mellow* Earth drama .....*The Earth Time/Space Bandits..... (and they are breaking all the rules and codes of ethics!)* Yes, every good *Melodrama* has to have one or two...And our 3-D drama certainly has more than it's fair share, and **these** villains..... **they're absolutely ruthless!**

They are tearing up the town. They have no respect or regard for anyone or anything, and give no thought to the consequences or outcome of their actions. They're just here, **"For The Hell of it!"** They are the Sneaky Snakes that think power comes from what you can do, and make.....or rather MANIPULATE..... with technology. They are power hungry little devils and will stop at nothing in their quest to become the BIGGEST, BADDEST, MEANEST, TOUGHEST, **RICHEST "GANGSTAS"** ON EARTH!

In their hunger and thirst for ultimate supreme power, their perceptions got distorted and perverted. In their fractured insanity, they began usurping, *or at least trying to usurp*, the feminine powers.....the sacred creative essence of the God-dess.....the Life Force that can only be created by the Feminine Ray.

In their foolishness, they believe that their technological power can reign supreme by overthrowing the very power and essence that created them, their Spirit, their being.....And the whole of the Universe!

This insane gesture is raising havoc not only in this sector of Time/Space, but is rippling into other areas of this and other Universes as well! (Not to mention the inter-dimensional rips and pollution it's causing.)

WHAT A HELL-UV-A MESS!!!......*or maybe it's so backwards it's a mell-uv-a hess?!!* What to do...What to do. There must be a Hero somewhere in this drama.....maybe we should put out a cry for help!?

**"HELP!  HELP!  SOMBODY SAVE US FROM THESE VILLAINS!!!"**

*(WHOOSH..... Enter our heroes...THE COSMIC CLEAN UP CREW. You know the ones..... "It's a dirty job but somebody's got to do it" crew?)* And their wages? Well, you couldn't pay them enough.....So .....I guess then you'd call it, **"Volunteer Work."** And their reward? They do it out of **love and devotion to the God-Dess!**

So here's the situation.  We have individuals and groups with some *serious* technology, who decide that they don't like our history ...it doesn't serve them.  So.....they take it upon themselves to change it.....go back and do some editing on this movie and **POOF!** A whole new history outcome and dimension is formed. (Have you ever been totally fascinated with the subject of time-travel, and absolutely enthralled with time-travel movies and multidimensional movies like *Sliders?*  Well, maybe there's a reason!?)

Basically folks, we're at critical mass here.  Because of all the holes, rips, ripples bleeding, and crossing of currents, what happens next is a *crapshoot!*  We have created a whole new element in this free-will zone that hasn't happened before, and that element is; **Any *one* and any *thing* CAN and DOES hack into this time /space/dimension, and as a result, things and beings and entities that have no business here, and theoretically shouldn't be here ...BUT THEY ARE SHOWING UP!!!**

I can see it all now; front row seats are a hot item this season in all the cosmic ticket outlets to view and *bet on* the outrageous events and conclusion of this earth game!  The cosmic bookies, refreshment-stand operators, and of course T-shirt & future memorabilia vendors, are all there cashing in on the last episodes to the live drama of the *Great Planet Earth Experiment!*  Beings from the farthest corners of space, taking off work, *or calling in sick* so they can come and witness first hand these **Earth-Shaking** events.  The stakes are high, anxiety even higher, and Planet Hollywood is there vying for exclusive movie rights .....this is sure to be a classic legendary blockbuster!

Now, back to our walk-ins/shove-ins saga. The rules and regulations have changed considerably and to put it bluntly, most of the rules and regulations have become extinct due to the lawlessness of "The Out Law" Gangstas.

The order and methodology of walk-ins and walk-outs is history, and now we have a new *Bully* type of situation that makes you take a microscopic look at our previous perceptions and the fine lines of "Free Will." Because of the irresponsible and many times unethical experiments at Montauk. We have a brand-new, never-been-tried before, reality game.....Or maybe it's better to say "**UN**reality Game."

What used to be an *orderly* process of walking in and walking out, has now become a process of *pure chaos!* What is happening now with the Gangstas, Outlaws and Bullies, is that at any **time,** any *where*, someone opens themselves up, even if its only a crack, and these bullies weasel their foot in the crack and expand its opening.....then with a *push or shove*, they evict the surprised and unaware resident being, and set up shop in their body!

Sometimes the original being is still attached and comes in but keeps getting kicked out again, or just "hangs out" watching and waiting for a chance to get permanently back in again! Other times they are shoved out with such force that they no longer have their attachment cord plugged into their body. In this case, they either hang around and follow the body, trying to devise a strategy to reclaim their turf or maybe give out an **"S.O.S."** for some assistance to get back in again. Sometimes they get so disgusted with what's happening with their anatomy and how it's operating *with a new boss,* that they say "to heck with it all, I don't have to put up with this." They'll turn around, walk away from their body altogether, and go find another game to play somewhere else.

If you are ever involved with a shove-in situation, you can be assured that it wasn't instigated or directed by a Light Keeper! (**Note:** *See chapter on Light Keepers and Light Distracters in* <u>*Kryahgenetics.*</u>) But don't think for a minute that you are powerless to do anything about it, no-sir-ree. There are a multitude of things that can be done to get not only reinstated, but also reinforced!

The first item of business here is to recognize that there is something ab**soul**utely not right here. You see all the telltale signs that point to an entirely new being in-bodying this body.

Don't let your love and compassion for the original resident being cloud your perception. If what used to seem as "just a phase" turns into a totally new personality with a new unfamiliar resonance, you could be dealing with a **shove-in**.

At this point, it is extremely important for you to get very clear and *neutral*. Separate your *self* from the illusions of *the body* and tune into the original resident being and their Higher Self.....*wherever it may be*. Make sure you feel the connection and guidance of your Higher Self and any other back-up support from other spiritual beings you are in alliance with that you ascertain could be of value and assistance to you in this matter.

Then go *directly* to this person's Higher Self to establish what *their* will and desired outcome is before you make any moves to assist them. **Remember,** *your will* may not necessarily be *their will*. Perhaps they are allowing it for a while to get some education.

When you are in this clean neutral space, you will be instructed how best to assist. Each case is different, and must be handled as a custom designed program. Maybe all you will need to do is **firmly** affirm their position as the resident being. It is very feasible that you can **out-create** and **un-create** a situation by putting a strong consciousness grid into the person's body and energy fields that "the big bully butt-insky does not exist in your reality or in the reality of the original being."

Yeah, this will probably most likely tick the bully off and they will rant and rave and pull ugly faces and make all kinds of threats. They'll try anything to get your attention and your agreement that they DO exist, and are the supreme force here...the **biggest bully you've ever met!** What they are ultimately trying to do is trick you into reinforcing their existence, their supremacy, and **your powerlessness!**

So if you just calmly and firmly maintain your position of deep peace and continue to affirm their non-existence, pretty soon their power and their butt-in position begins to dissipate like water in a hot frying pan. Turning on the heat makes the water leave the frying pan, change its position and its form. **Get the picture here?**

I personally have had some background and experience with this method. It wasn't easy at first, and I had my moments of questioning my capabilities and my sanity as I was dealing with one of the biggest, raunchiest, foulest, most vicious and aggressive scoundrels in the Universe.....and **IT** knew it.....and **IT** knew that I knew it!

What I attribute my success to was my consistent persistence in the matter. (Now this doesn't mean that I didn't get psychically beat up a few times and was left with a few physical and psychic bruises, but I was a determined little beaver! I would just continue to "ruthlessly and relentlessly" maintain my position of deep peace and also solidly maintain my own ability to create and un-create. I guess you could say that what I did was, "invalidate the **hell** out of **it!**) Pretty soon this bully started to loosen its grip, weaken its stronghold and gradually lost its power and position **in my reality.**

I have found that this method also works extremely well if you ever find yourself in a position of being put-out, or shoved-out. Never underestimate your power to create.

One more little hint when it comes to the fear factor... I picked this one up from one of our greatest teachers, our kids: One day several years ago one of my sons who was about six at the time, said to me, "Mom, you know what? ...*A ghost can't scare you if you're not afraid of it.*" I laughed and said, "*You know, you are absolutely right, a ghost* **can't** *scare you if you're not afraid of it..... And neither can a monster or a boogieman!*" (What would we ever do without the wisdom of innocence?)

At this time and space/place in this adventure game it is imperative that you maintain command and total ownership of your life on a constant basis. You must stay alert and not fall prey to victimdom. You must maintain your partnership, connection, and be in total alignment with the direction, wisdom, and advice of your Higher Self...your God or Goddess self. This is mandatory at this time when the strong control and absorb the weak.

All the reading, studying, meditating, philosophizing, practicing.....well guess what kids, it's *Show Time!*....And if you can't remember your lines, you'd better be able to hear or read the lips of your prompter (Higher Self.) In addition to this the script gets changed on a daily basis, so it would be way advantageous if you were a darned good *ad-libber*, 'cause other cast members are forgetting their lines, and this *Play* we're in could easily turn into a *Bad Dream* if we don't pay attention to what's going on around us, and what the other cast members are doing.

"Arrrrrrrgh, tha pirates ur a-scammin' tha seas maitees, so yu'd best be-a watchin' un a-takin' charge uv tha wheel.....ya hav ta be tha capt'n uv yer own ship now!

So yu'd best be-a qualifi'n yur shipmates un' don't let any skalley-wags aboard, kuz ya kan't afford any typ uv mutnee heer, now can ya?!!!!

If ya do, ya may find ye'rself a-blindfolded un' a-wawk'n tha plank on yur own ship...un' that wuud be a reel shame now wuudn't it Maitees!"

One qualification that is imperative now as you are taking charge of the wheel and steering through these uncharted waters is the ability to rise above it all in a moment's notice and take an uninvolved, unaffected bird's-eye view of your situation. Looks can be deceiving and you never know if the little floaty up ahead could actually be an iceberg! We don't always know what's "underneath the surface."

How many times do we experience something and automatically assume that we "know it all" and jump to a conclusion that is totally inappropriate and inaccurate, or observe someone else who is heavily involved in this *limited perception drama game?* This seems to occur most often when someone is activating our triggers and pushing our instant-reflex defense buttons and we are unwilling to see that we might not have all the pieces to the picture yet. Most often it's the people closest to us, i.e. our spouses, our kids, our parents, our co-workers that activate this **reaction game.**

Imagine yourself in this specific scenario. You are in a hurry to get to a meditation or a "W.S." (Weird Sh*t) meeting. You're in rush hour traffic in Phoenix AZ. It's hotter than "Hal" because it's the middle of August, AND YOUR AIR CONDITIONER JUST WENT OUT! If that weren't enough, there are lots of out-of-state tourists on the road who don't know free-ways or where they are going, and road rage is running amuck. (Get the picture?)

We can get so wrapped up and entangled in the emotions of it all that we delete all common sense and our ability to *respond* because we are so involved in *reacting.*

And what about when we, or someone else in our drama game has made a serious boo-boo because they didn't get all the facts? They may put something into motion that causes a lot of damage, hurts a lot of feelings, and creates a lot of harm that could have been avoided all together if some calmness and clarity would have been the first defense.

In case you haven't read between the lines yet, and you're still wondering and worrying about whether or not you're a candidate for a shove-in take over, I'll fill in some of the blanks for you. It is next to impossible for these hoodlums to gain access to you when you're in a state of: Joy, calm focus, deep peace, love, compassion, happiness, laughter, bliss, and self-confidence...NOT ARROGANCE! .....*That one rings a cosmic bell that says "come on in, this one's ripe 'n ready!"* Also, when you become solid in maintaining a strong personal relationship and alliance of love, communication, and camaraderie with your higher self .....this becomes a "Total-Coverage Insurance Policy!"

Some of the emotional states that attract a shove in are: Hate, Revenge, Jealousy, Rage, Resentment, Self Pity, and prolonged hostility and grief.

*Now this does not mean that shedding a few tears now and then will put you in jeopardy! Expressing sadness and grief at appropriate times is an important part of being human and being in sync with your emotional expressions. This is healthy and encouraged!*

I'm talking about the day after day gloomy grief that puts a dark cloud around you and those you live with.

And the anger? .....well, again, *little spouts and steam blowers every once in a while keep your nerves from fraying. Sometimes we need to get angry to cause change and let those around us know we're serious about boundaries!*

No, the anger we're talking about here is the constant and habitual kind where everyone and everything makes you angry.....and of course, someone or something outside of yourself is blamed. They have everyone and everything, tried, convicted and punished over and over! I'm talking here about habitual anger, or a prolonged state of intense anger. These are the states that put you at risk!

So many times it's the little things that rile us up and "disturb the peace" and change the energy of the dream into a nightmare!

If your favorite exercise is jumping to conclusions and your head's temperature tends to be *hot* rather then *cool*, remember again folks, It's show time, and it's time to put into action every thing we've studied and learned.

I know, it looks so good on paper, and feels so good to listen to tapes and discuss the benefits of all the different spiritual philosophies.  Whether it's Metaphysical, Eastern, Native American, Old age, New Age, New Wave, or what ever you want to call it, all of this information is so important, **yet absolutely useless if there is no application and action behind it.**

So the next time you start to get irritated and letting your fir stand on end, take a breath and allow the *passion for the reaction and anger* to pass through and be filtered *by your heart.* What will happen next is pure magic.  Either you will change your perception and disengage the energy of anger and conflict, or you will take a firm and commanding but calm stance with clarity that will bring truth and justice to the surface.

The ironic thing is....This may come **soul**-ly from your being able to hold the place/space for *deep peace and truth* to manifest!

"Haarrrrrrrrr,  Maitees,  heer me now, un' listen ta me words ya lads and lasses.  Yu'r travlin' thru sum strange waters heer un' th'r infested with sharkfish, un' snakes, un' crocodiles, un' pirates, un' all sorts a riff raff ya might never a-seen bee-for.  An maybe tha rules ta tha pirates game changes daily, an ya thinks thur's noth'n thut stays tha  same!

Remember yur just in a hologram for sum action pack't consolidated learn'n heer......un ya really can't get yurself hurt *cuz ya can't hurt-a Spirit!*

Arrrrrrrrgh Un' yu'r never alone, yu'v always go sum one a-wach'n out fer ya... an yur never inta a fix that-cha don't have tha wits ta get yer selv out uv!!!

So lets be a takin' off yur kufflinks un' a-roll'n up yur sleeves, un' see how well ya cun maneuver in thees heer challeng'n waves.....un' let's maken' dis tha best life yu'v ever had!

Ye'r tha dreamer heer Maitee, it's all upta yu now!!!!

.....Arrrrrrrrrgh"

# Chapter 4

# Indigo or Indigo BRAT!

Being a **First Wave Indigo** does NOT mean you have it in the bag, are "practically perfect in every way" and could lift off for ascension at any moment.

Many people have this grandiose, distorted image of Indigos. They see them as wondrous saviors coming to this planet with all their super powers and tremendous elevated spiritual awareness. They think that Indigos (like Christ) have come here to save them! This is simply not how it works. Indigos, like Christ, can only show you how to save yourself, and are not here to do it for you. I find that many First Wave's and Indigos are very repulsed at being labeled, and are quite annoyed with people's misperceptions of being their "Savior." They just want to figure out who they are, what they came here to do, and then develop/activate themselves so they can accomplish what they committed to do, to the best of their abilities.

As soon as the pressure is put on them to perform or if they are expected to accomplish someone else's demands on them, these beings want to shut down, clam up, and (or) retreat..... (much like how many of them respond to school pressure and authority). It is their nature. Because of their innate ability to tap into internal truth, they figure if it is not **Their Idea, Their Intent, Their Way,** then it has very little value or importance, and they will shut down, retreat, or rebel.

What I am about to tell you may come as a shock to many reading this, but there are numerous First Wave Indigos here that are very challenged by planet Earth and don't give a hoot what happens to them or anyone else. There are some who also have one foot firmly planted in Light, and the other foot firmly planted in the Dark (Ego) realms. Then there are some First Wave's and Indigos who even have BOTH feet planted firmly in the Dark (Ego) realms! All is not the fairy tale picture many have envisioned..... because much of what is written about Indigos only has one aspect of the whole "Indigo Picture."

With this information behind you, you can now understand why it would be naive to think every Indigo on this planet is here serving the Light and working hard to bring about balance and justice. There are Indigos who are spending time on "the other" team, and raising all sorts of needless and senseless chaos! The good news is (at least from the information that Hal has given me) that only about 25% of the First Wave Indigos on this planet are using their talents and powers to serve the tyranny agenda which is trying to take over this planet. It is my belief that of these 25%, there is at least 50-75% of them that can change their alliances and be converted back to their origins of Love, Illumination, Truth and Harmony. *(At the time of the printing of this book, only about 20% of the First Wave's and Indigos on this planet have awakened sufficiently to activate their true potentials, are focused and in hot pursuit of their missions here, and have their Altered Egos in check.)*

As I said before, there is a great deal of revernce and awe from people who think that just because someone is "Indigo," they have it all together and are some sort of Savior or God who should be bowed down to and worshiped. This puts much stress and anxiety on Indigos and makes them want to revolt. The truth is, Indigos have more than their share of dysfunction to work through and until they awaken and get themselves cleaned up, they can be extremely dysfunctional and messed up internally. Until Indigos get their Altered Ego released, they can actually play into the hands of *light distracters and light destroyers* and cause upset and discord for those in their environment. (See Kryahgenetics, the Simple Secrets of Human Alchemy by Laura Lee Mistycah, for more information on Light Distracters and Light Destroyers.)

It concerns me when I see or hear people buying into the idea that in order to properly raise an Indigo, and now especially with the younger Crystal children, that you should allow them to do as they please, all the time... thinking that they are "The chosen ones" and know best. I believe that this can be a dangerous thing and is fostering the prospects of creating what I call an "Indigo Brat!" (....which could easily turn into a future "Dark Lord!")

I have heard stories of parents who are raising their young Indigos and Crystal children with no limits or boundaries. They allow and even promote these children to always decide what THEY want to do, when they want to do it, and how they want to do it with no perameters. These kids then start dictating how the rest of the family operates with no concern or regard to others needs or wants. One mother waited nearly an hour for her little tyrant to decide to put on her shoes to go home from a friend's house late at night while her little baby sister was crying and fussing because she was tired and wanted to go to bed. The mother just kept saying... "Now honey, please go get your shoes on so we can go" as she was wrestling with a sleepy, cranky, infant. The little Indigo brat just kept playing with the Lego's, totally ignoring her mother. This kept up with the baby howling and the little tyrant doing exactly as she pleased with no regard to how her behavior was affecting those around her. In fact, she totally enjoyed the power she was given to NOT do as she was asked! Everyone in the house was getting really annoyed at the mother, and also at the father, for just standing there and not taking charge of the situation. Finally one of the hosts took the child, put her shoes and coat on, and helped escort the entire family out the door!

The disrespect got worse. This little tyrant would come over to her mother's friend's house and play with crystals and other fragile objects and ceremonial pieces from a sacred alter in a room that was off limits to children. She would also tyrannize other children that came to this house. When the hosts reprimanded the little girl, the mother got her feathers ruffled and said that if her children were not allowed to be free to express themselves in their home without getting reprimanded for it, then she would not be coming over any more. The host was secretly relieved and thought this was a blessing... and the friendship was never the same.

This story is typical of how some parents raise their Crystal children. They think that from what they have read, you should parent Crystals with no boundaries or restrictions, letting them "choose" when, where, and how things go down. I believe that the mother in the previous story truly believed that she was doing a grand job because she had so much patience and was so allowing.

Now, that doesn't mean that you can't give Indigo children options: "Do you want to brush your teeth now or wash your face first?" ... "Do you want to clean up your room or the play room first?" "Do you want to read before you go to bed or play with your erector set?" OOOPS..... Sorry.....These are the options you would give "normal children". For Indigos it would be more like, "Do you want to play with the fairies in the back yard or stay in and draw unicorns and gargoyles with your new crayons?" "Do you want to watch your Harry Potter video, or make a magick wand?" "Do you want to get out of bed and turn your night light off when your done reading, or stay in bed and practice using the powers of your mind to do it?"

Parenting Indigos requires a balance between logic and inspiration. There may be no hard and fast rules for every situation. You just have to be flexible and try to guide your Indigo in a direction that will have the best possible outcome.

My second son has always been a night owl. When he was three years old, many times I would get up to in the middle of the night to go to the bathroom and find the light on in the boys bedroom. There he sat, bright eyed and bushy tailed, playing with his toys. At first I was annoyed at this and would put him back into bed and turn the lights off. This went on and on until I finally decided that it wasn't a bad thing if there were some ground rules that were kept. "You DON'T wake up your brother, You only turn on the little lamp instead of the overhead light, You DON"T pour yourself milk from the gallon jug, and you DON'T go outside!" I got some remarks from friends and family who thought that children should be in bed by 7:30 or 8:00, but I figured that as long as he kept up his part of the bargain and didn't disturb anyone or get into things, it would be ok for everyone involved...and hoped it wasn't causing any psychological damage from sleep deprivation. I soon found that after an hour or two, he would turn the lights back off and climb into bed. (His capacity to stay awake at night and be creative turned out to be quite positive and useful in later years when he went to school full time, worked full-time as a waiter, and then had to go home at night and do homework for college. His ability to get up in the middle of the night with creative energy and focus, using short naps to regenerate, enabled him to adapt and get better grades!)

It is important to be able to follow your gut and know when to allow, and when to draw the boundary lines. I have a friend whose Indigo daughter constantly caused immense amounts of strife and conflict in her family. The child has her mother in a chronic fear mode as she tirades over the house and her younger Indigo brother with the style and power of a seasoned Dark Lord! Her mother is extremely frightened of her and is always trying to handle her with "kindness and love" and never raises her voice. This modality of parenting actually backfired because the child grew up with no boundaries or consequences. As a result the mother is being totally controlled and "whipped" by this young woman who is now in her late teens. This girl has some incredible psychic abilities, and has done some really despicable things with them. She now uses her abilities and powers to manipulate, control, and bring terror and chaos wherever she goes. She uses her manipulative powers, and temper tantrums, to get her way at any cost. She has a total disrespect for and despised any one or anything that she perceives to be an authority figure or.....any one telling her what to do. On the other hand, she also has an equal amount of despise and revulsion for those she considers "Underlings" (which would be most of the people she knows!) She even went as far as lighting the attic on fire, which quickly spread to the upper level of the house, causing some serious destruction and smoke damage to the rest of the house. Later she bragged about doing it on purpose to prove that there are no limits as to what she is capable of. She had her mother and younger

Indigo brother terrified, just the way she wanted it.  This is one situation where I believe that "Tough Love" would have been a better parenting skill for the mother to use from Day One.  Remember, Tough Love is still Love!

Now, on the opposite end of the scale, here is a true story of what I call a little "Power Crystal/Indigo."

I was at a health fair a few years ago and the woman in the booth next to me had this beautiful, amazing little girl.  She was 3 1/2, going on 43!  I had never seen anything like her!  She was kind, considerate, loving, gentle and very inquisitive.  She came over to my booth, and said "May I please look at your necklaces?" (So much respect and reverence for a child so young!)  I said "Certainly", and showed her some of the Aulmauracite Rocks too, letting her hold them, and told her how the Aurauralite pendants work.  After spending some time with her, I was inspired to "gift" her with a black cord pendant.  As she held it in her hand, she looked at it with sheer wonderment and delight!  She took the scroll I gave her, and all the information plus the "Aurauralite" story and scampered over to show her mother.....(who was sort of embarrassed that her child had made me feel obligated to give her one, but I assured the mother that I felt it was important that this gift was given.)  Then the little Indigo said with anticipation, "Mommy, will you please read this story to me?"  Her mother agreed, but first had to finish helping some people who were buying things she had on her table display.  After the crowds had dispersed, the mother picked up the little girl and sat her on her lap.  As she read the story, the little Indigo was comprehending and absorbing every word!  I was joyfully amazed and shocked at the aptitude and attention span of this little cutie pie!

The mother later told me of how she doesn't know where her daughter gets her information, but is constantly teaching her things.  One day the little girl was watching a cartoon about Gargoyles, and the mother said, "Honey, why don't you turn that off or change the channel.  Those are such ugly things.  I don't want you to get frightened."  The little master replied, "Oh, mommy, noooo, you don't understand, Gargoyles are wonderful, and very kind.  They are protectors and also my friends!" (Her mother had no idea that there was such a kingdom as the Gargoyle Realms, and still to this day I don't think she gives it any validity, since she is a very devout Christian, but honored that her little girl was not afraid and allowed her to keep watching. This incident actually helped the mother see a little better that, just because something looks ugly and different, doesn't mean it is scary and evil.)

Later on that day, I was doing some deep tissue body work on a man who was not inhibited to use tones and moans for letting go of stresses and energy while I was working on him. As he was vocalizing his release of energies, we were getting the attention of everyone around. The little girl looked over at us and was taking it all in. Finally she came over and stood right in front of him and said, "Is she hurting you?" We were both amused at her tenacity, and it was hard not to laugh. He said to her, "No honey, I'm just releasing energy this way." I then explained to her what I was doing and why he was moaning. I told her that this man was actually an old acquaintance of mine; his name was Jalinka, but we called him Link for short. She then, with all the grace of a queen, put her little palms together with her fingertips touching her chin. She closed her pretty eyes, and bowed... keeping her hands in place under her chin and said in a melodic voice, "Very happy to meet you Jalinka."

We were both floored! Her articulation was perfect! I have never, ever seen such respectful grace and charm as this little girl demonstrated, not even in adults! I later asked her mother if she taught her to bow like that when she met people, and she said, "No, actually, this is the first time I've ever seen her do this."

This tenacious, but charismatic little Indigo is a grand example of how young Indigos and Crystals can conduct themselves with grace and with style, enchanting all they come in contact with. The key is that they need the proper balance of love, respect, and boundaries in parenting. Part of the balance being to explain things they question, and also to command respect.

When they were getting ready to pack up their booth at night, the little girl was getting tired, and a little spunky, and said, "I want to go home now," and started heading toward the door. The mother firmly brought her back and told her to put her things in the box and to help her grandma get packed up. This was all it took and the little girl got busy helping her mother and grandmother get ready to go. I was happy to see this little incident for two reasons:

1- To know that the little girl could be headstrong and try to get her way, and

2- That her mother didn't let her pull a tantrum and knew how to set the perameters of acceptable behavior, doing it with firmness and love.

Since a large portion of First Wave Indigos are now having children, with a high percentage of them Indigo-Crystal children, it is important, now more than ever, to realize that balance must be in place for a healthy upbringing. If you go inside and follow your inner guidance or "gut" feelings, you will be more likely to raise these children in the way they require, instead of following the "rules" of our society. The trick is, to not allow ego or social consciousness to be a factor in your decisions and interactions with Indigos. If more people start doing this, the acceleration rate of Indigos awakening to their true nature will increase, and the planet will in turn raise its vibration to a new paradigm...one of Freedom, Justice, Truth and Enlightenment.

I for one, am looking forward to this, and like any paradigm shift, there is usually a lot of shaking and chaos that ensues while the Dark Lords of the past try desperately to maintain their turf.....but with Indigos waking up and balancing their powers with love and awareness of "Unity," the Dark Forces don't have a chance. It is only time that is between us and this new world. I have seen it... others have seen it...and when YOU see it, the shift will occur even quicker and with more ease.

May the love and power of all the Gods/ Goddesses of the Universes be with YOU always, and may we all join forces to bring Love, Light, and Laughter to our new realms.

So Be It!

## Chapter 5

# The Kryahgenetics Egg

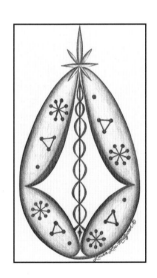

Some people will look at this Kryahgenetics symbol and think it's nothing more than an Easter egg or Christmas ornament, and then go on about their business, never giving it another thought. For them and their reality, it will seem quite meaningless.

Then there are those of you who have an innate awareness and understanding of things you have never consciously seen or heard before..... who can figure out symbolic encryption and language not only by the way it looks, but also by the way it feels. For you, the geometric shapes, tones and resonances that are emitted from this patterned image will have deep, ancient and perhaps even exclusive meaning and value to you from the moment you lay your eyes on it.

I would request of you now, to ponder as you study this piece of cosmic art/language, and ask yourself what messages are here for everyone, and what private communications it may have for you personally.

**NOTE:** *The above is an Excerpt taken from the book, "Kryahgenetics, the Simple Secrets of Human Alchemy", now in its second printing.*

When I first drew this symbol, I thought I was just mindlessly "doodling." Then I started getting intrigued with this piece of art I was creating as it seemed to just flow and it made me feel all warm and fuzzy inside. I kept picking it up and perfecting it because it just seemed like the thing to do.....but at that time, I still had no idea it was actually being channeled to me.....right down to the precise placement of each dot and symbol on the outer edge! I had no clue (and still may not have a clue) as to what a powerful, magical, interdimensional geometry I had just created!

I'm not even quite sure how it happened, but I started using it for a meditation device because it sort of looked and felt like some kind of Merkaba, and it expanded from there. At first I just gazed at it and got inspiration and information. Then I got the bright idea to imagine I was in the center of this egg, visualizing the DNA helix running through the core of my body... with the star at my crown, and the diamond at my base. This in itself was a wonderful experience, and I felt really safe and secure inside.  As I worked with this incredible geometry, sometimes the size would change, sometimes the color and texture would change, sometimes it would pulse, sometimes music would emanate, and sometimes it would spin... (but I never got dizzy!)  I was really intrigued at all the many different things I could experience when I was in my egg.  Then one day when it was spinning, I found that it was sucking out all the stresses and psychic debris that were imbedded in my body and auric fields!  Wowwww, what a rush!  I felt so light, calm and clean!

Well, one thing led to another and I soon found that the egg didn't have to spin.  It could suck out the debris from the DNA core just by giving it the command.  I could simply take a few deep breaths and then ask it to "turn on" and all the debris would get vacuumed out of me and stick to the shell, where it was instantly neutralized.  I was amazed.  It was as if the shell of the egg was filled with Aurauralite/Aulmauracite!  It had many of the very same qualities.  I found that when I was in my egg, I could get more clarity and it felt like the truth surfaced quicker, just like when using my Aurauralite pendant or Aulmauracite rocks.

I started experimenting with my clients using this egg, and found it extremely beneficial to begin a psychic reading or counseling session with an "egg meditation" first.  This internal and energy field vacuuming worked wonders.  It also kept the energy very stable when I had my clients stay in the egg for the entire session.  I discovered that being in this egg, helped to keep "undesirable" energy out.  I soon found that it could also be used as a "protective coating" when ever I thought I'd be in a place or space that might be surrounded by a lot of negative EMF/ ELF waves, or negative thought forms.  Well, this evolved too, and I found it was an invaluable tool when I suspected I was under the influence of:  psychic assault, radionic projections, H.A.A.R.P. (High Frequency Active Auroral Research Program), G.W.E.N. (Ground-Wave Emergency Network), & EMF / ELF (Electro-Magnetic Fields /Extremely Low Frequency) waves, or even spells and curses!  It was a place of refuge for me while trying to get some clarity on the situation and devise a plan of action.

I was amazed at how effective of a "protective coating" this was and how instant the results were.  I found though, that it only lasted about 24 hours, so I decided that in order to ensure no time elapsed without egg protection, I would put one over my body every morning when I woke up, and every night when I went to bed.  When I was cognizant enough to remember to put the eggs up, it seemed to cover the bases pretty darned good.....until about a year and a half ago.

I was under some brutal, extreme psychic assault via several different sources at once.....(similar to a class action law suit, like whoever it was that was behind this assault, collaborated with myriads of others to make their diabolical assaults more forceful, more potent, more encompassing and ultimately more debilitating.) It seemed that when I would put an egg up, 10-15 minutes later I would feel the assaults of oppression, extreme fear, and destruction that was previously being projected. This was like none I had felt before...(and trust me, I've had what I would consider more than my fair share of them!) It was absolutely debilitating with 3-D evidence to back it up! To make matters worse, I was really uneasy and confused as to why my eggs didn't seem to be working. I even wondered if the eggs could have been infiltrated and corrupted. This was very disturbing and I thought that perhaps I should completely stop using them...(which was exactly what the assailants were hoping I would think!) I was really uneasy about what was going down, so I held my Aurauralite pendant and breathed till I got stable. The Aurauralite gave me the assistance I needed to help me go as neutral as I possibly could under the horrific circumstances, and after some very difficult scanning, found that the egg was NOT infiltrated, and that it's integrity WOULD NOT and COULD NOT be altered. I got the brilliant idea then, to put some layers of eggs up...one over the other over the other... about 20-25 in all! This seemed to work very, very well! Ahhhhhh relief at last! I could now get some respite from the heavy bombardment I was experiencing, long enough to evaluate the situation and figure out how to handle it. Through constant "egging" of my house, my car, my self, my kids, and those closely associated with me, I eventually prevailed and am alive to tell about it.....(which really annoys them...whoever and whatever "them" are!) What I discovered is that this type of intense energetic bombardment wears down the eggshell and it needed to be replaced/recreated sooner. The layers make it more difficult for this energy to get through.....they wear one out and another is already there right underneath to take its place. After a while even the most relentless nasty buggers get tired and give up!

What I came to realize is that these magnificent eggs are not just a very powerful geometry, but an actual living organism! They have the same integrity and nobility as the Aurauralite/Aulmauracite rocks do. They are truly alive and ready to serve.

Recently one of my associates who is a trans-channel, (and an Indigo who goes by the name "Sunwalker",) did a spontaneous channeling in front of her partner, Noelle, and Archangel Michael came through. He told them to tell me that the Kryahgenetics egg and the Aurauralite/Aulmauracite rocks are "One." The Egg is the spirit or soul and the rocks are the body or the physical aspect. They both have many of the same functions but are in different forms. Noelle told me, "That is why when you tell the students in your classes, 'the egg shell neutralizes energy, sort of like it has Aurauralite in it' .....because IT DOES!" I thought, "Wowww, I innately knew they were connected but to hear it put this way really made sense... No wonder I felt they were so linked to each other!" My next thought was "Duahhhhhh .....It's so obvious now!"

The Kryahgenetics Egg, is a marvelous magical device/friend that can assist you in your travels here in "The Land of Make Believe."

I have found that these magnificent eggs can bring about accelerated transformations. I have used it for a "home base" when facilitating timeline and soul retrieval therapy sessions. I have used this modality to activate recent, ancient, and even blocked memories. It also induces profound Higher Self-awareness, wisdom, and healing.

Several moths ago I was teaching a class and decided to take the students through a quick 5-7 minute meditation using the eggs to remove stress and gain a stronger connection to our higher (God-Goddess) selves. We were near the end and each student was instructed to return to this reality and open their eyes when they were finished with their personal journey. The students were having their own private encounters, when we got interrupted by some annoying noises. They got jerked out of their shells so to speak, and came catapulting back to this 3-D reality. What happened next was fascinating to me. The students became very, very tired and groggy. All they wanted to do is sleep. After about a half hour of this extreme fatigue, I decided to take them back to their eggs, and continue where they had left off. Within seconds, I was able to guide them back in their warm fuzzy eggs from whence they came. When they were finished, the students reported that they had very profound experiences and couldn't believe how quickly they got into that altered state again. Normally this would take about a half hour.....but they were able to get into and continue to connect and receive information and healing from their higher selves in mere minutes! After this second "egg session" the students were full of vitality and returned to me with a deeper awareness of their authentic selves. I decided later that this needed to be a part of all my classes and lectures. I had no idea the eggs could be used to help facilitate such exquisite, intense spiritual experiences in others.....and in record time!

## Eggs Quarantine, Scramble Eggs, Egg Plants

## *... ahhhhh the things you can do with these eggs!*

The first time I realized you could put a "Quarantine Egg" around something, happened about two and a half years ago when my Ghostbuster partner Ronnie and I, were doing a Ghostbusting at the Amargosa Hotel and Opera House in Western California near Pahrump, Nevada. This hotel was out in the middle of the desert at Death Valley Junction and the closest town was about a half hour to 45 minutes away. The buildings were extremely haunted with a variety of very creepy energies and literally hundreds and hundreds of ghosts stuck there. I heard countless stories where people had either seen or heard ghosts, or been the unlucky recipient of "ghost hostility." One reason for all the nasty, bizarre things that were happening constantly was that a really foul, arrogant, tyrannical ghost was squatting there. He thoroughly enjoyed lording over the other ghosts and making their life, or rather their "after-life" a living Hell! This ghost was a jerk when he was living and was a jerk after he died.

It was on the full moon in May of 2002 ...the energies were perfect for what we were about to do. As I began to open the portal across the street from the hotel, all sorts of strange things started to happen. A man appeared out of nowhere and walked aggressively toward our circle, trying to interrupt us. When he was taken back to the hotel for a cup of coffee to keep him from interfering, he just "disappeared." Finally I thought, "This is just going to keep up because the hostile ghost knows what we're about to do and is not going to give up his turf without a fight!" So without thinking, I instinctively put a "Quarantine Egg" around this intimidating, diabolic ghost, and said, "Night, Night" to him as I lowered my hand from the top to the bottom of the egg, slowly anesthetizing him. His sprit was now in stasis, totally quarantined so he couldn't escape. As I was sedating him, he was ranting and raving and cussing and then all of a sudden, a horrible stench manifested. It smelled like rotten egg gas or sulphur or some such thing, and it hung around for several minutes and then dissipated when he was fully sedated. His quarantined slumber gave us the freedom we needed to help the other trapped spirits out of the hotel and into the shimmering portal to go back home to the light. Many angels were there assisting us and it took about 20 minutes to get them all out. (Some of them even came back out of the tunnel to say "thank you" ... which made our efforts totally rewarded!)

Now it was time to figure out what to do with the dictatorial ghost. I kept him in the quarantine egg, and slowly brought him out of his slumber.....and once again we could smell the horrible stench as he woke up and realized he was still quarantined! He was really angry at being confined as he was used to being the only one who called the shots and imprisoned others. When he saw the angels, he finally realized what was going on. This made him furious and he was NOT going to go to the light through this portal, and no amount of angels attending the portal could convince him otherwise. (He believed that since he was such a mean, cruel son of a gun, that the only place he would be going is to Hell, so he was just going to park his spirit and STAY RIGHT THERE!) Well, we finally figured out what to do. Ronnie got the bright idea to have one of the angels bring his Mother back through the tunnel and into the egg with him. This sobered him up and we were stunned at his countenance transformation.....he started to soften up. His mother poured her heart out to him about how much she loved him, and that he was NOT going to Hell. She said she knew he had a hard life because of how abusive his father was when he was a child and expressed her sadness that she passed away and was not there to love and protect him. This melted his steely cold heart. He trusted his mother enough now to take her hand. With this change of heart, the eggshell's energy fields opened, and he walked out of the egg and down the tunnel with her.

Whewwww, what a relief for everyone involved!

After the portal was closed and sealed, the heavy energy was totally lifted. We all simultaneously smelled another essence...this time instead of a nasty stench; we smelled the wonderful fragrance of Roses! (Remember now, we are in the middle of the desert, and there were absolutely NO Roses there!)

**NOTE:** *More details on this story and many others are revealed in the soon to be released book, "Got Ghosts? A Practical Guide to Ghostbusting" by Laura Lee Mistycah and Ronnie Foster*

After this quantum experience, I realized what a powerful device these eggs are for quarantining not just energies but also entities! **It is also important to note here that these eggs, like the Aurauralite/Aulmauracite rock, have a very strong code of ethics. You cannot use them for egotistical purposes or to try and hurt or injure someone or something with them.**

Now that you have been educated in **"Eggs Quarantine",** we will move on the next group of eggs on the menu, **"Egg Plants & Scramble Eggs."**

It has come to my attention that Kryahgenetics eggs can be of extreme value in dealing with different types of invasive implants. I have categorized them as:

*__Metallic__- These implants are mechanical in nature, with metallic compositions. Some include elements which cannot be found on planet earth. A number of these implants, believe it or not, were introduced to the body by some of today's designer drugs.

*__Organic__- These implants have live cells and can be detected, but many times are camouflaged.

*__Psychic__- These implants are projected and held in place by electromagnetic fields and thought forms.

**Metallic-** and organic implants can be physical and detected under certain medical diagnosis.....but also can be totally disguised and invisible. Psychic implants can become physical in 3-D if held and sustained long enough. All implants can receive and/or transmit information, programs, commands, data, holograms and emotions... which then can cause interference in thought processes, and also physical, emotional, spiritual, and psychic functions.

I have been aware of and dealt with these types of implants for more than 15 years. I have had numerous experiences with them both on a personal level and also with my clients. It seems that just when I think I'm getting a handle on how they operate, a new one comes out...(sort of like having to constantly design new anti virus software for new computer bugs!)

Recently I have discovered that there are implant varieties, which are similar to parasites in the body. When you scan for parasites, (I use kinesiology and my medical intuitive skills for scanning) these little buggers have their own consciousness, and will stop broadcasting their energy and go dormant to trick you into thinking they're not there! Through much stealth and perseverance, I have devised a way to detect them. Since they cannot change the past, you can go back in time and access accurate data on them. When I do this process, I ask my clients body if there were parasites setting up housekeeping in the body yesterday or even 15 minutes ago. If there were indeed parasites there yesterday or 15 minutes ago, it will show up in the scan. This way you can call their bluff and accurately identify their presence and their activities.

Some of these implants need special treatment and have to be dismantled in a certain order, similar to the protocol of disarming a bomb. I find it mandatory to use Aurauralite/Aulmauracite to find the truth about the implant and how to disarm and remove it, and the Kryahgenetics Egg to quarantine and hold it while I'm figuring out the proper removal procedure.

Most of these implants are designed to go off and debilitate you in some way when you start awakening to your spiritual path. Severe headaches and extreme physical pain of some sort is very common. They can also disturb your thoughts and your emotions. (While I am presently writing this, exposing their existence and designs, I am getting very dizzy, ill and foggy headed.....go figure!)

When I give Spiritual Contract readings, I find that for every contract you agreed to, you also have at least one (and usually several) implants that are trying to keep you from fulfilling that contract. These can be negative thoughts about yourself that have been reinforced by hurtful words, experiences and memories... (many of which are not even from this life time). This dynamic can make it really rough because unless you have excellent past life recall, all you have are the debilitating emotions ...which can make absolutely no sense. This scenario is prime bait for Indigos getting massively sedated and medicated either by self or by "those in authority".

Once an implant has been identified and quarantined, you can use the Aurauralite /Aulmauracite rocks placed strategically to totally scramble implants and render them useless. Then depending on what type of implant it is, you can either reprogram it, or eliminate it all together. When this is done, there is usually an instant physical sensation, and a release/relief soon follows. Sometimes these little buggers have other programs attached, like, satellites, repeaters, broadcasters, receivers, time-releases, pods, seeds, and new things that may not have even been invented at the time of this book's printing. When you rid yourself of implants, you also have to go after all the attachments for 100% clearing. After this process is complete, it is extremely important to fill in the empty spaces of what you just deleted from your body and energy fields with empowering elements/programs .....and especially a stronger connection with your Higher Self/God-Goddess Self.

I find that with Indigos, all they need is one or two "implant removal" sessions and they can take the ball (or implant in this case) and run with it. They innately know what to do and how best to do it. I encourage this! I tell my clients that if they get stuck though, not to hesitate to contact me for help. It is not a shameful thing to need a little help once in a while.....in fact, some implants require someone else's assistance for full resolution.....and some implants are designed to not allow the recipient to take them out themselves without serious repercussions.

The up side to all of this "Implantation" is... that it makes the host much tougher and wiser for the experience. You gain a more profound "intimate" understanding of these types of sinister operations, and with this education, you activate wondrous aspects of your being that you didn't even remember existed. Also, once these implants or programs have been removed, it seems that you are so happy to be free, that you face life with a new zest and joy in small things many take for granted.

To give you an idea of some of my personal implant challenges, here is a recount that might help you understand a little better, how they operate.

About 20 years ago, when I started waking up spiritually, I became aware of a strange response I had that centered around my kids. I found that I was very uncomfortable demonstrating any type of physical affection to them in public. My energy and actions seemed stiff and robotic. I could do things like dispassionately pat them on the head but not hug and kiss them. When I was home, I was a regular "mother goose" ...however in public, I felt very awkward and uneasy. This bizarre anxiety bothered me for years as I tried and tried to figure out what my idiotic problem was!

Then one evening in a meditation I heard this authoritative, conquering voice in my head that made my blood run cold. It said something like..... "If you start waking up spiritually, and fulfilling your contracts, we will hunt down the ones you love and ANNIHILATE THEM!"

I knew then that this warning had subconsciously been running in the background of my mind and affected nearly every aspect of my life. This threat was backed by some extreme, intense fear frequencies and also imprints from some of my past existences where this very threat actually happened! At that time I had no idea what an "implant-imprint/program" was and no idea how to remedy it.

I worked for many more years to finally get rid of this foul controller. I realized when I was on the other end of it all, that this threat dissipated slowly as my awareness increased of who I am and the empowerment of knowing what I am capable of. Had I known about the Aurauralite/Aulmauracite Rocks, and Kryahgenetics Eggs at that time, this implant could have been identified and removed in 15 minutes or less. What a relief it is to have these wonderful life forms here to assist us!

WE DON'T HAVE THE LUXURY ANY MORE OF TAKING THAT MUCH TIME TO RESTORE OUR AUTHENTIC POWER!

# Music of the Kryahgenetics Egg

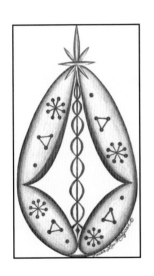

I am searching the globe for musicians and vocalists to do the Kryahgenetics Egg Meditation and then really listen while they are inside the egg to hear and feel what they perceive to be "cosmic music from the egg." This music can change and morph, and may sound different to different people; it is all perception. I know for certain that the Kryahgenetics Egg does indeed emit healing and code activating music/tones/vibrations.

I have a vision of musicians from all over the world recording their renditions of this inspirational music, and sending it to me for a new CD I will be producing. I would like to have these submitted to me by Jan. 2007 so that it can be produced and available to the public by Valentine's Day. If you (or someone you know) would be a candidate for this project, please pass the word along and help me make one of the most cosmic CD's on the market.

For those whose music is chosen for this CD, I will send them a complimentary Aurauralite pendant. In addition, I will print their story of how they felt when they were creating this music, as well as their contact information or web site on the jacket if they have other music they are marketing. This music will be a "gift" to Mistyc House, and will NOT be copyrighted. Just like my books, if someone wants to copy it to enlighten themselves or someone else, then this is divine order to me and I will have achieved my goal.

If I continue to get exceptional music from global musicians, then there may be subsequent CDs produced.

Send your submissions to:

**Mistyc House Publishing**
**816 West Francis #244**
**Spokane WA. 99205**
**(509) 487-0151**
**Knights@MistycHouse.com**

For questions or comments, write me at:

healing@mistychouse.com

***We need to wake up NOW and Do/Be what we came here for. Game On!***

# Chapter 6

# What is the Indigo/ Ultra-Violet Ray?

**NOTE:** *I have been instructed by my Spirit Guides not to actively investigate or research information on what I term First Wave Indigos (FWI's). If something is sent to me, I just put it in a "for future reference file" or skim it quickly. The reason for this is to keep my information as clean as possible and not allow myself to be influenced by other authors. Not that information from other authors is invalid or disreputable, because there are some really good articles, books and websites out there on this subject. But rather to keep this particular aspect of First Wave Indigos as pure as possible from the standpoint that my information has come from:*

*My own memory banks.*

*Data from my cosmic informant, Hal.*

*First-hand accounts from FWI's themselves.*

**T**he Indigo/Ultra-Violet Ray has many definitions, facets and aspects. I will attempt to impart an explanation that **may not** completely define this Ray but will provide you with a solid foundation and provide directions to go when you turn to "Spirit" to understand the magnitude of this magnificent energy. (You truly do have to turn inward to the Spiritual and Higher Self or "God Within" aspect of your being to really understand this vibration.)

The Indigo Ray or what I call *The Indigo/Ultra-Violet Ray* is a very noble, very evolved, and of a very high vibration. As stated before, this ray resonates at a higher octave unheard on this planet before. It can be understood by literally comparing it to the difference between white light and florescent black light. Both give off light, but florescent black light, or ultra-violet light has a very different illumination capability and function than white light. Black light will actually illuminate other colors and give them very different vibrations and emanations when viewed under its rays. Ultra-violet lights also literally make white look whiter and give off its own **luminescence**. For instance, when you look at a white sheet under a black light, it literally emanates light! You can take that sheet and it will shine on things that were previously dark and shadowed. It has its own luminescence, almost like shining a flashlight on these objects. Ultra-violet lights also give other colors a different character: more brilliant, vibrant and effervescent. Under the influence of these rays, everything takes on a different dimension, a dimension that at first seems surreal.  Everything it shines upon creates an almost magical environment, and from my experiments with Ultra-Violet light, it is a very healing and powerful light.  It can, in fact, scatter radiation from computer screens, TV's and other electronic equipment!  I have found that if I run energies of white light and ultraviolet light together or oscillate back and forth when doing healing work, it creates a balanced polarity and healing time quickens!  I have recently done experiments using black and white light randomly while simultaneously oscillating Ultra-Violet and white light to maintain balance and security after an implant clearing-session.    Another aspect of Ultra-Violet light is that you can see things that were previously hidden or concealed before.  For instance, there are certain colors that are only seen under ultra violet lights i.e.; a certain color of ink is put on currency that can only be seen under a Black Light...or, you can have your hand stamped for entrance into a club or event, which is invisible until it is exposed to a black light.  Get the picture?

Ultra-Violet light also has characteristics of both Royal Blue and Electric Purple.  When you look at a black, florescent-light globe or tube, it looks Dark Royal or "Indigo" Blue.  However, when you see its reflection on something, it has Electric Purple hues infiltrated with Royal Indigo Blue.  ***Black Lights embody both colors.....and when analyzed, personify the qualities of First Wave Indigos!***

**Violet:** Regal, Dignified, Assured, Spiritual Strength, Nobility, Emotionality, Sensitivity, Intuitiveness, Channeling Information & Energy.

**Indigo Blue:** Royalty, Loyalty, Responsibility (able to respond) Managerial, Directorial, Intellectual, Wisdom, Discernment, In Charge.

I got these definitions from different colour therapy books and it appears that these color descriptions also define left- and right-brain functions.  Putting them together creates a balance of assertive, intelligent power and calm, intuitive strength.....like a balance of left and right brain.  I have observed that Indigos, in general, have a great balance of left and right brain + masculine and feminine energies, particularly when they are awake and know who they are.

**NOTE:** If you have always had an affinity to florescent Black Lights, now you know why. I would highly recommend that every First Wave Indigo invest in one or more florescent Black Lights. *(Make sure they are the florescent ones and not the backlight bulbs. Unless they are florescent bulbs, they do not have the same luminescent effect and are also a serious fire hazard!)* Florescent black lights are fairly inexpensive and will shed new light in your life...literally! (I have several in my home and leave them on 24 -7. They are very durable and some of mine have been going nonstop for over four years!)

The first time I really got in tune with the Ultra-Violet energies of the Black Lights I had in my bedroom, was about 1995. I first experimented by taking pieces of white printer paper and noticing that different brands of paper varied to the extreme in their illumination qualities. Some hardly illuminated. Some were ultra-white and iridescent. But under regular White Light you could hardly tell there was any difference. I started using the brighter irides-cent white paper for my Journal....I would shut off the overhead light and only have my black light. It was amazing how bright the paper was, enough so that I could clearly see what I was writing as long as I didn't cast a shadow on the paper. My journaling took on a different essence when I wrote this way. My experiments continued and I discovered all sorts of colors that illuminated better than others (but I found that my teeth were not on the "high illumination list"!)

After playing with the colors, I decided to go deeper and find out what the black light "felt like." I got the inspiration to lay unclothed on my bed with the black light shining down on me. I turned on some soft music, put an Aulmauracite rock in each hand, focused on my Aurauralite pendant around my neck, and started to breathe deeply and absorb the energy.

I was not prepared for what happened next.

I started to flash back to powerful memories and deep feelings of love that came from another time and place. I began breathing with more intent as I absorbed the rays, which in turn acti-vated more encoded memories. Deeply imbedded emotions began firing off. I could feel the rays penetrating my body and waking up recollections that were hard for my mind to catalogue...but the emotions were so prominent that I couldn't deny the truth of what I was feeling. The energies escalated to such intensity, that I burst into tears of both joy and agony. It was then that I began to remember and recognize my existence and position in the Ultra-Violet Realm. The emotions were so passionate, that it was hard for my nervous system to handle the vast amount of information coming in. All I could do in order to balance and try to comprehend it all, was release my innate response to cry.

The crying eventually turned into sobbing as I fell into a deep, profound sleep. Several hours later I regained consciousness, feeling like a different person. I remembered a very important piece to the puzzle of my life.....my existence in the

"Ultra-Violet REALm" ...which was and is as real to me as where I am at this moment in time on Planet Earth.

I encourage each of you to do your own "Ultra-Violet Light" experiments... because only then will you understand what I am talking about.....and when you do, may you embrace what happens next. It is time..... you have waited your whole life for this awakening of memories and personal power.

It is time for the X-Men and Women to "WAKE UP"!

It is time to remember who you are, what fields of expertise you brought with you, what you came here to do, and to stop being afraid to express and BE WHO AND WHAT YOU ARE!

The Indigo Ray, like ultraviolet rays, can seem as unearthly and as surreal as ultraviolet lights. It is like going to another reality. How would you try to explain a black light to someone in the 1800's who has absolutely no point of reference. It would be next to impossible.

This is how difficult and frustrating it has been for these First Wavers to relate to people, and the environment around them. They have the capacity to see, comprehend, and emanate both *black light and white light*...and how to function in **both** realities. Sadly, for most of the First Wavers, it takes years to wake up from their amnesia and finally understand that those around them do not see the world through their highly-evolved "ultra-violet black light" *and* "white light" perception. Therefore, most of them do not understand why others cannot see or comprehend what was *so obvious* to them.... they do not know that others are privy only to the "White Light" reality!

FWI's usually have some type of past life recall, (which may or may not include this planet) and about 65% have had a great deal of previous experience on this plane. Approximately 35% of First Wavers are from other sectors of space, and have had very little experience as to how to operate physically, socially and/or psychically on Earth. This can be useful at times, but more frequently makes things extremely difficult and complicated, especially when they have not opened their memory banks to who and what they truly are, and understand their spiritual contracts here.

All FWI's are on what I called in my book, **Kryahgenetics,** "The Cosmic Clean-up Crew".....or the "C.C.C." This "Clean-up Crew" is a cross between a *Service Organization and a Cosmic Special Forces.* This group has been equipped and trained to go to the most dysfunctional and perverted places in our Universe, and clean up energetic/thought pollution/distortions and the destruction which have been left behind. Their focus and goal is to restore balance and synergy to systems/societies in constant chaos, corruption, devastation and debilitating decay. In other words...to places that are *"really messed up!"*

It is my understanding that all First-Wave Indigos went to the "Ultra-Violet Realm" for intense training, and earned their Ultra-Violet Ray before coming here to do their jobs. This realm is in another time, another place, and another dimension. A place that also has access to and uses the Aulmauracite-Aurauralite Stone of Truth for energy, focus, strength, healing, broadcasting and internal code activation.

**NOTE:** *There are other training facilities for the Cosmic Clean-up Crew which are very significant and credible. I am honored whenever I am in the presence of anyone who is a member of the "C.C.C." I have worked with and given spiritual contract and other readings to many impeccable and talented beings who were trained at these other facilities or academies. The C.C.C. works together in harmony, and each respects the expertise and skills of the other.*

The difference between FWI's and the rest of the people on the planet, is that they have taken on /absorbed the Indigo/Ultra-Violet Ray before they came here **this time**. This Ray, has to do with the high frequencies of unconditional love and compassion, is only attained by very evolved souls and ***had to be earned!*** The job of these Beings is to bring new vibrations, new information, new technology, new wisdom, new life, and a newly expanded-consciousness to the corrupt and unloving frequencies which are imbedded here and guarded by tyrannical systems that keep their agendas intact. It is not a job for the weak and wimpy... (although some of the Indigos may feel weak and wimpy because of the misperceptions and labels that have been placed upon them, and the imbedded implants that are running false information.)

First Wave Indigo Beings are here now anchoring their rays of love, compassion, balance, unity, higher consciousness and freedom into this planet, and it is changing the earth grid systems permanently. If it weren't for these robust, impeccable Beings making the commitment to come here and transform the energies of our earth, the new subsequent ray of Indigo and Crystal children that are here now as infants and small children, would not be able to express their hyper-intelligence and psychic abilities. The FWI's came first to neutralize the hostile energies that repel and reject higher frequencies.

In many ways, the First Wave Indigos were (and are) the trail-blazers, the wake-breakers, the morphogenic-field shatterers, the Bravest of the brave... the Toughest of the tough... and the Boldest of the bold on this planet.

I honor and give tribute to all of you FWI's for your valiant efforts and commitment to your contracts and sacred agreements here, to transform the path of spiritual evolution and history on this plane. Your example and presence here is influencing the future of this planet, and will forever change the course of the corrupt and tyrannical systems we have been enslaved in for soooo long!

The Indigo/Ultra-Violet Light = **FREEDOM!** ....or Freed Om?

May you be blessed in all your Noble Quests.....

## ~*Lady Mistycah*~

# The Legend of the Ultra-Violet Realm

**O**nce upon another time and space, there was a beautiful, majestic, loving planet. This Celestial Body was host and nurturer to many different species of plant, animal, mineral, aquatic, and human life. Everything on this plane of existence ebbed and flowed with the rhythms and balance of the Goddess herself. Each kingdom had honor and respect for all other kingdoms and life forms that they co-existed with. Life on this planet was a synergistic masterpiece.

No one (save the Goddess herself) would have suspected what was about to happen. An experiment got out of control, and treacherous viruses were released on this planet. They spread slowly at first, but rapidly began to multiply throughout the land and sea. They soon gained forceful momentum, taking on a shape and form as had never been experienced on this or any other planet before. These ever-expanding viruses and those infected with them were filled with "consumption, greed, and obsession for supreme power" believing that they could devour and overthrow the very essence of the planet and control it all. In their insanity, the infected even believed that they could create an artificial technique for the power of creation to eventually usurp and overthrow the Goddess herself..... and ultimately become the Lord of it all!

It was apparent that the infections of these consuming viruses were out of control. If nothing was done to correct the distortion and destruction left in their path, they would consume the whole of the planet (inside and out) and in the end, there would be nothing left.....just empty space, and the residue of terror, suffering, desolation and an out-of-control virus.

The imbalance these viruses caused soon began sending ripples to other dimensions and star systems. They too were in jeopardy of being polluted, distorted and knocked out of balance.

Just when it looked like things might be beyond repair, there were some experiments done by some virus-crazed men on this planet. They were playing and tampering with what they perceived to be *The Ultimate Powers* (next to the Power of Creation) .....the power to control life-forms through their thoughts and emotions.....and then control events through manipulation of the Time-Space Continuum. Through the use and abuse of some of these sinister experiments, they aggressively started ripping holes in the very fabric of Time and Space!

During one of these experiments they opened up a portal that allowed an intruder in .....a nameless "beast" that was not from this Universe, and had no business being here. It morphed and soon became more lawless than those who had let it in!

At this point, the planet and all of her inhabitants put out an urgent "S.O.S." to the Universe *(and other Universes as well)* to come to her aid. If something wasn't done soon to stop this infernal insanity, the entire planet and others connected to it would be affected/infected with this insidious sickness and destruction.....and in the end, all would perish.

In a realm far, far away on the other side of space, in another Universe, the cry was heard and quickly responded to. This realm was (and still is) known throughout the cosmos as the "Ultra-Violet Realm" which was renowned for its superior training academy of *Inter-Dimensional Knights*.....Knights that, after their commencement, would be eligible to join the Cosmic Clean-up Crew. When knights were trained in this academy, each graduate was awarded a unique colour for their superior achievements and valor. That color was a deep blue/electric purple mix or Indigo-Ultra-Violet (IUV).

The Knights of the Ultra-Violet Realm were educated and trained to be strong, yet flexible in the most intense, adverse conditions in imagination ...for it is the imagination that creates new game rules. Many simulators and holo-decks were programmed and reprogrammed to equip these aspiring Knights with every thinkable, and especially the *unthinkable* situations of darkness and corruption that could exist in all of Creation. Countless cadets, both male and female, from many different species, come from all over creation to this academy with fond hopes of graduation...but only approximately 5% make it through the intense training to see their graduation and earn their Indigo-Ultraviolet color that is presented to them ceremonially, and permanently imbedded in their energetic/auric field.

One of the benevolent species that assists in the training of future IUV Knights in this realm, are a clan of kind, noble and courageous dragons.

They teach how to stand tall in the face of opposition and find alternative routes to resolve conflict. They teach how to go neutral in an instant (especially in the midst of chaos) to find your source of Truth and Inner Strength. They teach grace and dignity when enslaved in hostile, vulgar and humiliating environments. They teach how to see through the illusions that others project onto and into you. They teach how to anchor and broadcast Love, Light, and Laughter from the core of your being in environments that are void of these. They teach that fear is an illusion of the mind and how to reverse this mind game. They teach that all life forms in our Universe are connected and how to love unconditionally. And.....they teach that "tough love" is still "love."

The Emperor and Empress of this realm are a gracious, impeccable couple who would not ask any of the cadets, servants, or anyone in the Royal Court to do anything that they would not or could not do themselves. No job was too lofty or too lowly for anyone, including the Emperor and Empress. They demonstrated this on many occasions and the entire Kingdom knew they were in the best of integrity at all times. This is one reason they were so highly revered and respected. They were icons to inspire others.

As Royal Overseers of the UV REALm, the Emperor and Empress, were the final filter for "quality control." With their collective and diverse psychic/intuitive abilities, they knew if a knight was qualified to receive their IUV Colour. Many a Knight made it through the intense training, but did not make it through the strict examination from the royal couple. With the alliance of "The Stone of Truth" the Emperor and Empress went straight to the knight's core to know if a pure heart, unconditional love, innate wisdom, psychic powers, passion, stamina and inner strength were at optimal enough levels to earn the IUV color. Sometimes it took eons to get through this final qualification.

As legend has it, the Ultra-Violet Realm is training and qualifying Inter-Stellar Knights to this very day. If you visit Planet Earth in the 21st Century, in all its chaos and tyranny, you are likely to encounter some of these Grand Knights..... those who embody and emanate the IUV Ray. Many don't even know who they are.....but the sleeping Knights are waking up. As they do, the outcomes change. Futility turns to hope... and hope turns to optimism...and optimism turns to trust ...*which turns to knowing that balance and justice will soon be restored!*

# Chapter 7

# Indigo Dimensions

1.

The Modern Age . . .
When vacuums and toasters,
Transistors and automation,
And a host of scientific gadgets, widgets and whatnots,
Were poised to transform Modern Man
and Modern woman
From slaves to Masters
and mistresses . . .
Ended with a whimper
Thirty years ago.

A glitch,
A missing magic spell,
A disappearing subatomic quirk,
Doomed the Modern Age.
The Fifth Dimension sang,
But the Fourth Dimension darkly beckoned.

Mother Gaia noticed,
Taking pity on her wayward Favorites,
And conceived a brood of children with indigo lights –
The Indigos.
Astral children born of a higher octave,
And stamped with a stubborn genealogical temper.
Children infused with a planetary mission –
Sent to stem a consumptive rush,
And reopen cosmic channels for global balance.

2.

An Eastern wind blows through the deserted sky palace,
Where Jealous Yahweh,
Good God Almighty,
And Allah the Merciful,
Used to reign together as the One.

Mother Gaia just waited,
And smiled her secret smile.

Scattered voices in the desert cry –
A warning from a visionary vanguard:
Make way their paths!  Make way their paths!
The old roads will not hold them;
The Elders' schools will not teach them;
The Indigos have other lores to learn.
They will not compromise
Nor honor lame conventions
Forged to preserve dishonest truces.

They will break the foolish laws of rigid men.

3.

Yang and Yin awake in separate houses,
Drugged with tales of futuristic pleasures –
Dissipating echoes of intoxicating mantras –
Whispers of a kingdom just beyond the light;
A Kingdom Come that never seems to come.

Into that crumbling world came the Indigos.
Children who, rejecting the rational myth,
Were born to fight,
But not for goods nor money.
The Indigos will not resuscitate an obsolete Modern Age.
The Indigos will fight for Mother Earth,
And a radical, emerging stewardship
Of organic, planetary consciousness.

## 4.

A century of voices so foretold –
The keepers of the watchtowers saw the signs:
"God is dead," spake Zarathustra.
The scientists cross-sected and dissected,
Reducing matter into nothingness
And finding nothing –
The scientists concluded:
We are nothing.

So the sacred rituals lost their holy purposes,
After passing from Pope to Priest to Penitent.
And beneath the eye of a Godless microscope
Jesus died again.

Yang and Yin feel betrayed,
Sensing each other's numinous majesty
In a rational world gone mad.

The scholars exhumed and examined the Dead Sea scrolls
And concluded with a start:
The Hebrew rabbi worshipped as "the" God –
The alpha and omega –
Was just a man.
He was simply what he simply claimed to be,
Like Siddhartha five hundred years before him.

Jesus Christ!
(He wasn't a Christian, you know.)
A life of pure example.
It should have been enough.
The best that humankind has yet to offer:
It was enough.

5.

The Third Eye is open;
The Indigos are here.
The Indigos recall a glorious heritage
Of divinely pagan gods and goddesses.
The Indigos worship not just the One,
As in the days before the Modern Age.
The Indigos have come to let us know:
We need them All!

We need to learn to worship in the moment,
And look inside ourselves to find the Sacred –
For if we cannot find it
Inside our beating breasts,
We will never, never, never
Find it elsewhere!


Namaste!
The Divine in me sees the Divine in you.
A pantheon of living gods and goddesses.
All around us!  In us!
An infinity of ways to worship –
Limitless expressions of fertile creativity
Thrive all around us!
Yet few – so very few – can see it here.

So Gaia sent the Indigos to guide us.
Confused at first –
How could they not be?
Witnessing dead rites with catchless phrases –
Utterances by somber, shackled bishops,
Whose supplicants stare back with vacant faces,
All mumbling about pies in the skies,
While the real feast before them
Lay untasted and untouched.

The Indigos have come to show the way.
Inventing and discovering joyful practices.

New – yet somehow old – Yes! Somehow ancient!
Summoning back a Golden Age
When Ra and Mut, Isis and Osiris, Nut and Geb,
Filled with boundless love and creativity,
Walked among us –
They were us!

Yang rises, Yin inhales –
A unity of opposites delights
In present possibilities.

6.

Spent and dying,
The Age of Pisces thrashes weakly
Like two broken sharks beached on a dusky shoal.
The Age of Aquarius dances in the dawn:
The electric age of energy has come!

It must be spoken: a dark side they have,
These promising Indigos –
Like all humanity, though more evolved,
They are dangerous.
Mother Gaia only gives with one hand,
What she is willing to take back with the other.
But the dark side of the Indigos is not like ours.
Our kind pillaged and plundered for profit:
Taking from the Earth,
Polluting the Skies,
And poisoning the Oceans,
All without remorse.
Unchecked, the darker Indigos will turn upon themselves,
And then they'll come for us,
All without remorse.
The dark side of the Indigos hums paradoxically
Of cold electricity.
Their dark ones exist in quiet corners,

And if misunderstood, neglected and ignored,
They will short-circuit.
Where the dark ones of our days
Had faulty hearts led by absent minds,
The darker Indigos have faulty minds,
Led by absent hearts.


Yet still and all much hope abides;
For the Indigos take roads that upward wind
Along the climbing contours of the land.
The Indigos will show us how to live:
How using only what we need,
And needing less than we've been using,
How preserving and renewing and replenishing,
Will save the Earth, the Oceans and the Skies,
And restore Mother Gaia to her temple –
Terra!
Her children's blessed home and only refuge.

7.

Yang sees, Yin knows,
Apart they seek, apart they flow,
Each toward the other.

We must learn again to love our Holy Selves,
In equal measure, we must worship Thou,
The Other, as Ourselves.
In the present moment we must trade our talents,
Instead of hoarding them
Like empty promises for a senseless future
And a Christian burial.

The time is now! The place is here!
This is where we are and where we be!
We must love and feel and taste and touch each other.
We must learn again to worship
In the here and now.

Yang and Yin at last,
Bodies touching lightly,
Join their souls together,
Breath in joyful breath,
Legs intertwined, yin and yang,
Cheek on breast, rise and fall, rise and fall,
Hand in hand they worship.

M.D. Gales

(Printed by permission)

## About M. D. Gales

M.D. Gales is an exceptional vanguard Indigo I have known for over 4 years.

M.D. has been a practicing trial lawyer for 20 years in Spokane, Washington. He has a Bachelors of Arts degree in English Literature from Seattle University. *Indigo Dimensions* is part of a collection of thus far unpublished poetry.

His background includes almost 16 years of Catholic education – eight in the Jesuit tradition. Mr. Gales explains that he is "probably inoculated" against all religions by virtue of his years in the Catholic system. However, he says he remains keenly interested in all facets of religion – especially insofar as it attempts to plumb the essential depths of spiritual experience. His lack of allegiance to any particular religion frees him to explore, practice and participate with any religious group willing to accept his non-committed yet respectful existential bent.

Mr. Gales describes his poetry as an unintended outgrowth of dream journals he started in 1999. For several years he kept track of his dreams in prose. After about two years, he found that his practice of dreamwork journaling branched spontaneously into poetic expression, independent of the dreamwork. The dreamwork also sharpened his sensitivity to other art forms, and that heightened his overall sensitivity to intuitive and spiritual phenomenon.

He has two children, ages 10 and 15, both of whom he says are advanced far beyond their years, and both of whom are well able to speak for themselves. His observations of them over the years led him to understand they were radically different from himself and most of his generation in their orientations to what he calls "waking reality," and what others may describe as "empirical reality." In consulting intuitive masters, he was advised that both of his children are classic Indigos. They are extremely bright, artistically inclined and radical in their own ways.

In addition to the lessons from his children, Mr. Gales says that *Indigo Dimensions* was inspired chiefly by the following sources or personalities, in no particular order: Carl Jung, Joseph Campbell, Gary Zukav, Carolyn Myss, Soren Kierkegaard, Freidrich Nietze, Sigmund Freud, Albert Einstein, Neils Bohr, Allen Wheelis, James Joyce, the Sixties, Jesus Christ, the apocryphal Gospel of Thomas, Buddha, Mohammed, Ovid, John the Baptist, Lao Tse, the ancient Druids, the ancient Egyptians, the ancient Greeks, and the modern Wiccans.

# Chapter 8

# Indigo Contracts

It has been my responsibility and pure pleasure as an Indigo Activator to give what I call *Contracts/Talents/Sacred Agreements - Psychic Readings.*

With each reading, I can "Feel the Force" grow stronger within the Indigo I am working with, and also within the entire Indigo Collective Force Field. When I am finished with each reading, I have to take a few minutes and lie down so I can absorb and adjust to the energy of this newly realized Indigo transformation. Many times it leaves me tired, thirsty, hungry, and mineral depleted. I can only do 2-3 readings a day as it takes an immense amount of psychic energy to give these readings, but the rewards and results are well worth it.

Here is a sample of some of the contracts/talents/agreements that these Amazing First Wave Indigos (and others on The Cosmic Clean-Up Crew) have committed to do in order to bring balance and a higher frequency and vibration of love to this planet. It is important to note that when I give these readings, it does not mean that this is the only talent or aptitude they have, because Indigos and members of the Cosmic Clean-Up Crew have many other abilities and passions to bring to the table so to speak. These are just the ones that they have "committed" to do..... (and even these contracts are not always set in stone, and can be renegotiated.)

It is also interesting that when I give these readings to people who are not on The Cosmic Clean-Up Crew, they may have 2, 3, 4, and maybe 5 things on their list, but The Cosmic Clean-Up Crew has 12, 13, 14, and maybe up to 17 contracts. Indigos generally have from 16 -19 contracts, and I am finding that many of them are coming back for "the rest of their contract reading" ... (which before this, I had no idea that there were more! I just have to go with what is flowing at the time and always be open to changes and expansion.) Indigos have about 6-10 times the contracts as others on the planet have. The reason is that they are better prepared and equipped to do more because of the intensive training they had before they came to this world.

**NOTE:** *There is about 20% of the population that have NO spiritual contracts at all...they are just here for the heck of it and have no prior "REAL" spiritual commitments. If they do anything to up the spiritual equation on the planet, it is a bonus. Then there is another 20% that is actively trying to snuff out true authentic spirituality here and have the advantage of extreme wealth and financial backing to make their agendas a reality...many of which are in the inner network of organized religions.*

As you read this list, understand that this information came to me in words, phrases and metaphors....many of which were very specific as to how they were written and the placement of the words. There were some that seemed to rhyme, and some of them made little sense to me at first, but after getting the "bigger picture" and having it explained to me...(sometimes not in words but pictures, emotions, and impressions)... then it made total sense. Many times I felt I was totally off base and questioned myself over and over again. Then my client would relate something to me that totally reinforced its validity.

When you are finished reading this list, you will realize and be comforted in knowing that we truly have **_Real Life X-Men (and X-Women) on this planet who are in hot pursuit of activating their benevolent powers to transform the world!_**

## *Indigo Contract*

## *Sample List*

Fairy Kingdom Assistant
Anthropology Re-Designer (food-geometry-education)
Harmonizer (food, color, other)
Quiet Undercurrent (make big waves - when you come to the top, everyone takes notice)
Stability/Centerer-Director (calmness, send stability vibrations out)
Tone Healer (sing a tone-make music-heal with laughter tones)
Animal Liaison – Ambassador
Compassion Teacher/Be-er/ Eminater (permeate others, change perceptions, plants included)
Concentration-Focus-Go Neutral... (then activate creation)
Chemistry Creator (formula withheld in this printing)
Clairvoyant, Clairaudient, Clairsentient (with plants too)
Light Protector
Crystal/Rainbow Children Teacher
Catapulter (take things/energies quickly from one place to another)
Runner-Forerunner
Quarantiner

Heavenly Being (noun and verb)
Fairy-Diva-Elemental Communicator/Protector
Quadrant fixer
Light Ship Navigator
Bridge The Gap.  Indigo Waker-Motivator
Cosmic Clean-Up Crew Waker-Motivator
Magick Maker/Activator
Christed Energy Anchorer
Compose-Create Divine Music
Peace Keeper
Re-instater
Mystery Breaker
Telepathic Healer
Interdimensional Liaison
Earth Grid Balancer/Stabilizer
Truth Catapulter
Candlestick Maker (Tesla Technology)
Aurauralite Wizard
Goddess Energy Broadcaster (balance, wisdom, power)
Energetic Garbage-Debris Recycler
The Domino That Stands-Up
Vibrational Tone Healer/Transmitter
Joy Junction ————*
$ Launderer
Forgiveness Exemplifier
Serenity Maker
Indigo Assistant
Animal Protector
Telepathic Communicator
Capitol Keeper/Re-Distributor
Order-Rememberer-Stabilizer-Broadcaster
Spirit Assistant-(animals too)

Compassion Teacher

Interplanetary Communication – (in engineering)

Child Advocate (help create scholarships)

Lime Light  (expander/extender)

Simple Inventor

Creative Genius

Tone Hearer/Interpreter/Fixer (also hear pain and suffering-hear interstellar too)

Prosperity M-Field Breaker (especially for Indigos)

Love Emanater/Broadcaster

Truth Definer-Refiner (expose the truth-take fear away from seeing the truth)

Interdimensional Animal Communicator/Steward

Redirector/Reflector (Light and other things)

Heal Thyself-Know Thyself (know past lives-serenity trademark, grace, poise)

Take The Mystery Out Of "Women's Mysteries" (make head-dresses, dance. Sing/tone take energy to the planet, experiment with star fire)

Empathic/Telepathic (people and animals)

Hands On Healing/ & With Aurauralite (vibration of balance)

Liaison (medical and metaphysical-indigos and crystals- women and goddesses-men and women)

Crystal Children Steward

Anchor Broadcaster, Emanater  True, Pure Goddess Energy/Power)

Uncover Lies, Deceptions-Bring Truth To Darkness

Karma Creator (make instant karma)

Life Enhancer...(all life forms)

Fairy/Diva Communicator

Simplifier

Animal Steward/Protector

Earth Energy Conductor

Peacemaker/Chaos Breaker

Counterfeit Detector

Interstellar Liaison

Compass Keeper (internal)

Energy Accelerator/Director

Interest Activator/Instigator (on many levels)
Power Cleaner/Conductor (cleansing and orchestrating the cleansing of power)
Stability Eminater
"Be Yourself"
Divine Activator (self and others)
Clear-Audient (living and dead)
Clear-Voyant (any time and any where)
Clear-Sentient (through time and space, all life forms)
Remote Viewer (find truth, any time, any where)
Goddess Eminater (embody Goddess Energy)
Self Absorber (Higher self)
Apathy Reverser (self and others)
Fairy Steward
Cinderella Maker (you are your own Fairy God Mother)
History Maker/Breaker (break paradigms that change history)
Compassion Holder/Teacher
Power Converter-Broadcaster (self and planet)
Frequency Disrupter-Cleaner-Reverser
Passion Rekindler
Joy/Humor-Being Spreader
Sing Your Own Song (literal and figurative –others may hear, or not)
Bring Yourself & Others Home (what ever, where ever that may be)
Animal Healer-Communicator, (tone healing, radionicaly, and healing with images)
Lens Crafter/Perfector (telescopic vision-eye lens-long range, short range-camera lens
Vibration and Tone Maker/M-Field Breaker (healing –sonic waves)
Telepathic Healer (mind - radionics)
Time Keeper-Rip Mender
Bridge Maker (consciousness, realities, people)
Reality Bender (bring reality back)
Dragon Kingdom Liaison
Inner Earth Liaison
Peace Keeper / win-win maker

Knights Code Exemplifier
Surveillance Expert (implant detector, chips, psychic energy)
Light Hands-hands of Light
Green Peace (balance to all plant life)
Water Spirits/Tender Protector/Commander
Keeper of Records/Organizer/Filterer/Distributor (archeology, Indigo, interstellar)
Music Tone Translator-Math (tone healer-voice, drums maker. 5 other instruments Play-2
  Other Instruments (make them)
Higher Self Absorber/Integrator
Light Conductor
Joy/Laughter Emanater
Phantom Energy Disburser/Clearer
Loving Presence (in the mist of fear and pain)
Money Manager
Breath Enhancer (life force, ...plants need us)
Capitol-Capital Lies Exposer
Dragon Realm Protector
Indigo Advocate (wake up Indigos, help those already awake)
Crystal Children Protector
Truth Exposer
Animal Communicator /Ally
Mineral Kingdom Coordinator /Interpreter (can move mountains if necessary)
Seer-Past/Present/Future (see timeline/manipulation can make corrections)
Group Leader/Motivate /Instigator (difference in leader and tyrant)
Strength In Numbers/Strength In Oneness (teach)
Peace Keeper/Director/Calmer (relationships, meetings, outbreaks)
Rekindle Ultraviolet Flame (rekindle purity, life and passion of flame)
Simplify The Complicated/Clarity To All (spiritual, scientific)
Connector/Adaptor
Treaty /Contract Writer (business conflict resolution-international)
Love Enhanser/Understander (self, others)
Apparition Understander (ghosts, visions)

As You Wish   ...(so it is)

Tele-Healer

Mineral Kingdom Assistant  (communication, help grid of planet with minerals, replace-
  activate certain minerals)

Indigo Activator

Light Spreader

Inventor (make patents)

Instructor (specific method to be followed)

Interplanetary Communicator (have a one-on-one relationship with the planets)

Earth Telepath

Vibrations Master (drumming, making vibrations)

Connector (people to people, energies, fix broken connections)

Vision/Visionary (see future, make positive changes to alter future)

$ Cleanser/Transformer (transform money energy, up vibration to free instead of enslave)

Psychic Counseling/Hands On Healer

Fairy Kingdom Steward

Light Broadcaster/Anchor

Bring Order To Chaos

Manipulate Reality

Alchemy/ Physical Body  (physical plane, spiritual matter)

Heal Self (and in doing so clear the distortions in ancestors' codes)

Help, Interact, Assist Unseen Kingdoms, (i.e. fairy, divas, gnomes, leprechauns, dragons, etc.)

International Information Net Worker

Morphogenetic Field Breaker

Overcome Fears (self imposed and projected)

Empath

Charm Maker (make charms and magical things that really work!)

Compass Direction Finder (physically, energetically)

Calendar/Time Reviser (consciously changing YOUR reality)

Nature Nurturer / Command Nature

Energy Reverser (people and things)

Wake Breaker - Universal Wake Breaker (also direct swirling movement into stagnation)

Truth Displayer (display so well, no one can deny authenticity and validity)
Interdimensional Communicator (feel vibrations of dimensions / communicate - then
  teach others)
Encryption decipherer
Error Corrector
Information Release Monitor
Center For Control (many levels)
Caring Discipliner
Refuse Cleaner/Recycler (all levels)
Truth Emanater
Secret Technology Developer (Tesla is Sprit Guide)
Trans Medium/Channeler
Pollution/Debris Transmuter
Fairy-Diva-Elf Liaison
Win-Win Energy Activator
Interstellar Liaison
Catalyst (energetic and chemical changes in the environment)
Upper Region Lifter
Earth Speaker (4 others like you)
Love Transformer
Reformatory (things and people-needs absolute integrity!)
Quantum Healer (in ways others have not discovered yet)
Quest Realizer (will see evidence of diligent works)
Element Commander
Subliminal Art (overt and covert healing with black and white & color modalities)
Humor Healing
Lock & Sealer
Writer/Re-writer
Catastrophic Stabilizer
Love/Compassion Broadcaster
Seed Planter (Earth seeds & seeds of truth and understanding)
Capitol-Capital Delegater (have command of where large amounts of money is spent)

Earth/Fire/Water/Air Commander
Memory Activator (self, others, mass-consciousness, past life, encoded unique memories)
Mistake Corrector (even through time)
Quantum Leap Instigator (self /others)
Inventor/Creator
Philanthropist (Money/Energy/Time)
Nature Steward (plants, animals, elementals)
Calibration Specialist
Chronic Relief Agent (people and places)
Tesla Tech Re-Designer/Creator
Fairy Diva Earth Spirit Communicator/Steward/Comrade
Time Line Manager/Fixer
Garbage Sifter/Gem Finder
New Ideas/New Solutions Creator (personal, professional, global, interstellar)
Compute – Er (self local cosmic – making sense out of nonsense)
Parasite Identifier/Corrector
Center Gravity/Gravity Center-er (levitate)
Metamorphosis Activator (self &others)
Secret Technology Displayer (Tesla is a spirit guide)

# A Hal-atious Indigo Reading Story

One evening I was intently giving an Indigo phone reading and feeling really confident that I was "In the Zone" and "With the flow," when unexpectedly I just kept getting the word "Cannibal..... Cannibal..... Cannibal....." over and over! I would wait and see if there was something before or after it, or if it was a "sounds like cannibal" kind of thing...(sometimes that is the way information comes through.) This puzzled and confused me as I just kept trying to figure out what was being sent or transmitted to me. After about three or four minutes of this, I got so annoyed I just skipped it and went on. (Four minutes can seem like an awfully long time when you're a client and there is nothing but dead silence coming from my end of the phone!) Well, later on in the reading, I'll be darned if the "Cannibal" thing didn't keep coming up again and again. It just wouldn't go away! By now I was getting really irritated and frustrated, thinking that some how I was getting some sort of psychotic interference! I decided that since it wouldn't go away, I would just go with it and see where it took me. I kept saying it over and over again, changing inflection each time to see if there was some other meaning. Finally I got it! It came out "Can-Able!" Whewwwwww.....what a relief! I was really beginning to wonder what in the heck was wrong. Can-Able ...it has several meanings, such as "Help others take back their power" or "Be their cheerleader." (And what a joke! I thought that Hal must have been lurking in the corners or something with his off-the-wall sense of humor and play on words!)

I started laughing and laughing. Of course my client was dying to know what this joke was that would give me my daily laughter quota in one sitting. I told the woman what had just transpired in my head. She laughed too and said she understood, but I could tell that there was still some real uneasiness and tension.

I wanted to make sure that things were ok with her so I made it a point to keep in touch with e-mail. Here is some correspondence we had.


Monday, June 14, 2004 3:07 PM

Dear E.

(Body of letter edited out)

P.S. I still crack up when I think of "cannibal/Can-Able" ...that was such a hoot! I could not get it out of my head and thought I was nuts! It was really distracting to me and I was almost uneasy about going back to it. It just shows that if something needs to get through, it will find a way even if you have to leave it and go back later.

Laura Lee

Monday, June 14, 2004 4:40 PM

Hello Laura Lee

It is funny that you mention the cannibal thing in your last letter because that continues to puzzle me. I assume it is the job of a "cheerleader." I think I understand it but I don't know why it came through like that. Cannibalism is such a disturbing idea for me.

Thanks again.

With Love,

E.


Mon 6/14/04 10:55 PM

(**Note:** *Notice the time this was sent. I did not do this on purpose, but only realized it right now as I'm editing this story!*)

Dear E.

I too was weirded out about the cannibal thing, but then knew that there was some sort of hidden meaning to it all.....(just like a play on words for "can-able".) I knew it was a "Good Thing" .....so I went to my World Book Student Dictionary to investigate further, and found **"cannibalize"** to have several meanings.

**1-to strip (old or worn equipment) parts for use in other units.**
**2-to take personnel or components from (one organization) for use in building up another.**

Now THAT is even making more sense! .....I knew there were hidden meanings to it....and I feel that there are still more that you will be made aware of in your meditations on that contract.

This is toooo funny and I will fur-sher use it in the book for the chapter on what some Indigos have on their Contract list. I tell ya, I thought I was loony tunes when it just kept coming back and back and back.....(this is sooooo how Hal works.....I bet he is one of your guides!)

Ok, hope this helps you feel better, I just couldn't rest till I got this cleared up, it has been bugging me all night but I had other things that had to be handled first before I researched it.

Much Love and Laughter to you.....

Laura Lee


Friday July 23, 2004 3:30 P.M.

Dear Laura Lee,

Yes, I did receive your email about the cannibalizing. I can identify with the "recycling" mentality. Instead of throwing things away, see what can be built out of the rubble. I have really accelerated quite a bit with my Geometry Healer, Tone Healer, and Manifesting ability. It is so wonderful to wake up but it is funny how you have to be diligently careful to stay on the path because it is like there are cliffs to accidentally fall off of. It's all about awareness. And I am becoming much more psychic.

I can't wait until the book comes out.

Love

E.

# Chapter 9

# Insights into the Indigo Mind

### Tales of my own Mutant Children

Since I have had the unique opportunity of "Living in an Indigo House," I've acquired scores of astounding tales to tell. Some that may be hard to believe, some that I can hardly believe, and some that I promised to change or withhold the names to protect the guilty!

Just to set the record straight, I have never thought of myself as "A Mother" in the traditional sense...not B.C. (Before Children) or A.D. (After Denial). I never could quite picture myself playing that roll, so instead I had the approach that my children are not "MY Children", "MY Property" or "MY Possessions"...but more "My Stewardship."

This mind-set was apparent, several years ago, prior to my leaving organized religion. I was attending a church meeting and after it was over, I was chatting with some of the other women when one of them said, "Let's see Laura Lee, you have four kids now, don't you?" I was shocked at what I had just heard! This was shortly after Xavier was born and sleep deprivation was the norm for me at the time, (so my mind wasn't quite right any way,) but it truly hadn't dawned on me till that moment that I was A Mother With Four Kids! What a jolt! This is when I decided with even a firmer conviction that I wanted to be a "good steward" for my children, which in my perception may not necessarily be the "molly coddling, doting mother hen type" that you might meet at a kids' soccer game or a PTA meeting. My kids learned at a young age how to cook their own food, operate the washing machine, mop floors etc. They think I'm a "neat freak" (which is a joke...I can only wish...) because they perceive my demanding excellence in their work, i.e., cleaning the kitchen includes wiping the counters and sweeping the floor, cleaning the bathroom sink includes getting all the grime off the porcelain and shining the fixtures with a towel, and mopping the floor doesn't mean using a mop and pushing the dirt around, it is getting on your hands and knees and scrubbing with a rag to get the gunk out of the corners. I tried to make work fun by putting on "cleaning music" (our favorite rock station) and all pitching in at once. We got more work done in half the time that way!

I also tried to make things outrageous. Not many kids are going to prefer "Healthy Food" to "Junk Food" so I disguised their rations with different names. I concocted something that might be similar to an "everything" omelet and called it "Skexi Food" (if you have ever seen the movie "The Dark Crystal" and the scene where the Skexies were eating **Crawlies,** you will get a good visual image of what I'm talking about.) Since the omelets had ground-up carrots, broccoli, turkey dogs and whatever I had in the fridge, it looked colorful and the things sticking out of it were definitely assumed to be "the crawlies." There was also "dinosaur food," "weevil mush," and an assortment of other gourmet dishes they thought were staples of life. When their friends would come over and the kids told them what we were having for dinner...they wanted to eat at our house too, and...well, that's another story!

With my stewardship of these kids, I also felt it my responsibility to make sure that I taught them some of the Universal laws such as "action and reaction," "cause and effect" or, in other words, how to play the game "What Happens Next?"...(which by the way, I have found that many, many people have grown into adulthood and beyond, never quite figuring this game out!) I felt it was my duty as their "steward" to make sure that when they displayed or created *inappropriate actions* there was an *equal and opposite reaction*, or **Karma.** I have always been a big advocate of Karma, especially **INSTANT KARMA.**

I believe that this type of Karma is the quickest and most efficient way of correcting inappropriate behavior or imbalances, no matter who it is, how old they are, or what their social status is...(which especially includes heads of governments and heads of corporations!) If time and space collapsed, so that cause and effect were closer together, this world would be a different place. Karma coming back around days, months and years later can make the effect seem unrelated to the cause and in most cases, ineffective...especially if you can't remember the cause...(such as if it happened many years prior, and particularly if it was a past life which many people are unaware of).

Here are some examples of how I helped Karma in my kids' life be a little more *instant.*

**Cause:** Teeth marks of sibling #1 on the arm of sibling #2.

**Effect:** Sibling #2 has the option of having their teeth marks in the arm of sibling #1.....(which I found that option was gladly exercised, but only once and the behavior was not just modified, but eliminated!) Now I know you're thinking, "But this sounds like an eye for an eye and a tooth for a tooth" ...and you may be right. However, I tell you what...it worked, it worked well, and it worked permanently! A child has no idea how much pain and damage can be caused by sinking their teeth into the warm flesh of another soft body, and no amount of scolding or "time out" works nearly as quickly or effectively as an intense but brief tactile example..."Ok, here is what you did, and here is what it feels like!" To the biter, it is just a way of retaliating on a spongy body, with little awareness as to the extreme pain and injury they caused... but when it happens to **them,** there is an instant registration that goes off in their little head and they suddenly **"get it!"** I know that there are lots of Child Psychologists out there and also Peace Advocates that may not agree with my protocol. It is my belief however, that this is the kindest, most loving way to get instant results and extremely effective behavior modification. It is also my conviction that the sooner the behavior is responded to, the more likely it is to be resolved permanently...three or four days later is not as effective. It needs to be at the time when the emotion is there and memories are fresh in their little minds. I have often wondered how differently our government and corporate officials would act if they themselves were to be right in the middle of the trauma their decisions and orders caused, and also in the middle of the clean-up or restitution.

What if oil executives whose companies made oil spills, had to be there to see the sea-life dying and feel their pain and suffering? What if they had to stay there with their sleeves rolled up, cleaning up the mess till it was all fixed, and environmental harmony was in balance?

What if corporate executives of companies that create toxic waste, were forced to feel the effects and illness that their waste caused the plants, animals and humans?

What if Heads of State had to be in the middle of the wars they sanctioned and feel the terror, pain and desolation their war had caused? What if they were to be the ones who had to look their *"enemy in the eye"* before shooting them? .....especially if the enemy were an innocent child! What if they were in the center of that war-torn country, to feel the grief and see the blood and devastation from their bombs and weapons? .....then they would truly know the meaning of "Weapons of Mass Destruction!" Perhaps, if they were forced to *be in the middle* of the "War Game Hell" they caused instead of in their air-conditioned luxury offices, their luxury homes and hotels, with fine dining options for every meal .....the rules to their "War Games" would change dramatically.

What if corporate heads had to live a full week as one of their own "lowly employees," feeling like a number, a commodity, an expendable resource or a faceless robot with a microchip in their hand for identification and surveillance?

I believe that we are coming into a time where **Instant Karma** is the only thing that will bring back balance into our out-of-balance world. Waiting for another life-time to do penance just isn't cutting it .....if you don't remember what Karma is for, then it is pretty darned useless and only causes more imbalance. Instant Karma is the most loving thing I can think of to bring full understanding and restitution from whatever pain, suffering and damage you are putting out to the world. What do you think?

**Cause:** Original artwork on the walls with crayon or permanent magic marker.

**Effect:** Scrub until your little hands hurt and then keep scrubbing until you can't see it any more, or until it is barely detectable. Or in some cases, paint it over and over and over because the color RED bleeds through white walls easier than any other color. Or, pack your bags and go live in the scary, haunted-looking, tumbled-down old barn at the end of the block where it doesn't matter if you write on the walls because it's dark and creepy and no one would notice or care since no one ever goes there. (This descriptive option cured my oldest son when he was 5...he never actually went to the creepy old barn, but just the thought of it cured his "wall art" instantly. Then we moved to another neighborhood where there wasn't such a place, so I had to resort to the other means of correction for the rest of the kids.)

**Cause:** Selling old junk from our garage (without permission) to the neighbors (for candy money) and convincing them that these **"Junk Items"** were a **"Must Have"** in their life, and if they ever decided they didn't want them any more, they could just sell them to one of their friends for double the amount that they paid for it and make a profit!

**Effect:** Returning all the $$$ that was swindled and apologize for the Hard Sale. The guilty one's name will be withheld, but I will give you a hint, he is the #2 child....and he was in Kindergarten at the time.

**NOTE:** This backfired though, because the neighbors got so sucked into his *pathetic little face, with heart-rending, sad eyes* that when he came to return their money, every one of them told him that he could keep the cash! Most of the junk that was sold went straight to the local landfill on garbage day, so we got very little of the *junk inventory* back in our garage.

**Cause:** Sibling #1 using their tyrannical authority of being older and at the top of the pecking order, making sibling #2 always have the smaller piece of cake or pie when it is divided.

**Effect:** Ask Sibling #1 to divide the dessert as evenly as possible.....(which was not even remotely close to being even!) then telling sibling #2 that they can have the first choice!   This only happened once and you can't even imagine the lengths they would go to, to make sure that the desserts were exactly symmetrical!

OK, now that you know that my children had a mother who was a little unconventional in her parenting, you can correctly assume that the stories I am about to tell will be entertaining ...but true and candid.

Just like the grand awakening when I realized I had four children, another grand awakening happened about 3 years ago when I was receiving information, instruction and inspiration about writing this book on First Wage Indigos.  It hit me like falling into a Swedish ice plunge .....”Oh my Gosh......all four of my kids are **First Wave Indigos**......no wonder my life with these kids has been so challenging and bizarre!”

From that moment on, my perceptions changed and I had some very important revelations come to me, which I am sharing with you now.  I hope  they will be beneficial to you as you begin to understand the Intrigue and Magic of interacting with First Wave Indigos.

I have said many times, "For every rule on this planet there seems to be an Anti-Rule."  This also is the norm for interacting with Indigos, and for them..... in their world, generally the "Anti-Rule" RULES!

When my oldest son Reuben was about 10 years old, I was doing some research into how people perceive and evaluate their lives.  This research was put into a set of questions that I would use in my counseling practice.  As I was perfecting this system, I was using it to help me understand my own kids and how to communicate with them easier.....(like how to get them to take out the garbage the first or even second time.....ok...the third or fourth time would

106

have even been acceptable...but 14-28 times was way beyond my abilities to maintain composure!)  In this evaluation form, there was:

**Audile,** (interacting and learning through hearing, tone, music, voice etc.);

**Visual,** (interacting and learning through observation, watching videos or TV, reading etc.); and,

**Tactile,** (interacting and learning through physical touch, feeling, hands on, etc.)

As I was working with this fascinating communication tool, I decided to start this procedure with Reuben, since he was the oldest of the brood, to see how my offspring perceived life.  I used Kinesiology and my psychic ability to scan him for his percentages in these 3 perceptual dynamics, so that I would know which was 1st, 2nd, and 3rd in his reality.  In the middle of the evaluation, he said, "Mom, what about the other one?" I looked at him confused and said, "What other one? These are the three ways people perceive life. Which other one are you talking about?" He replied, "Mom, you know.  The **Other** one. The 4th one." I said, "Hmmmmm.  No, I don't know.  What is it?" "Well", he said, "It's just **Knowing.**"

I was stunned. He was absolutely correct!  There was one more...***the internal Knowing...innate knowledge...perceiving by what is inside, not outside!***  It is this very thing, this "internal knowledge" that Indigos feel the most comfortable using, and if they had it their way, would use it at least 80% of the time!

**I**ndigos seem to believe deep inside that, for the most part, the rules to this planet do not apply to them....and...for the most part...they are correct.

There are exceptions to this *"Anti-Rule"* which can sometimes cause much anguish and grief.

I will now tell a tale on my second son, Micah *and as you noticed, I am not going to change the name to protect the guilty on this one!*  Micah was about three years old when this "anti-rule" incident happened.  We had just moved to a new home and I was busy trying to put things away and get some order in the house.  Being four months pregnant with Ma' Lady, my

3rd child, made it a little more challenging to get the job done as quickly as I wanted to. I had the electrician at my house fixing some of the wiring on a ceiling fan which had not been installed correctly, when Micah came up from the basement, tapped me on the leg, and boldly announced, **"Hey Mom! I drank that poison downstairs and didn't even die!"**

I was mortified, but tried to maintain my composure as I bent down, held his shoulders, looked straight into his little mischievous eyes, and said as calmly but firmly as I could..."What poison?!" (I had always been extremely conscientious about keeping Mr. Yuck stickers on anything even remotely poisonous, including the plants! I also kept the really fatal things under lock and key because I knew how exploratory my kids were.)

He looked at me straight back and said, "The one that has the Mr. Yuck Stickers all over it. You told me if I drank poison I would die. I just drank that poison downstairs and I didn't even die!" (I knew he was thinking... either I had been lying to him about the effects of poison just to scare him... OR... "Nanny Nanny Du-Du, I just got one over on you." In his mind, he had over-thrown the laws of nature and he was standing there rubbing it in my face! *Now, I am not saying that it was not possible that he could have used the powers of his super-consciousness to over-ride this physical plane...but it was just a little unnerving to have him so pompous about what he had just done!)* I took his little hand and said, "Come and show me. Where did you get this poison?" He led me downstairs to the room with all the boxes that needed to be unpacked and pointed to a box with all the most toxic cleaning chemicals I owned. He then reached over and handed me a spray bottle covered with Mr. Yuck stickers. "Here it is", he declared proudly, "This is the one!"

My heart sunk. This was by far the most poisonous substance I had in the box. It was some industrial-strength carpet germicide/deodorizer that I had gotten from the carpet cleaners in the last house we rented. There had been severe pet odors in that house and they got so tired of coming back to spray it that they just gave me the spray bottle so I could do it myself.

My problem now, was to determine what the chemical in this spray bottle was and how diluted it was. I immediately called Poison Control and alerted them to the situation. I then proceeded to call the previous landlord to find out the name of the company that had cleaned my carpets...my mind had gone blank and I could not remember who it was. It was close to 5:00 pm and nearly closing-time. I knew I was on a time crunch. At that moment my gabby sister-in-law called and wanted to chat. I told her I had to get off the phone because Micah had swallowed some poison and I needed to make some calls. She instantaneously went into chat mode and wanted to know all the details. I said I didn't have time and I needed to get off NOW! To my dismay she kept asking questions and I was getting so frustrated that I hung up on her. I have never done that to anyone in my life! Several seconds later I picked up the phone to call the carpet cleaners AND SHE WAS STILL THERE! I finally got rude and told her to get off the phone NOW! She finally hung up and I got the carpet cleaners just as they were closing. I explained the situation and they just happened to have my name and the name of the chemical and how many times they had come to my house in their records. What Luck! Now, the remaining problem was to find out how much it had been diluted.....the guy who cleaned my carpet was not working for them anymore and may not have remembered anyway. I called Poison Control back. They said they would investigate it and to take Micah immediately to the Hospital Emergency Room.

I called my husband at work and told him to meet me at the Hospital Emergency. I got one of the neighbors to take Reuben for a few hours and sped off to the hospital. When we got there, Poison Control had already alerted the Hospital Emergency Team. They had a room for him and were waiting for us! I was impressed. I had never had anything but negative experiences with hospitals, till now. They were busy calling Poison Controls around the country to find out about this toxic chemical. When we got into the room, they put Micah in one of the little cages.....I mean cribs.....(it looked like a miniature metal cage to me because the bars were metallic and several inches taller than the one I had at home. I secretly envied such a device, only I would have improved upon it by putting a lid on top!) He looked so cute sitting there in his little flannel shirt and overalls...people would come by the hall and say..."Ohhhh look, isn't he so cute"...*and I'm thinking..."It's a darned good thing he's so cute or I'd...Well, it's just a good thing! " Then I thought, "Maybe he deliberately tries to be cute so he wont get into trouble when he does stuff like this!"* (For some reason I don't think I'm too far off on this one!)

They first gave him some ipecac and a little bowl to throw up in. This he did with no problem, as by now it was almost a form of entertainment to him. To my dismay, I had caught him before, bent over the toilet. This was being instigated by the daring and taunting of his older brother Reuben and their friend Joel, (who is also an Indigo) chanting, "Puke,

Micah, puke! Puke, Micah, puke!" He had this trick down pat by now and could almost hurl on command. He showed me the bowl, and said with a sort of bizarre pride, "Look Mom, I puked!

This went on for about 30 minutes, and then the nurse brought in a paper cup full of liquid charcoal. She handed it to Micah and told him to drink it, and she would give him a sucker. He took one sip, closed his eyes tight, put his hand in a fist, and shivered for several seconds. Then he gave the cup back to the nurse. She said, as she returned it back to him, "Here honey, drink the rest." He held it, looked at it for a moment, and then once more returned it to her and said in a very polite little voice, "No, thank you. You can drink it."

The nurse and I both had to turn away and try to conceal (and repress) our response to burst out laughing. He was so courteous and generous about it; I was wondering how in the world she was going to get out of this one. The nurse stepped over to me and said quietly, "This is the worst tasting stuff, try some yourself, it's really nasty!" I turned my back to them, took a little swallow and just about gagged. It was hideous! It was gritty, thick, black, and tasted like someone had swept the chimney, put it in a cup and then added a little water. It was absolutely GROSS!

Finally, with some coaxing and a tremendous amount of bribing, (bribery always worked very well with my kids) the nurse got Micah to take a few swigs and then stuck an all-day-sucker in his mouth till the nasty taste went away. This cycle went on for about an hour till nearly all the charcoal was gone.

We finally got word from the Poison Control in Denver who confirmed that we were giving the right treatment to him and his chances of survival were good. The difficult thing was the fact that we were not sure how much he actually drank, as he was really vague about this, changing the story each time. The first time, it was a lot. Then, he was confessing that it was only a little squirt.

**NOTE:** *This incident was a year before I learned the incredible and most valuable art of M.R.T. or Kinesiology to test the body for nutritional deficiencies and for truth and lies. After I learned this precious ability, it was amazing the "True confessions" that would surface when I threatened to "test" my kids for the truth about how things got broken, treats that were eaten without permission and who hit who first!*

The hospital kept Micah there for about another hour for observation and then released him. Their conclusion was that he hadn't had enough to do any serious damage and if we just kept an eye on him for 48 hours and if there are no symptoms, he should be fine. (Again, I'm eyeing and envying that metal cage visualizing a lid on it! Keeping an eye on him for 48 hours seemed like an impossible task.) But, I did it and he is fine and alive today to have me remind him of this and many other tales that might be revealed in this book. He is over 21 and legal now, so I am breathing a sigh of relief. Somehow I kept him alive to adulthood and now he is on his own. When he came home from college for a Christmas visit 2 years ago, I took him out to dinner. After taking a walk down memory lane, reminiscing about his child-hood and the "anti-rules" he lived by, I showed him some of the gray hairs in my bangs. I said, "Micah, see these? **They have your name on them!**" We both laughed, but he knew I spoke the truth!

This little tale is just one of many that I might make public.....(ahhhhhhh Micah, Karma is finally on my side, and now I have the opportunity of helping it along.)

One remarkable quality of most Indigos, is that they can calculate solutions to problems in their head quickly and effortlessly. *(Except when it comes to resolving conflict with their siblings...then this innate ability seems to go dormant!)* Here are a few examples.

When Xavier was in kindergarten, I was stressing over what to do about our oil-leaking car. We were getting ready to move, and I had just cleaned the driveway of oil spills. There was no place to park on the road, and I didn't want to get the driveway spotted again. Xavier came in and saw that I was upset. When I explained the situation to him he said, "Mom, listen, I have a plan. Just get a big piece of cardboard, drive the car over it so when it leaks, it will leak just on the cardboard. Then, when we move, you can just throw the cardboard away and the driveway will stay clean!"

I was dumbfounded. It was too simple! Why didn't I think of this? His immediate solution to my problem was the simplest and the most efficient. This is typical of how Indigos think.

**I**ndigos display totally different perceptions in life and how to follow instructions. I remember going to Xavier's Kindergarten parent teacher conference and when the teacher saw me, she just started to laugh and snicker while she was finishing up with another parent. I just took a deep breath. I knew it was going to be an interesting conference! When she was ready for me, she said, "Ooooooohh, I have been waiting for this conference with you." (I didn't quite know what this meant so I quickly started thinking of excuses to leave and have my husband do this conference instead!) She said, "Come on in and have a seat." (I couldn't think of any viable excuses fast enough so I was stuck). The teacher proceeded to tell me what an interesting and amusing child Xavier was, and then told me about how she had the children introduce themselves and their world to the class. Part of this assignment was to make a self-portrait. She said all the kids got their papers and crayons out and began to work. Xavier sat there for the longest time, and then came up to her desk and said. "Miss...(name has been withheld), I don't know how to draw Humans"...(not "I don't know how to draw myself" or "draw people," it was "I don't know how to draw **Humans!**") His teacher thought it was amusing that he would be so adult and biological in his language, and she said, "Well honey, just go sit down and do your best." Xavier walked back to his desk and picked up a crayon. The teacher noticed that he kept looking under his chair, and thought that he must have dropped something. A few minutes later he came up to her desk and inquired, "How do you spell Ninja Turtles?" She was not quite sure of the connection between Ninja Turtles and a self-portrait, but she complied and wrote it on a piece of paper for him. "Thank you very much," Xavier said, as he once more returned to his desk.

A little while later some of the kids finished and handed in their art assignment and began other projects while they waited for recess. When the allotted time expired and all of the portraits were handed in, Xavier asked if he could have more time. Wondering what the problem was, the teacher walked over to his desk and viewed his project. She said she was absolutely intrigued, impressed and amused at what she saw. Xavier had meticulously drawn two feet wearing Ninja Turtle shoes, and the stubs of two legs were in progress. In his mind you had to start a project at the bottom and work up. He was doing this art project, paying extreme and meticulous attention to every detail!

*Again, very typical of how the Indigo mind operates differently than those in society's mainstream.*

At this conference, another family story surfaced. When Xavier was only 2 days old, I had just brought him home from the hospital and had him sitting on the floor in his infant seat (never on a table or counter...always the floor so he would not get "accidentally" knocked off). I had to go to get the clothes out of the dryer and when I came back I noticed that his mouth was moving and he was sort of gagging. I ran over to him and fished out something soggy and gritty. I asked his sister Ma' Lady, who was barely 2 years old, what was in his mouth. She proudly replied, "He was hungwy so I fed him." I was really uneasy about what this might have been, and I responded, "What kind of food?" Ma' Lady marches to the cupboard and points to the opened bag of tortilla chips! I took a deep breath and said, "Ohhh, Ma' Lady— he can't have any of that kind of food yet. Look (and I opened his mouth exposing his gums)...Do you see any teeth?" "No..." "That's right, he doesn't have any teeth yet so he can't chew! Don't ever give him any food till he gets teeth.... Ok?" She said "Ok, Mommy." I gave her a hug and said, "I want you to watch and make sure that NO ONE gives Xavier any food without my permission, and if they do, you come and tell me. Ok?" (**NOTE:** *This little job of authority over him seemed to carry on through childhood and teendom to present day.....she is STILL telling me if Xavier gets into any junk food!*)

Ok, so now you have the story.....but it got a little twisted when Xavier related the incident to his class. As he was in the spotlight showing his self-portrait, and telling his class about himself and his family, he said....."And when I was a tiny baby, my sister tried to kill me by feeding me a 'Torpedo Chip'!" The teacher thought it was so funny she could hardly tell me the story. This is typical of how Xavier displays his "drama-king" abilities, and somehow uses his powers of vocal alchemy and persuasion to make people love and adore him.

Another account of how Xavier's "Indigo Mind" works: When he was 6 or 7, I was busy trying to get some journaling done and had asked Xavier three times to get ready for bed. He walked into my room and by now I'm a little annoyed at his not responding to my request to brush his teeth and go to bed, and asked, "Now what!?" He replied in a very casual but direct manner, "Ok, Mom. I will, but first—could you please teach me all about quantum physics?" I was floored! Now I'm thinking, "This is one of the best strategies he has ever come up with yet to stay up for a while longer! If I say 'NO!' then I am losing the golden opportunity to educate my child (which he knew would be hard for me to resist)" I felt quite confident that, in his mind, he didn't know exactly what quantum physics entailed, but it sure as heck sounded like it would take awhile to explain...and might even be interesting...what a bonus for him!

Indigos seem to be "in their own little world" sometimes, and my oldest son Reuben epitomizes this. He would, for no apparent reason, get up and just wander around, looking up at the sky or ceiling or whatever the environment was. This did not sit well with his 2nd grade teacher who would severely reprimand and humiliate him in front of the class. I'm not quite sure what happened in school that year between him and his teacher, (even though I was there from time to time volunteering as a room mother) but he had a definite personality change that year.

The next year his 3rd grade teacher wanted to put him on Ritalin! I had a fit and absolutely would not allow it. I was appalled that this was considered an option! Reuben was not mean and hostile to the other kids. He wasn't hyperactive. He wasn't necessarily disruptive. He would just get up and wander in the back of the classroom. If he was asked to sit down, he would. I asked some of the other teachers I knew what he did during recess and they said he would go into the forest and just wander there until the bell rang. This was so typical of him. Instead of playing contact sports with the other boys, he opted to commune with the trees. I was telling one of my friends this story a few years later and as we were talking she said, "Where is Reuben anyway?" I went to the window to see him eating a piece of toast, looking up in the sky and wandering around the back yard. We both just looked at each other and laughed.

This eating and wandering thing never quit. To this day he doesn't sit down to eat very often. I remember one day we had Thanksgiving at my house and there weren't enough chairs. Well, you can guess who had no problem with that. Reuben willingly volunteered to stand...the guests were concerned that he had to stand with his plate in his hand, but we both assured them that it was no problem...I know it was hard for them to understand, but he actually preferred it. (Too bad this refined talent isn't something that could be put on a résumé!)

Male Indigos seem to be very intent on "pushing the envelope" when it comes to knowing what the rules are and exactly how far they can get those rules to bend. Two of my boys had this one down to a precise science. When Xavier was in the 8th grade, he didn't really care for his math teacher, so he retaliated by constantly missing assignments. When the notes would come home from his teacher (or phone calls because most of the notes never got to me) he would swear that he did the assignments. (Later I found out that he did, in fact, do the assignments, but neglected to hand them in! In his perception it was a good way to flip off the teacher...do the assignments and then keep them in his binder and not hand them in or else hand them in late!) Well, this went on until the end of school, and the awful thing I warned him about was now going to become a reality. He was going to have to do the dreaded "Summer School!" I thought this wretched replacement of his summer video game-time would cure him of his blatant retribution. I felt that, even though it was a super inconvenience for me to have to get him up in the morning when I didn't get to bed till the wee hours of the morning myself, he was now going to have to learn some responsibility for his actions, or rather ***"non-action."*** I would ask him how summer school was and get the pat answer of, "Fine" which I thought was his way of saying ... "Just fine, now stop trying to rub it in and leave me alone." The strange thing was, he didn't seem to be THAT upset about it, and a week later when I asked, he told me that he loved summer school and wants to do it again next year!

I was in shock. Either he was being super sarcastic with me or something was seriously out of place, and I needed a reality check! I finally got up the courage to call his teacher and got the answers I was not prepared to hear. Xavier was actually acting as her assistant and was helping tutor the other kids in the class! She said, "Xavier is a delight in class, and I'm really glad he is taking summer school. He is such a happy kid and really takes some of the load off of me."

I then asked what I thought was a silly question, "Is he handing in his assignments?" She replied, "Oh, no, he actually doesn't, but in summer school, (and the kids don't know this) it is not mandatory, you just have to show up." (Somehow he got wind of this confidential information and milked it to the max!)

And here I was thinking that the only reason he might remotely be ok with summer school was the free snacks. They were a bonus!

Now I'm about to tell another tale that could have been on one of the TV news stories about amazing kids. I was talking on the phone to one of my clients when there was some commotion in the kitchen. (You have to understand that commotion in the kitchen at dinner-time was NOT an uncommon thing at our house.) I didn't think much of it and just kept conversing with my client till Xavier said, "Moooooooom....Ma' Lady just puked all over the floor!" I quickly got off the phone and ran in the kitchen. There was Ma' Lady hunched over totally traumatized and Micah standing next to her with his arm around her shoulder asking if she was all right. I assumed that she had just gotten sick, but found out that was not the case. Ma' Lady (who was about eight years old at the time) had some how gotten some chicken stuck in her throat and was choking. Micah, (then age 12) saw that she was in serious trouble and holding her throat, so he stood her up and tried to do the Heimlich Maneuver on her. The first try didn't do anything and caused even more fear and hysteria in Ma' Lady.....so he did it again, which still did nothing except now she was really in trouble and horrified. So he did it again with extreme force and instantly dislodged the chicken (and everything else in her stomach) onto the floor. His quick response, and his calm "take charge" attitude along with the knowledge and self-confidence to do the procedure, had saved his sister's life! Before I even knew what was going on, he had taken responsibility and just handled the situation. Then he sat back down and finished his own chicken like it was no big deal and happened all the time. It took several months however, for Ma' Lady to recover because she had a very strong fear imprint of having anything the least bit bulky in her throat. She lived on protein drinks, soups, milk, and eventually soggy cereal and watered down mush for several weeks while she gained the confidence to take in larger things like soggy toast, mashed carrots and potatoes.

After reminiscing about this and other experiences, I came to realize that my children were not "normal." However, at the time, I did not know exactly how or why.

Many Indigos have no problem when it comes to defining our language, telling others when they have misinterpreted their words, and being bold and honest in their evaluations. Such is the case that happened several years ago when I was on a hike with my kids and my now ex-husband. We were nearing the top of a steep hill that looked and felt more like a steep mountain than a hill. Xavier was lagging seriously behind since he was the youngest (about eight or nine at the time) and his legs were shorter than everyone else's. Finally, totally frustrated at being on the tail end and having a very difficult time keeping up, (and being the drama king that he was) he stopped and yelled, "Hey, did it ever occur to any of you that I could use a little help back here?!" With that my ex-husband and Micah immediately called back. "Come on Xavier, you can make it, one foot in front of the other.....you can do it, just a little further to go now, your doing good, just keep going!" Xavier didn't budge but got totally aggravated and yelled up at them, " I said I needed HELP, *not* ENCOURAGE-MENT!!!!"

I about busted up laughing. It was so funny because his reply was absolutely accurate from his point of view. (I have to confess that I too have felt that way when asking the "higher ups" such as my guides and guardians for help!)

Another incident happened when Xavier was about five years old. We had a healing clinic in our home in the lower level. This was good in many ways, (a quick commute in the morning from the kitchen to the second level of the home) but also had its challenges with the kids there. One day one of our regular clients pulled up to the curb and got out of her car. Xavier was outside playing and ran up to meet her and walked her to the door. As they were chatting, he boldly asked her, "Are you going to pay my Dad for your massage when you're done?" Amused at his tenacity, she said, "Yes, here's my check book, I always pay him for my massages, why?" (I can only imagine what was going on in her head with our son interrogating her like this!) Then Xavier explained, "GREAT! ...You see, my Dad owes me a dollar and he can't pay me till you pay him. Now I know he has the money!" Then he ran off to play with the other kids. I never would have known about this but our client was so amused and impressed with his reasoning, that she related the story to us. (I have no idea what other stories our clients had that they didn't feel as free as this woman to reveal...and I'm not so sure that I want to know!)

Indigos in general have very strong empathic abilities, and also abilities for "self correction." My daughter Ma' Lady seemed to take this to the next level when it came to her relationship with me. There were countless episodes of her picking up on MY emotions, MY stresses, and in many cases, psychic assaults that were directed toward and intended for ME! (The phenomena of her being my "front man" has since been modified and corrected, but it took a while to understand it and handle it).

This trend became crystal clear to me several years ago when Ma' Lady was still in grade school. An energetic shift came on suddenly and within a few hours she developed an animosity and distain for me that was soooo out of character for her. It was almost like she had turned into someone else. This went on for a couple of days and I was wondering if it was some new breed of "pre-teen PMS" or something! Nothing I could do was right. I couldn't brush her hair right, I couldn't help her with her homework right, I couldn't have any kind of conversation with her without it turning into a big drama. This was in May. It was getting close to Mother's Day and Ma' Lady was calculating diabolical things she could do to wound me. She got this brilliant plan that she was sure would do the trick. She went to the Dollar Store with her friends, bought me a candleholder, wrapped it up, and then planned on giving it to me early...before Mother's Day so it wouldn't be "special." (This goes to show what a loving little girl she was if the worst thing she could think of to upset me and hurt my feelings, was to give me a present at the wrong time!)

I was in my room on the bed reading when she came home. She darted over to me, shoved the present in my face while ripping the wrapping paper off, and said in a sinister little voice,

"Here, I'm giving you your Mother's Day present early!" I thanked her for it, but at the same time was quite confused at the vindictive and hostile energy around this "gift."

I would soon find out.

Not long after this incident, I was trying to help her put barrettes in her hair, and she got livid. She screamed at me and said every spiteful thing she could think of and told me to leave her alone... I was ruining everything! I became really weirded out by this whole scene, so I went to my room and shut the door. I heard her Dad say to her, "Ma' Lady, why are you being so mean to your mother?!" What I heard her say next made my blood run cold. She said in a nasty, hateful voice... "Because I want her to HURT!"

This shocked me and I knew there was something serious going on that had nothing to do with how Ma' Lady really felt about me. I sat down on my bed, and asked my guides to please give me some clarity. What I was shown made total sense to me, but it wasn't an easy road to reconcile.

My husband and I were in the process of separating, and his new girlfriend thought I was The Devil! She despised me and was always throwing psychic spears and poison at me. Some purely on her own volition; some she had help on. Her anger and extreme animosity toward me, I believe, made her a perfect conduit through which other energies/entities to assault me. I think she was "being used." When I identified this problem and attempted to show my ex-husband what was really happening, I was perceived as the "whacko, psycho psychic weirdo who was so jealous that I was losing my reality." (Jealousy on my end was not the problem. I was trying to be as evolved as possible in my thinking about this relationship, and was more accommodating than a room full of politicians that had just been paid off!)

The new girlfriend was a very left-brained, educated woman and was constantly criticizing and ridiculing me for the "Weird Shit" and "WooWoo" I was into. This made her the perfect decoy. No one would suspect that she really did know something about dark energy because she had the perfect disguise. She would say things like, "All I do is send Laura Lee love, and I don't know why she is saying these horrible things about me. I will just keep sending her love though and maybe it will help her stop being so hostile toward me."

There were many, many instances of this scenario, and I thought it would never end. (It did...but took about 9 more years!)

After I could see what was happening on a psychic/energetic level, I grabbed my Aurauralite pendant, closed my eyes, and said... "Help me show my daughter the truth."

I called Ma' Lady into my room and said, "I know what the problem is and how to fix it." Ma' Lady was stiff and cold at first but soon relaxed and softened as I continued. "Remember how I told you that since you are so close to me and we love each other so very much, that sometimes you get TOO close to me, and the energies that are meant for me get stuck in you? Dad's girlfriend despises me and is using you to get to me and hurt me." Ma' Lady looked at me in shock and total realization, which then turned into regret and grief. Her eyes started to water as she said, "Oh, Mommy, I am sooo sorry I hurt you! What can I do to fix it?" I showed her how to take some deep breaths and disconnect. This was accomplished within minutes and I had my little girl back again! All she needed was the truth and she had the innate understanding and wisdom to know how to quickly fix the problem...even at such a young age.

Ma' Lady then told me how terrible she felt immediately after she ripped the wrapping paper off the present while shoving it in my face, and then dashing out of the room. She said she didn't know why she did these horrible things, but just did what she felt she had to do. I hugged her and said I understood, and a new bond of camaraderie was formed between us.

Many, many times this woman had been the conduit for other energies and entities to identify and target me. Using her seething animosity toward me as an amplifier, they were able to beef up the already enraged energy daggers to new and lethal levels.

About a month later Ma' Lady was caught in another crossfire while she was away visiting her cousins.

I was hoping to sleep in since it was summer and had been up late the night before. I was awakened though by the phone. As I turned over to pick it up, it suddenly felt like someone had hurled me across the room! Instantaneously I was impaired with dizziness!

I quickly got off the phone and lay there trying not to move. The slightest movement or motion would put me in a spin—I couldn't move my eyes back and forth without getting dizzy! I did everything I could think of to counteract it...deep breathing, herbs, vitamins, minerals, electrolytes, reflexology, sunlight, positive thinking.....nothing seemed to make a difference. A horrible fear descended on me that this condition would never stop and this was how my life would end! All I could do was hold my Aurauralite and petition its assistance. After several hours of this I started to get upset and worried that the Aurauralite wasn't working, (but I found out later that it was indeed working... and working overtime!) I know now it was shielding me and protecting me from the majority of the energies assaulting me, and if I didn't have it by my side, assisting me, I would have been so knocked off balance and terrified that this fatal attack would have permanently taken me out of the game of Earth Life!

It was devastating. There were kids to take care of, a business to operate, and besides all that, we were in the last few days of promotions for a Kryon event I was hosting...I didn't have time to get dizzy and sick! I felt like crying most of the time, but couldn't even do that because it made me dizzy too! I tried to go to the bathroom by myself once.....BIG Mistake! It felt like someone literally threw me onto the tub and hit my head so hard it nearly knocked me unconscious! I felt helpless, hopeless and trapped. It was soooo depressing and scary.

Upon careful evaluation, I knew two things for sure: One, it was some sort of psychic assault or dark magick, and two, that I was going to find the answers!

After several days of holding the Aurauralite, going to my core, and trying to stay calm, I started getting a little stability back and progressed to semi-functioning again. I could not however, tilt my head back, even slightly, or I would go into a spin!

I kept thinking, "Thank Goodness Ma' Lady isn't here and getting sucked into this mess" .....but what I didn't know is that Ma' Lady was caught in the crossfire and picked up this energy too.

She was staying with her cousins on top of a mountain with no electricity and telephone. About the time that I got hit with my "Dizzy Spell," (Spell being a truly appropriate word here) Ma' Lady got a terrible nosebleed that lasted for hours. It scared her, as well as her aunt and uncle. All she could think of was that she needed to come home and be with me. It was about 4 more days before Ma' Lady and I reunited, and when she told me of her horror story, I knew there was a connection and turned into a Mother Bear! "You can go after me, BUT STAY AWAY FROM MY KIDS!!!"

After relentless scans and searches, I finally found the solution to this bizarre ailment. I discovered that when I left the house for more than 36 hours, my symptoms dissipated. Within 12 hours of returning home all the dizziness returned. I realized that there was "something" in the house that was broadcasting and making me sick! It didn't affect anyone else.....just me. I looked and looked for whatever it was, but never found it. Five months later I moved to another house and the symptoms completely and permanently vanished.

**NOTE:** *A longer version of this story will be in the upcoming book "Got ghosts??? A practical guide to Ghost Busting" by my Ghost Busting partner, Ronnie Foster, and I.*

Ma' Lady is such a close friend and ally that sometimes I think she is my Guardian Angel on Earth! I tell her, "Every mother should have a "Ma' Lady!" ...(Yes, that is her real name; the name that is on her birth certificate...but THAT is another story!)

And this is how it was, to the best of my memory, growing with and raising this brood of "Indigo Kids." (Yeah, I know. You're thinking, "She couldn't even remember how many children she had. How accurate can this be!?")

Well, I guess you could ask my kids, and when they answer, muscle test them using Kinesiology the way I did to see if they are telling the truth!

## What My Indigo Children are doing now:

**Reuben:** Joined the Navy and is stationed in Honolulu, Hawaii, working with, maintaining and troubleshooting the hydraulics of missile-launching systems. When he gets out of the service next year he plans on going to school in Seattle and, after graduating, is hoping to create new and innovative computer games.

**Micah:** Graduated from DeVry Computer School in Phoenix in February 2004 and is now working for Micron, fixing robots. He just got engaged to Ma' Lady's college roommate Kaylin. Micah took jobs as a waiter to put himself through school. While there, he lost his car in a crash and had to work extra hours to pay for a car he didn't have, lost at least five bicycles to thieves, and still maintained a good GPA, his sanity and his sense of humor.

**Ma' Lady:** Is a junior at Washington State University majoring in Physical Therapy and works part-time and summers with the USDA. She helps me with my Cutting-Edge Healing Labs, and is my very best girlfriend! I can always count on her to make me laugh when my humor quota is down. She is a free thinker and is constantly expanding her views on world religions and spiritual beliefs.

**Xavier:** Just graduated from high school. He uses his creative mind and unique brand of humor to buck the system and do as little as possible to get by. He joined the debate team and was selected to go to State and Nationals. Debate was a perfect and appropriate place to display his quick wit and "smart mouth." His last stated goal was to attend law school so he could buck the system on a grander scale. As always, that's subject to change.

# Chapter 10

# You Might be an Indigo if...

It all started one crazy evening in my Knights' Chat Room on "Indigo Night" when we were sitting around chatting about how "odd" we all were and how other people just didn't have a clue as to who we really were and how we thought. One thing led to another and one joke lead to the next, and then I got the bright idea.....Hey, lets do a spoof on Jeff Foxworthy's "You might be a Redneck if".....

It turned out to be one of the most enjoyable and humorous evenings I've had in a long time. Here is a sample of what came out of the chat room that night! I have given credit to these creative authors by using their chat room handles. You don't have to be a psychic to figure out that these all have validity and most likely actually happened!

< Frank S>You might be an Indigo ...If you try to explain what you are thinking to someone, and they look at you like a dog being shown a card trick.

<angelboy>You might be a Indigo if... you're arguing with yourself and someone answers.

< Frank S>If you get in more trouble for being right than for being wrong, YOU MIGHT BE AN INDIGO!

<sunwalker>You might be an Indigo... if you really think you can fly.

<angelboy>You might be an indigo if... you bring back an imaginary friend and he reprograms your VCR.

<Yeshiva>You might be an indigo if ...you get sudden urges to hug trees in the middle of Central Park and people stare at you like you are crazy.

<Frank S>If you're the one everyone calls to figure out what the heck just happened to their computer, YOU MIGHT BE AN INDIGO!

<sunwalker>You might be an Indigo if ...your teacher calls your mom to have conference with her at school because you were talking to a man in the window that the teacher could not see.

< Frank S>If you're the one who the teacher says "Anyone else can answer the

question but you", YOU MIGHT BE AN INDIGO!

<Yeshiva>If no one can follow ur topics, u might be an indigo...

<angelboy>You might be an Indigo... if you heal the rip in your pants.

<sunwalker>You might be an Indigo ...when no one thinks your humor is funny.

<tmann>You might be an Indigo if... you talk to infants less than one year old.

<Yeshiva>If u can see colors on people's head and can see things breathe even after hitting your head against the wall to make it stop... you might be an Indigo.

<Frank S>If the most common phrase people say to you is, "You're weird", YOU MIGHT BE AN INDIGO!

<Dean>You might be an indigo if ...you start diving into swimming pools to save small insects from drowning.

<angelboy>You might be an indigo if ...you put your crystal in water because you thought you heard it tell you to.

<Frank S>If authority figures refer to you as a "walking disruption", YOU

MIGHT BE AN INDIGO!

<Yeshiva>You might be an Indigo if ...you're caught hitting the table for ants to leave it before you clean it so you won't kill them all.

<little tiger>You might be an indigo ...if when you go into a forest to practice meditation, all the little birds around you suddenly stop flying and look at you.

<angelboy>If you take Prozac so often that you collect the dispensers because you think they will fetch you a profit on eBay, ...you might be an Indigo.

<Yeshiva>You might be an indigo... if they have to ask you to leave the room in

ethics class cuz the teacher can't advance since u r interrupting all the time to say what u don't agree with...

<Dean>You might be an indigo if ...you end up being a street sweeper tidying up after messy people.

<Misty> Hahahaaaa, just one more job for "The Cosmic Clean Up Crew"

<Frank S>If you go to a party, and you'd rather talk to the pets than the people there... YOU MIGHT BE AN INDIGO.

<tmann>You might be an indigo ...if you teach your two year old mantras.

<angelboy>If you lay in bed at night trying to switch the light off by mental powers... you might be an Indigo.

<Dean>You might be an indigo ...if you end up having your wedding in a barn instead of a church.

<tmann>You might be an indigo... if you talk to your vegetables before you eat them.

<little tiger>You might be an indigo if you can hear the trees talking to you.

<sunwalker>You might be an Indigo if ...you know the lines to movies never seen.

<Yeshiva>You might be an Indigo...if u stare at dogs and give them orders mentally and then wait till they obey u.

<Frank S>If you know who Georges Gurdjieff is, and can't understand why nobody else knows who he is, YOU MIGHT BE AN INDIGO!

<angelboy> If your unity candle goes out mysteriously at your own wedding... You might be an Indigo.

 <angelboy> (... that's info you can all learn from)

<myah>You might be an indigo if ...a bird calls you outside at night to talk.

<Yeshiva>You might be an Indigo...if random lights go on and off in the streets as u walk by.

<little tiger>If you have started reading Spinoza when you were 15 years old then you might be an Indigo.

126

<Sunwalker>You might be indigo if...The rest of your family wonders if you were adopted.

<Misty>You might be an Indigo ...if your MOTHER wonders if you were adopted!

<angelboy>You might be an Indigo ...if you can confuse a cop after being pulled over to get out of a ticket...

<Dean>You might be an indigo... if you cheer and clap when the Ents from lord

of the rings stick up for them self.

<Yeshiva>U might be an indigo... if you taught ur parents how to raise u.

<angelboy>If the word concentrate means to roll your eyes to the back of your head and chant....You might be an Indigo.

<little tiger>If you can heal yourself only by deep breathing techniques then... You might be an indigo.

<Frank S>If you collect books of "forbidden knowledge" like some people collect "Beanie Babies", YOU MIGHT BE AN INDIGO!

<angelboy>If you have ever wished to manifest a fire ball and then change your mind because you may not be able to turn it off... You might be an Indigo.

<Yeshiva>You might be an Indigo...if homework time means following every fly that passes you by... or counting the lines in the wood, or looking at a random flower out the window, or counting the dots on the ceiling.

<sunwalker>You might be an Indigo... when you bring home big rocks, and say "but mom, it followed me home."

<angelboy>If you find yourself arguing with your spirit guide because you didn't like what they had to say...You might be an Indigo.

<little tiger>You might be an indigo if you think the Elves from the Lord of the Rings are real.

\<sunwalker>You might be an indigo ...if you eat Aurauralite.

\<angelboy>You might be an Indigo if you no longer go by your birth name...

\<tmann>You might be an indigo... if your friends ask you how you did something and you say, "I manifested it."

\<Dean>You might be an indigo if ...for Christmas you asked your mother and farther for a book on Physics and got a book on wrestling instead.

\<sunwalker>You might be an Indigo... when you start sentence with "Energetically speaking."

\<tmann>You might be an indigo if... you have a dream journal next to your bed.

\<little tiger>You might be an indigo... if you can actually see the elves from the Lords of the Rings novel all around you when you walk alone in the forest.

\<Frank S>If you listen to microtonal music and "The Residents", and can't understand why others don't like it, YOU MIGHT BE AN INDIGO!

\<sunwalker>You might be and Indigo if ...Your family is glad when you go home to your own house.

\<Yeshiva>U might be an indigo if ...u have complete conversations with fairies and unicorns, and say it out loud with "normal" people around.

\<angelboy>You might be an indigo ...if people leave your party because you and another Indigo are playing with an energy ball.

\<tmann>You might be an indigo ...if you feel a pain in your back and think it is your heart chakra.

\<Frank S>If you compose songs in the key of D++, YOU MIGHT BE AN INDIGO!

\<angelboy>If you pick your friends by what color they project... you might be an Indigo.

\<tmann>You might be an indigo... if you raise the frequency of your water before you drink it.

\<sunwalker>If you can understand this chat room, you must be an indigo!

128

<little tiger>You might be an indigo if …you think you maybe could have been Paul in the "Dune" novel from Frank Herbert.

<Yeshiva>You might be an Indigo if u leave a cafe because the "energy was making u feel Uncomfortable."

<Frank S>If you play a musical instrument that most people have never even seen, YOU MIGHT BE AN INDIGO!

<angelboy>If you choose what you are going to eat by the dream you had the night before… you might be an Indigo.

<tmann>You might be an indigo… if you choose what color outfit to wear for the day by which chakra is buzzing the most.

<angelboy>If teletubbys scare the hell out of you… you might be an Indigo.

<Frank S>Heck, if television scares the heck out of you, you might be an Indigo!

<tmann>If you haven't watched TV in over two years, you might be an Indigo.

<angelboy>If you can remember the cabin # of your room on the titanic… you might be an indigo.

<tmann>If you can remember the harmonic frequency to open the door of the great pyramid at Giza, you might be an Indigo.

<Frank S>If you walk into a cafe, and find yourself listening to five different conversations simultaneously, YOU MIGHT BE AN INDIGO!

<tmann>If you can type faster than you can read, you might be an indigo.

<Dean>You might be an indigo if …you start lecturing pump stations on how oil is messing up the planet.

<Frank S>If you were fixing household appliances when you were five years old, YOU MIGHT BE AN INDIGO!

<sunwalker>You might be an Indigo if... you see the royal family as other than human.

<Yeshiva>If u look at the stars and talk to them sending messages to your "other family" ....you might be an Indigo.

<Dean>You might be an indigo if ...you spent the last 10 years in anger management.

<Frank S>If you look at the belt of Orion in the night sky, and dream of someday "going home", YOU MIGHT BE AN INDIGO!

<little tiger>If you think that you are an alien child coming from outer space and being adopted by humans then You might be an indigo.

<angelboy>While leaving your body you find that your nose itches and your astral body scratches it for you...you might be an Indigo.

<Dean>If you worship yoda you could be an indigo,

<Frank S>If you watched "Eraserhead" in the theater, and laughed so hard the ushers threw you out, YOU MIGHT BE AN INDIGO!

<sunwalker>You might be an Indigo if..... you always get parking spot in busy parking zones with time still on meter.

<Yeshiva>If people don't laugh at ur jokes until they think about them...you might be an Indigo.

<angelboy>If you can tell the exact time you got mad because your battery fried...you might be an Indigo.

<sunwalker>You might be an Indigo if the movie "Contact" was great to you.

<sunwalker>You might be indigo if you call healers in the middle of the night saying, "They're after me Again"!!!

<Misty>You might be if you have as many lives as your cat.

<Frank S>If you don't get any better in group therapy, but you end up driving everyone else crazy, YOU MIGHT BE AN INDIGO!

<Misty>If the "powers that be" keep trying to destroy you.....you might be an Indigo.

<sunwalker>You might be an Indigo if....you scare your Medical Dr.

<angelboy>If you can tell everyone around you is lying to impress the other people...You might be an Indigo.

<Adonis>You may be a red-necked indigo if you think the bottoms of broken beer bottles have crystal-like qualities.

<tmann>If your friend says "my neck hurts" and you put your hand on it and the pain goes away ...You might be an Indigo.

<sunwalker>You might be an Indigo ....when you keep looking at clouds and they melt.

<angelboy>If you see a ghost and try to corner him...You might be an Indigo.

<sunwalker>If you say, "sorry for the weather" ...you might be an Indigo.

<Frank S>You may be a red-necked indigo if ...you try to rewire the refrigerator on the front lawn into a Tesla transformer.

<windfire>If you're addicted to Star Trek you might be an Indigo.

<tmann>You might be an indigo if...you can't find the keys to your Merkaba Vehicle.

<Frank S>If you're addicted to Star Trek you might be a nerd. If you are building a Star Trek warp drive core in you basement... you might be an indigo.

<angelboy>If you bless money then give it away in the hopes that it will come back ten fold... you might be an Indigo.

<little tiger>You might be an indigo if... you think that you have been sent all alone on this world.

<tmann>You might be an indigo... if you say "But captain, we don't have enough power!!"

<angelboy>You might be a Indigo if.... you play chess with dead people.

<tmann>You might be an indigo if... you have teleported your cereal box onto the kitchen table.

<windfire>If you started talking a whole other language suddenly .... you might be an Indigo.

<Misty>You might be an indigo if ....you are there and you understood that language!

<Dean>You might be an indigo if ...you turn you microwave in to an anti-gravity unit.

<tmann>You might be an indigo if ...you think Spring Equinox is New Years'.

<angelboy>If narcolepsy means journeying and day-dreaming means channeling ...you might be an Indigo.

<Dean>You might be an indigo ....if you make your family disappear into another reality.

**And Now,
Here are some Jokes...**

And Now, Here are some jokes channeled that night by Sunwalker, (and one by Frank in retort.)

<sunwalker> How many ascended masters does it take to change a light bulb?...
(None .. they illuminate themselves.)

<sunwalker> How many illuminati does it take to screw in a light bulb?
<angelboy> How many?
<sunwalker> none, they Hate the light .... they broke all the bulbs!

<Frank S> OK, how many guitar players does it take to change a light bulb?
101- One to do it, the other hundred stand around saying how much better they could do it.

# Chapter 11

# Vital Indigo Info!

In the past couple of days, some important information has come to my attention that needs to be revealed in this book.

I have been aware of this phenomenon I am about to tell you for several years, but for some reason it didn't find it's way into this book, (until now, just as the book was about to go to press!)

About 50% of Indigos, are wired totally different than what is standard protocol .....even for Indigos this wiring is somewhat abnormal. When many of you read what I'm about expose, you will breathe a great sigh of relief and say YES! I knew there was something terribly wrong!

Have you ever been in a meditation class or listened to meditation tapes and they tell you to "imagine a ball of white or golden light at the top of your head (crown chakra) and slooooowly bring it down through your head, through each chakra, to the bottom or root chakra, filling your body with love and light" .....and so you try and try and try.....but it just doesn't work!? It makes you feel like a loser and totally inept since everyone else seems to have it working and it is effortless to them. They may tell you how they get connected to The Source and feel warm and fuzzy inside and may even start to have visions. When YOU try to do the same thing ... NOTHING HAPPENS!

If this has been your experience, try this: Go directly to your heart/heart chakra and imagine that it is filling up with intense love and light, both white and Ultra-Violet.....this light can mix with each other or oscillate, white light and then the Ultra-Violet light. Then send half of it up to your crown, and half to your root. When all of your body is filled completely, send that energy up through your crown and let it spill out around you like a fountain.....and continue rising up and spilling out to the furthest regions of the Universe! Then direct the generated heart energy the other direction down into the Earth, blessing it and all the inhabitants with your powerful love/light. This protocol can also be done simultaneously so that it is a smooth even flow going up and down. You may have noticed that sometimes your heart chakra literally hurts! The reason may be because this intense love/light vibration needs to be expressed, and needs to be expressed the way YOUR particular outlets flow, with YOUR unique wiring. This type of wiring is truly "Heart Centered" where your entire Being operates, generates, and re-generates from the heart.

Since Indigos are literally wired differently, you may have encountered body workers, energy and reiki therapists that seem to do more harm than good because they are assuming that your energy is supposed to flow in a certain pattern. When they try to change and alter you to that pattern, it throws you out of balance and almost into shock! This can be very frustrating because this usually happens when you are fatigued and need the most help.....(that's why you went to the therapist in the first place!)

I would suggest that if this happens in the future, you do the "Heart Center" meditation I just outlined, and also get some Aurauralite/Aulmauracite and use it to do a "custom re-wiring job" the way YOU need to be wired.....back to your authentic self!

In the future I hope to have a list posted on my web site of qualified practitioners that understand Indigos and can help you when you get out of balance. Right now I don't know that many, but I'm sure I will be led to Indigos that have 'Indigo wiring/re-wiring" on their contract list!

# Chapter 12

# The Indigo Mind

## Thoughts and Insights from Real life X-Men (& Women)

## ...The Misfits in our Society

The series of stories you are about to read will give you an idea just how varied and powerful the First Wave Indigo experience is—and the quality of individuals that make up the Indigo Nation.

The one thing you can truly say about First-Wavers is that you really can't generalize about these unique individuals. Well, you can, but you can't – as you will see when you read through this cross-section of experiences submitted by Indigos from around the world and around the block.

These stories offer a view of what it's like to be a First Wave Indigo in a world oblivious to any spectrum of light not offered by a GE Soft-White bulb. The brave, wonderful Indigos who wrote their stories for inclusion in this volume range in age from recent high school graduates to Generation Xers to 'Tweeners to tail-end Baby Boomers.

And while their stories include tales of abuse both physical and mental, as well as of lives wrought by challenge and misunderstanding, they all demonstrate a miraculous ability to grasp the meaning and the mission connected with being a First Wave Indigo.

In this Indigo World of unique individuals, First-Wavers show a remarkable similarity in this regard. Indigos come from all walks of life. Their experiences are as varied as their personalities, which you will find when you read this chapter.

However, there are common threads that appear throughout these stories. These are incredible people whose feelings are as intense as is their belief that the world is currently inside out and backward. It is my hope that, as you read these collected stories, you will find both comfort and inspiration in your own life.

# Careening Off of the Guardrails

Like most Indigos, my childhood was chaotic and unstable, with a tempestuous and unstable family life. My father left when I was five years old. I did well in school academically, but poorly from a social point of view, never being popular with the other kids. The most common thing people had to say to me when I was a kid was, "You're weird." When I was old enough to leave on my own, I did. I soon broke off ties with my family—not out of malice, but out of a need to preserve myself and my sanity, having never seen eye-to-eye with them on anything.

After my first few years of adulthood, a pattern began to emerge, that pattern being one of wild oscillations from one extreme to another. ...From liberal to libertarian to objectivist. ...From believer in the supernatural to hard-core skeptic. ...From compassionate bleeding heart to icy-cold self-centered technocrat. Never one to be moderate in anything, my course consisted of being as far out on the fringes as possible in whatever it was that I was doing at the time.

I've been an integrated-circuit layout designer, a radio personality, a singer in a punk rock band, a musician, a poet, a stand-up comedian, and a professional photographer/videographer and documentary producer. The most important thing I've learned over the years is how to be totally self-sufficient. It has been my experience that the moment you depend on others for anything, they will let you down every time. Learn to believe in yourself, learn to trust yourself, and learn to forgive yourself when you screw up.

Having seen how our society is run at the very topmost levels, I can say without hesitation that our society is corrupt, and entirely money driven. This corruption creates injustices that will eventually result in severe social and political instability. Do you feel like you are working harder for less and less, and that no matter what you do you end up losing? It's not your fault. Trying to get ahead in this society is like trying to win a jackpot in a rigged casino. You do all of the things you're supposed to do, work yourself into a tizzy trying to get ahead, and one torpedo comes along and sends you back to the starting line. Here's the bottom line: You're trying to beat the house, and the house consists of people who were born in the winner's circle, who laugh at you for your sin of doing such a poor job of choosing your parents.

No matter how powerful the corporate overlords become, no matter how wealthy and well-connected they are, they can't own a sunset. They can't take your capacity for joy away from you. They can't take away the pleasure one gets from listening to good music or sharing a laugh with friends. They can't take away your capacity to love another person. And, that is the one thing they don't have. The wealthy and powerful are loveless people. They have chosen to sacrifice their capacity to love on the altar of wealth and power. This feeds their greed and makes them become ever more addicted to acquisition and domination of others to make up for their lost capacity to love other people. For all of their money and power, they don't have love in their lives. For all of their wealth, they are the poorest of all. Their poverty makes them mean, and that meanness makes them want to make everyone else as miserable as they are. So, they elevate money to being the most important thing in the world, and they try to convince everyone else of this.

The only way to really win is to not play. The things that we are supposed to aspire to are priced too high, and are not worth the effort it takes to get them. The things we really should care about are denigrated and despised by those who want us to dance to their tune. So quit dancing. Stop letting them call the tune, and start dancing to your own tune.

Frank S. (Age 43)
Spokane, Washington
sheridan8502@mac.com

# Surfing the First Wave

It was my great pleasure to meet Laura Lee socially before I ever became aware of Indigos, first-wave or otherwise. To be frank, there could have been no more wonderful way to be introduced to this hidden nature than in a one-on-one setting with the gentlest of spirits.

I am a journalist. I've worked in the news and information industry for most of my adult life. I make my living interviewing people. Over the years I've interviewed politicians and priests, the famous, near famous, the infamous. I've talked with people with indomitable spirits and people of highly questionable moral fiber. After focusing on sports writing as a career move, I've spent a great deal of time talking to coaches, agents, athletes as well as their families and extended entourages. In summary, I've learned to read people over the years. I have a pretty well developed bullshit detector. I can tell when someone is being evasive and when they're flat-out lying in a professional setting (in my personal life, I'm as vulnerable as the next guy – go figure).

So sitting in a Thai restaurant over chicken with Thai basil, I listened while Laura Lee unfolded an incredible story about the Ultra-violet Realm, who First Wave Indigos were, and that how she was rock certain I was one. To go from thinking an Indigo was an off-shoot of one of those color charts that tells you whether you should wear winter or summer colors to accepting her words as an unequivocal truth was a pretty big jump. When my personal bull-shit detector did not go off, I knew I should pay close attention to what the pretty lady was saying.

To start with, Laura Lee told me a great deal about myself that she had no way of knowing. She knew about feeling alienated as a child, about always feeling outside the mainstream. Let's just say it was a lot more than small talk.

I remember being quite alienated as a child. I remember being fascinated by the voice inside my head and contemplating whether or not everyone else had a similar voice and if it was possible to make an exchange for one that would eventually sound more like James Earl Jones. I grew up thinking that I was probably just one slight slip away from being hauled away by the men in the white coats.

Much of what other Indigos have written about themselves on these pages applied to me, so I won't repeat those experiences here.

Let me put things this way. One of my pet analogies is to liken the creative process to one of those little clown puzzles we played with as children, turning the clown's head so that bee bees roll into his eyes and mouth. It takes a steady hand and a great deal of patience to make it all work, and the thrill of getting one of those little steel balls to drop is the moment that I refer to as the "Aha!" I aspire to in my work. I had that moment a hundred times over learning about why my life had unfolded the way it has through my first 47 years on this planet.

Someone once explained to me the way astronomers find black holes. They watch the way planets orbit suns and the way solar systems make their way through the Universe. When they find something moving in a strange way with nothing to explain the odd behavior, they know they've found a black hole. Discovering that I was a First Wave Indigo was like discovering my own personal black hole. Suddenly the strange, entire orbit of my life makes sense, and my future, my mission, my social contracts assure me of a rich, rewarding future, with many, many stories to bring back and share with others who share my purpose.

In the days and weeks since learning about my own identity, I have learned to embrace the many, varied facets of my life that had remained somewhat hidden for the greater part of five decades. Embracing them has made for radical changes in my life and I look forward to an incredible ride minute-to-minute for the remainder of my life.

Laura Lee, you have never been as hidden as you thought you were. But to find you, one must actually search. You are entirely worth the lifetime effort and will be a most treasured part of my life forever. Bless you.

Steve C. (Age 48)
Spokane, Washington
SteveC99212@hotmail.com

# The Sky's Not The Limit

I am a newly-awakened 49-year-old Indigo and am still discovering my true identity. I am a recently divorced mother of three girls.

As a child, I always had a fascination with ESP and the spirit world. I used to play a game called "Kreskin's ESP." Kreskin was a famous psychic back in the 1960's. The game tested your ESP abilities. I used to score very high, indicating that I had a lot of psychic ability, but I didn't really give it much credibility. I had scattered psychic incidents throughout my life, but I did not think that they were an indication of anything extraordinary. I also always had a hidden "knowing" that I could somehow transfer energy with my hands.

I became more aware that I probably had a little bit of a psychic gift when my youngest daughter began to exhibit amazing psychic abilities. When she was around 11 or 12, we realized she had special talent. We were watching a magician on T.V. named David Blaine. He was doing a card trick where he could "read" the cards. My daughter proceeded to say, "I can do that." My family all said, "No way!!" She went and got a deck of cards, kept them face down, shuffled them, cut them, and then laid down on the bed and buried her face for a couple of minutes. She then stated a card, suit and rank, which was correct. She continued to be able to identify the cards down to about the 5th or 6th card from the top. We asked her how she knew she could do this. She said she had no idea. She just knew that she could. Over several years, she continued to perform this feat. My daughter, now 18 years old, is an Indigo, but she does not want to have anything to do with her talents at this point in her life. She does not even have any knowledge of what an Indigo is. She is aware that she and I, and her two sisters, have capabilities that most people don't have or are not aware that they have.

Another incident that happened around the same time, was when the whole family went out to dinner at a Japanese restaurant where they cook dinner on a teppan grill in front of you. We were waiting outside for our table to become available. A young couple pulled up in a limousine and walked past us into the restaurant. My youngest daughter looked at me and said, "They are going to pay for our dinner." I started laughing and couldn't even fathom what possessed my daughter to make a statement like that. When we were finally seated, we were at the same table with the young couple. Not only did they pay for our dinner, but the man gave each of my three girls a $100 bill!!!!!

At this point, I still had no idea that I had a lot of "special" capabilities. I was in a very oppressive, verbally-abusive marriage for many years. I was very unhappy. I remained in the marriage because I felt it was in my childrens' best interest to do so. Then the kids began expressing that they too were unhappy and they also wanted to leave. In March of 2003, I became very ill with a severe relapse of Chronic Fatigue Immune Dysfunction Syndrome. I had been fighting this illness since 1987. I would have relapses a couple of times a year. It would sometimes take weeks or months for me to get back to a functional level by using vitamins and herbs. This time, I was so sick that I knew if I didn't find a way to get out of the house and the marriage, I would slowly die. I was afraid for my safety and also the safety of the girls, if I tried to talk to my husband about leaving. We had to plan to leave when he was out of town. At this point in time, I began working with an incredible spiritual healer. I was so ill that I could barely walk. Within three days of seeing her, I was on the road to recovery and back at work. It was a miracle. She worked with me and helped me process through all of the issues in my life to facilitate my healing.

In March of 2003, after I made my decision to leave, I began to experience synchronistic events - signs from the Universe that I was doing the right thing in leaving my marriage. These events occurred with regularity and continue through to this day. We had to wait about four months after I made the decision to leave, for my husband to go out of town. I was trying to decide if I should take the kitchen dishes with me. They were given to me as a gift. But I was very afraid he would get extremely angry if he found the dishes gone. I finally decided to take them with me. The day that I made the decision that I would take the dishes when I left, my husband came home from work and said, "You'll never guess what happened to me today." He proceeded to tell me that he went to the store to purchase new tennis shoes. They told him that if he purchased four pair of shoes, they would give him a free set of dishes. So he purchased four pairs of shoes and brought home a new set of dishes, which we didn't need at all!!!

I continue to receive these signs from the Universe almost daily and whenever I am in any doubt that I am doing the right thing.

Here is another example of Universal signs indicating that I am on the right path. This is a story from Memorial Day 2004, when I went skydiving. My friend wanted me to go skydiving with her up in Big Sur, California. It took me a month to make up my mind if I wanted to go or not. I was going back and forth about whether or not I should do it. At 49 years old, most women don't go jumping out of airplanes at 15,000 feet!!! What finally made up my mind was another synchronistic event. I was reading the book "Angels and Demons" by Dan Brown. One of the main characters was talking about his experience of skydiving. He said it was like flying with God. At that moment I knew that I needed to do it. When the time came to go and we were driving to the skydive site, I found myself thinking, "Why on earth am I doing this?" Right after I was thinking this, the answer came to me: "You are going to fly like a bird." Immediately after this thought came into my head, we were at a red light and I looked out the window to my left. I saw a single cloud formation, in an otherwise completely blue sky, in the shape of a bird soaring. I quickly grabbed my camera to take a picture. You can definitely see the bird in the picture, but the picture doesn't show how it looked EXACTLY like a sideways soaring bird in flight. We were all laughing!!! Then to top it off, right before I actually jumped, the instructor that I jumped with told me I needed to put my arms back and "fly like a bird." It was the most incredible experience of my life!!!

Another story I would like to relate for entertainment purposes is an experience I had with Aurauralite rock.

Two of my friends and I were connecting into a national medicine wheel grid ceremony that took place in May 2004. I was setting up a circle of crystals around a very large quartz crystal cluster. One of my newly acquired Aurauralite rocks seemed to jump out of the bag I had it in! I think it got very excited to have its first real job!! In the center of the cluster, I put one of the Aurauralite rocks along with some amethyst and rose quartz, and the other piece of Aurauralite was one of the stones in the circle around the crystal.

We were doing our ceremony and we had some purple grapes on the table that we were snacking on. One of my friends, my very gifted telepathic healer, is very in-tune with rocks and crystals and she communicates with them all of the time. The Aurauralite rocks communicated to her that they wanted grapes!!! She wasn't able to determine exactly why they wanted grapes, but she gave them some anyway!!

My friend was surprised because she has never had a crystal communicate to her that it wanted food. I had told her previously that the Aurauralite was a much more sentient stone and entity than other "normal" crystals. She feels that there was some significance to the fact that they were purple grapes. (Laura Lee's comment upon hearing this story was: "Ya think that the 'purple grapes' could be actually 'Indigo Grapes' or 'Ultra-violet' grapes?")

My healer put one grape on either side of the Aurauralite that was on the crystal cluster and one by the Aurauralite that was in the outside circle. She said that made them happy.

Another process that has helped me immensely in my continuing Indigo awakening is past life exploration. By going back and reliving some of my past lives, I have gotten a lot of help with issues in this life. I highly recommend this avenue of exploration to assist anyone in developing all of the capabilities they have available to them in this lifetime.

One thing that has been very difficult for me is the fact that I seldom "see" or "hear" anything. I do have an unwavering knowing deep inside of me that whatever I think will happen. I have done a lot of work with Laura Lee to help heal the planet. She verbalizes to me what she sees when we do this work together. Not being able to "see" or "hear" what is happening as I participate in this healing work is extremely frustrating for me. Almost everyone around me can "see" or "hear". However, I almost always get some type of 3D validation of the results of our work. I have been diligently working, since my awakening in 2003, on activating my spiritual vision and hearing. I have come to the conclusion that I have to stop trying to force these abilities to actuate. We are each unfolding at our own rate and the Universe will assist us in bringing forth our gifts at the appropriate time.

HAL gave me the following analogy: "If you take out a watercraft with a hole in it, it will take you twice as long to get to your destination." In other words, you have to heal the necessary things in your life before key events can happen. If the appropriate things are not in place, it will take you much longer to get your life to the position where you want it to be.

My advice to other Indigos is:

Have confidence in yourself. Know that you can do ANYTHING that you set your mind to. Always listen to your higher self and don't allow outside judgments to influence what you know to be the Truth. Pay close attention to the synchronistic signs from the Universe.

When things are not going well, use those indicators to your benefit and change the direction of your life until you get positive reinforcement from the Universe.

As Indigos, it is our job to make humanity aware that each human being is fully responsible for creating their own reality and that each of us can have **H**eaven here on **E**arth.

Ann L. (Age 49)
Los Angeles, California
luminosa8039@yahoo.com

# *An Indigo Journey*

In 1977, a four-year-old girl sat at the table with her imaginary friend. This occasion was unremarkable due to the regularity of its occurrence. Suddenly, her cup flies towards the door, shocking her grandmother who had seen it from another room. "Traci, why did you do that?", said her grandmother. "I didn't do it. Uncle Bill did," Traci said, as she pointed to an empty chair. Her grandmother slaps Traci's face and grabs her shoulders. She shakes little Traci so hard her teeth rattle. "What the devil has gotten into you?" "Quit lying and apologize this instant," said her Mamma. "I'm sorry Mamma," the weeping four-year-old cries. "I won't do it again." From the empty chair uncle Bill looks on as his sister sent her heartbroken granddaughter to huddle alone in the room he had died in two years before her birth.

It sounds like fiction, I know. But this tale is all too true. I was raised in Texas. My family, both racist and misogynistic, attended a Southern Baptist church. They spoke fervently of God and Jesus' saving grace. Domestic violence was expected, just business as usual. So much so that it was discussed at the dinner table. "Your cousin David stole my watch. I beat the crap out of him. I'll probably kill him one day. Pass the peas."

But the darkest undercurrent of all was incestuous assault. It remained a dark looming specter, strangling the life from us all.

I recall waiting in fear for my bedroom door to open, announcing another drugged interval as my stepfather's child prostitute. I cringed in the daylight waiting for the times where my brother would use me to try out all his newest tricks. I remember the beatings, screaming, cursing, and name-calling. I remember how they told me I was mentally deficient because I was born female. I was called tacky and rude for speaking up since children should be seen and never heard. What made this situation even more frightening was their declaration: "Outsiders are dangerous. Don't speak of family business because 'Blood is thicker than water."

Even at school the abuse did not end, because in every unsupervised moment, the other kids would descend like a pack of hyenas. They smelled the blood of wounded prey. Like a trained victim I curled up and hid, too silenced to even beg for them to stop. The only time I had any peace or sense of security was under the teacher's watchful eyes. Even then, there was a lingering fear. So I would leave my body for other realms. I would watch orbs dance and zip around the room. I would watch energy shimmer off of everyone in sight. My teachers labeled me as Attention Deficient and I was prescribed Ritalin.

At church I was told only virgins had worth, and that all sinners would go to hell. I was told that I should respect my elders, and never, ever question their words. God had put them in charge to teach me wrong from right. The Biblical passage "Thou shall not suffer a witch to live" rang in my ears at church and echoed madly through my family at home. Every time it was said with such passion and force, I just knew they were speaking of me!

I developed a fascination for the Salem witch trials and the Spanish Inquisition. In second grade I scoured the library's adult section for every scrap of information on these subjects. I learned about possession and witch dunking. I learned abut being locked in a dungeon and tortured. I wondered what it felt like to be burned alive. A vulnerable child can take only so much, so I buried it all... my memories and my gifts. My childhood story was tacked together through snapshots pasted with "ought-tos" and "shoulds." In a time of innocence lost, I could only pretend to play. Still, even in the midst of this violence, a part of me cried out. Something deep inside me knew this to be wrong, knew I had been wronged. That part of me curled snug around that Truth and hid deep within, awaiting the time to spring forth and be reborn.

I spent my teenage years with my father who was a deacon in a fundamentalist church. While the physical and sexual assault ended, mental, emotional and spiritual abuse still remained a daily reality. All my life my father had given me the impression that he never really had much use for a girl. Now I was left with the lasting impression that the only reason I was there was because he had rescued my brother. To do any less for me would be unchristian. My father soon had me weighed and measured. He found me severely wanting. Overeating was a deadly sin. No mention of health was made. All I heard was how my being fat made a poor example for personal appearance... his appearance! To continue to be fat was disobedient to my father as well as counter to my primary purpose as some man's wife. Although I had no memory of it, my fatty insulation had saved me from a pattern of sexual assault. And with one of my primary offenders in the same house, my resistance was mighty indeed. I hated my body and refused to live in it. I would view life from a hazy, distant cloud. It was as if opiates numbed my pain, both physical and emotional. I used this trick to distance from my father's tirades. He soon began to call me other things than fat. "Lazy" and "Spacey Traci" became things I heard almost as often as my first name. And when he lost his temper, he called me my mother, a woman he hated with the greatest of intensity. He waged a holy war against the very skills I had used to survive my war-zone of a family. I was charged with dishonoring my father, a sin that in ancient times was cause for public stoning. He thought with more effort and Bible thumping he could get me to change my sinning ways. Rather, it just caused me to become even more unreachable.

At school I was still the pariah. Intimidated and threatened, I had no friends. I had learned long ago that my peers could not be trusted. At church I was told never to question the Bible or the men who ran the church. They were made in God's own image and spoke His undiluted truth. Because I was born a woman, I was told I was their spiritual inferior. I absorbed faithful recitations of how Moses and his band of holy refugees raped and murdered their way thru the Promised Land. They slaughtered all but the virgins; those they kept as wives or slaves. These crimes were declared holy because they were "ordered by God." I would hear heartfelt renderings of Hebraic law that held women responsible for their own rape. If they were not forced to marry their violators, they were murdered at their father's door, because as the root of all wickedness, the daughters of Eve were mindless pawns of Satan who tempted Godly Men away from their Holy path. This had only confirmed what my rapists said. It was my fault all along. I would shiver in terror and pray, "Jesus, wash

146

away my sin.  Holy Spirit, lead me on the path of right.  And God, forgive me my sins.  Please don't cast me into Hell to be tortured for all eternity."  If a part of me knew this was wrong, I could not hear it.  I was lulled into believing abuse was only when blood had been spilt.  No mattered how hard I pretended, I felt dead inside...like a hollow, plastic person, barely breathing in and out.

As I left my father's house at the age of 18, it was to the sound of him yelling, "Don't let the door hit you in the ass as you leave."  From the age of 18 to 30, if I darkened the door of a church, it wasn't for long.  I felt God had waged a war on me my entire life.  So I returned the favor with a two-bird salute by the light of my full moon.  For a while I was Atheist, then Pagan, then Buddhist.  But each time I found set systems that did not ring true.  In college I found my niche in the realms of anthropology and philosophy.  I sought value in being smarter and seeing more than those I came from.  I thought, therefore, I had worth.  And most of all I was Right!  About what you might ask?  Any topic I was speaking on.  I would even switch sides and every time I just KNEW I was right.  Anytime someone disagreed with me, I took it as a personal attack.  My identity was a sand castle built upon a painted veil.  This illusory strength left me achingly vulnerable.  When a drug dealer entered my life wearing the mask of friend, I bought the act hook line and sinker.  Drugs soon over took my life.  I soon began to have some of my first adult psychic experiences on weed.  I would see things a second before they happened.  And then came speed.  It shot me into a place I could barely remember, a place of peace.  I saw white lights move out from my third eye in expanding circles.  One night I felt a benevolent presence and experienced the most achingly pure feeling of unconditional love.  I got high, time and time again, looking for that feeling.  I never even came close.  Like many seekers who turn to drugs for their glimpse of the transcendent, I crashed and burned in a most explosive way.  What I was later to discover to be a spontaneous kundalini awakening soon took me on a truly unpleasant ride.  I had severe mental breaks that left me in the hospital on more than one occasion.  I began hearing voices once more.  The colored orbs I had once seen came back in numbers.  In truth they practically swarmed me.  The doctors took this all as symptoms that needed to be medicated.  I accepted because I was scared out of my mind.  The only part of this kundalini experience I found joy in was I that had discovered my ability for hands on healing.  But the medication changed that.  I took so much I was stumbling around in a drugged stupor and running into walls. All interest in healing was gone, but at least I found relief. The voices were silent, but so was my spirit. Of faith and hope I had nothing. To love I was lost.

The years since have been a fear-drugged haze. Then just four short years ago, I began a journey of releasing the pain of my past and discovering my inner world. I learned to gradually decrease the medication I was on. As the voices and orbs came back, there developed an uneasy truce between us. Even if they were not real, I was unwilling to go back to my former drugged state and forfeit the progress I had made. Then came the dreams where a loved voice sent me messages. And dreams where I was repeatedly told to go back to school. It got to the point I was having lucid conversations, arguments with the ones who spoke. I came to understand that I was meant to continue on my Path. Part of me was still invested in being disabled and crazy. But part of me knew this was what I had always longed for: a return of the gifts of my child hood. I began studying the orbs and found wings and points of light, much as the chakra systems I myself had. I listened to the voices to discern what they said. I developed a practice of divination and dream study. And through this, I journaled my discoveries.

One day I decided to make my peace with the church and God. I felt drawn to the United Methodist Church just a couple blocks from my house. While I never bought the party line, I knew I was there for a purpose. I argued in Sunday school and I spoke out for women's rights. Not only was I welcomed, I was told I was a valued member. Women were respected; I was respected. Then my grandfather's impending death triggered the return of my memories. Flashbacks swarmed me. And I didn't know where to go, so I turned to my pastor. I spoke to him about my painful past. I found no blame, no admonitions to forgive and forget. He told me that his mother and his wife shared my pain. He told me that God never sanctified such behavior no matter what my abusers had claimed. It was then my lingering doubts towards God vanished and when the pastor retired in December, with our contract fulfilled, so did I.

I began writing poetry, marking the milestones in my path; poetry of dark inner rage and deep inner spiritual-yearnings. I called forth memories from my darkened mind and wailed my anguish to a still-distant God. Always present was the demanding cry, "Why ME?!!!" In that same December, I found my way to my first psychic fair. The woman who read me told me I was an Indigo.  I didn't have a clue what she was talking about.  There wasn't much time in fifteen minutes to explain, but the short of it was that my abuse issues, depression, and toxic reaction to organized religion were trademark.  And the voices I was hearing, well, it seems I am a dead people magnet.  Lucky me!

I was sent home with a list of books to read. But the problem was that they all seemed so insistent I should be a teenager.  And even though they did give me a general idea what an Indigo is, I was left with an overwhelming sense of "Now what?  So I am here to change the world... care to explain how?  I have all these psychic 'gifts.'  Most days I wish I could return them.  And if this is my Awakening, where's the snooze button?"

In a world where I was always outcast and alienated, I felt that I was never on the same page. I didn't even feel like I was in the same book.  Now I've been ejected from the library altogether.  I find myself pretending that I'm not seeing, hearing, and feeling the things I am.  I go to counseling for recovery from my abusive past.  Even though my councilor is open minded to chakras and such, when I mentioned the voices I heard, she wanted to check my medications.

Now I found a group where, two times a month, I can be myself without wondering who's going to call me crazy.  There, I explore my gifts and practice healing.  The last psychic fair I went to, I was asked by this same Indigo psychic why I wasn't giving readings there that day. The truth is, I've grown accustomed to never belonging and thinking of my self as less than worthy.  Even though I asked for signs to clarify my Life Purpose, I just ignored the energetic and clairvoyant upgrades, as well as my own inner promptings.  Though I now know increased self-acceptance and love, I am still overset by an ever-present fear.  Fear of my family finding out.  Fear of reaching a point of no return.  Fear of completely losing the "me" I thought myself to be.

In the midst of it all, my only moments of peace come when I am deep in meditative bliss.  I put my mind on hold and I follow the paths of energy as they circulate in my body.  I release emotional blocks and the results are seen in my life long after the rings of light are gone. Two months ago I began to notice angels trying to get my attention.  I began to work with them and their energies of pure Love.  Through my relationship with them I am building a relationship of trust with the Divine.  I gradually extend my trust and devotion to a God of

MY understanding.  I practice a daily ritual of prayer and cleansing.  I commit myself to the development of the spiritual gifts I was given.  I ask for my fears to be illuminated by the light of Divine Love.  I find forgiveness for those who wounded me, but it comes in layers.  I constantly find myself exploring the same issues, though different angles and different chakras.  But the real humdinger of all is a truth that seems beyond belief.  Though I wrestle with it daily, I have yet to get the knowledge that I chose my life and my family, to migrate from my head to my heart.  It is in these moments of contemplation that I find myself believing that my Soul Self is truly the crazy one.  This roller coaster ride is enough to get me tearing out my hair and screaming some days.  But one thing I know, the inner self I once buried now stretches and bursts forth with green growth. With slowly increasing volume this inner I demands to be heard.  It demands, nay requires,  that I commit to my Path.  So I have made the commitment to read at the next psychic fair.  Although I am still at loss to say where that Path will lead, I know it begins  with where I am, and deep within a knowing rises up and through every level of my being.

I am God's own holy child, and who I am is perfect.

**Traci N.  (Age 30)**
**Spokane, Washington**
**Sherezia@AOL.COM**

# At Least It Doesn't Hurt to Talk about It Now.

## (I just shake my head.)

## Who WAS That Masked Woman Back There?

I feel so different from the person I was when I first heard you on the radio and then contacted you. My life has not changed a great deal externally, but how I respond to my reality has changed tremendously, as has my perception of myself. I no longer have any desire to go back into my painful and abusive past, but I feel that I must use it as a reference point for the Indigos who still feel that it would be easier to check out. I almost did that eight years ago.

I had spent years taking psychic classes, using healing modalities, and taking care of and healing everyone around me, all the while trying to figure out what was wrong with me... why I always felt so alone and isolated. I had experienced suicidal thoughts since my teens. I moved a lot – I even moved to the U.S. from Canada when I was 24. I felt such a deep pain, an agony that never went away no matter what I did. Then eight years ago I crashed, bottomed-out as the saying goes... *I just couldn't find any good reason for putting up with the pain any longer.* I found myself a thousand miles from anyone I knew, with no one to turn to and one step away from destitution. I felt completely hopeless, a total failure... how I could have screwed up my life so badly after the nice, comfortable life I had created for myself in California? So I laid my plans to check out. The thought of who would take care of my four feline companions had always stopped me when I thought about it in the past. It was not something I ever admitted to anyone but myself, just how bad it felt to be alive. I had reached the point that I was prepared to put my cats in the car with me when I stuffed the exhaust with the rags.

I couldn't even get a phone line where I was living, so I had to go to a pay phone to make calls while checking on jobs. For two weeks, I had always gone to the same place to do that. As I was about to leave to make a last call to a friend a thousand miles away, who was in no position to stop me and who understood my desire, a voice (I now know was my guides) spoke very loudly in my head and said, "Go to the truck stop," not once, but three times until I finally said back to them, "Alright for Christ sake, but what difference does it make where I make the call?" A man I'd never met, overheard my phone conversation and came up to me and said, "You can come with me to North Carolina. I have an extra bedroom and there's lots of work there." He took me with him and took care of me until I got a job and could take care of myself again and find my own place. A total stranger in THIS life, but someone I must have done a big favor for in another life! So, if not for the extreme intervention of my guides and guardians sending this man in my direct path, I wouldn't be here to say, "I'm still alive and kicking." He told me when we got to North Carolina that he didn't know why he said that to me. He said, "It just came out of my mouth." (I think it came from his heart as well.)

I have since found out from working with Laura Lee and remembering who and what I am, that the main source of the agony and hopelessness was a series of implants that were pro-grammed to "slap me down" every time I came close to remembering who and what I am, or feeling good about myself and taking on my power. So when I say, "Don't let the bastards get you down!"......I know of what I speak. I truly am discovering that even in the Dark's attempts to destroy us, there are still great gifts and a lot to find extremely funny. The sweetness of life is something I can never take for granted. The beauty that I am rediscovering within myself, that is within each of us, continues to astonish and inspire me.

I am not a Power Indigo yet, but becoming one is my constant focus and my most passionate desire. The doldrums are over. What a relief to no longer wonder what I'm supposed to be doing with my life! And most of all, to know that I am never alone, I always have help and I am always being guided.

Love always,


Carolyn C. (Age 49)
Greensboro, North Carolina
ccoates@wcsr.com

# Music Soothes the Savage Beast

**I** just discovered the Jeff Rense website, a wealth of information and eye-opening events. I was browsing though the archived radio programs and found one called "Indigo Children." I didn't think much of it at the time, but I decided to visit the Mistyc House website and listen to the show.

To my surprise, it (First Wave Indigo Profiles http://www.mistychouse.com/Knight's-code/Indigos.htm ) pretty much described my feelings and thoughts exactly. I believe most of the traits on the list fit me... many of them pinpoint me accurately.

I was born 3-15-1982. From an early age I was labeled as special or gifted to some extent. Early on, I understood depth and perception in art, drawing, and such. I can easily assemble most electronic and mechanical items with little or no instruction. I have never enjoyed the idea of an "English Class" in school. To me, that idea makes as much sense as learning how to breathe. I agree that to learn anything however, one should obtain a good base of information. I believe "Experience" and "Doing" are the best teachers.

From an early age I had great interest in "Paranormal" and "Out-there" studies...however, it was subdued due to the lack of material. With the advent of the Internet, it was like the sky had opened up to me and I had looked upon the great "Library Of Pandora." With that, I tried to absorb as much info as a sponge could hold.

I am naturally very quiet or calm, however, not shy.

From the age of 11, I began to gain weight until the age of 21. From this weight gain I developed few friends, and even fewer love interests. At times, I felt happy to be in solitude, but the H.D.D. (Hug Deficit Disorder) Laura Lee describes made loneliness unbearable. One reason it was so hard for me to make friends was that I found their thoughts and mentality cruel and alien to me. I was the odd puzzle piece in a game of chess. I didn't belong there.

At my present age of 22, I look back at my years and see myself as crippled...not really different. I even had the notion that a "soul-mate" idea was for everyone else, not me. I would stare at my hands at night wondering, "Why?" "Am I an alien?" There was a faint aura of despair that surrounded my soul.

I have tried on-line dating. Each person I met, ended before they could start; I could never feel any "connection" with them.

These days, however, I teach guitar/music (after 2-3 years of study) to people and kids of all ages...it makes me quite happy. I have no problem with the very young or old. I can blend like a chameleon with the personality of the students. (This can be a problem however, if they are very tired and not interested in music - it drains my energy.) I spend long hours trying to construct the "perfect lesson" for each student.

For all my time in this space, I have always felt the need to do something good, something to help others even when I was in my most cynical mood. Yet, still my role eludes me. However, I have found a "training job" in teaching music/guitar.

My teaching methods circle around showing the student the basic structure of what makes a song, a melody and a phrase. I may not use "proper" musical terminology for what I teach, but "why teach what they can't understand?"

When I was 22 years old, I lost quite a lot of weight. People tell me I look years younger and sometimes think I am the youngest brother of three. In general, I feel much better and truer to myself. Still there is much more work for me to do to really be happy in this life.

Looking back at all the mistakes, problems and even failures, I see lessons laced throughout them. I see that without them, I probably would be somewhere I wouldn't want to be. These lessons exist at even the smallest level...it is difficult to explain.

Thanks for putting out the word of Indigo Children. Any help you can offer is appreciated.

Thank You,

**Alexander S. (Age 24)**
**Brooklyn, New York**
**AlexzndrLS@aol.com**

# Correspondence

These letters are correspondence I had with a wonderful Indigo, Robert Johnson. Robert's insights and perceptions are wise beyond his years.....but so typical of how Indigos think. I am reprinting these letters with his permission, as I felt they would be profoundly inspiring to all those who read them.

Sun. 4-11-04 12:00 A.M.

Dear Laura Lee,

I was recently at your web site after hearing about Indigos on the Jeff Rense program. Allow me to give you a little background on myself.

My name is Robert Johnson. I am 23 years old, born January 8th, 1981 in Erie, Pennsylvania in a beat down ghetto neighborhood. I rarely got to go outside because of all the drug wars.

I have always known that I was different in some way from other people around me. In school I often felt like an outcast and seldom had any friends. I didn't follow a clique of any kind as I believed them all to be the same and I preferred to just be myself and not care what others thought of me. (But inside I really did care; I just didn't let it consume me.)

When I was 16 I was advised by my guidance counselor and vice principal that it was in my best interest to leave school and get my G.E.D. Not that I was being disruptive, I just couldn't conform to their standards. I did do this when I was 16 and thought they knew what was best, but now I regret that decision as I am hungry for knowledge about things that interest me. I am predominantly self-educated on issues ranging from income tax code (which I have found no American has to pay income taxes) to Zero Point Energy. I am now teaching myself the necessary math skills to get into physics, as I am greatly intrigued by the inner mechanics of the Universe. I was very bright and intuitively gifted in areas that interested me, but was not at all able to follow things I felt were irrelevant...and just when I started getting interested in something, the damn bell would ring and the class would be over.

I was diagnosed with Tourette's syndrome, but I don't know if that's a bad thing. When they tried to put me on meds for it (Prozac), I refused to take them because they made me feel less like me and more like a shadow of myself. I have always been opinionated and verbally open with my views, and that has gotten me into a bit of trouble in school because I was always able to articulate my feelings with great ease. I've researched all the symptoms I feel and I am very in tune with my body. I know I am obsessive compulsive about certain things and attention deficit on others, depending on what interests me, and what does not.

I am always completely frank when I speak and I don't beat around the bush. This has made it hard to get a job, and when I do get a job I often lose it quickly because my immediate supervisors feel threatened by me. They are afraid I will take their jobs. They never voice these concerns...I just feel them. I just recently learned that being able to feel what other people are feeling isn't something that most people can do, but I can feel the slightest amount of tension in a room to the largest amount of joy. I've often congratulated women on their pregnancy before they even knew they were pregnant. Later they asked me how I knew when they found out they were. I could never explain it...I just felt it as easily as any other emotion. When I am confronted and backed into a corner, my whole body shakes like I'm an emotional lightning rod feeling someone's anger. I flee often and have rarely been in a physical fight. The ones I have been in I walked away unharmed and did just enough damage to the other person as was necessary to get him to go away.

I found the Jeff Rense site because I was sick of the media's lies and spin on events. I can smell a lie like a fart in a car and could tell something just wasn't quite up to speed on their reporting. I rarely watch T.V. The only show I watch is Star Trek. I'm much more entertained by the Internet and video games.

As far as religion goes, I have always been in a big controversy because I just didn't buy the "send me your money, God needs a new car" mentality of the typical faiths. I am Wiccan and have been since I was 15 years old. It was the only religion I found that allowed me to interact with and feel the Universe. I have never been able to grasp the concept of averting my eyes at a God that I am supposed to worship that loves me, but will send me to hell if I don't blindly conform. To me, God is so much more than any kind of human preconception of an omnipotent being, so much more than is humanly imaginable, and so much more compassionate. I do not believe in the concept of hell unless it is what we are living in right now. I cannot trust someone who demonizes all of the facets of human nature, and calls them sins and claims to be the only place a person can go to be absolved of simply being human. They call them the seven deadly sins, but I have found anything in moderation is good for you. I call them the seven living signs. I don't know how an All Mighty Being could create us in its own image and then punish us for being how we were created, like he's looking in a mirror and doesn't like what he sees. If there is a God and it is like the typical faiths suggest, then this omnipotent being has a severe personality complex.

I have never been able to conform to society and I am still an outcast. My significant other (of the opposite sex) is the only person I really talk to. I have no friends and don't really want any. I view society as a plague to the planet because it has become so corrupt. We have a government that facilitated the terrorist attacks on 9/11 just to keep people afraid so they could take away more fundamental rights. We have a president that speaks as if he were Jesus proposing a ban on homosexual marriage when who the hell is he to say what is right for other people. I am not homosexual and I may not agree with their lifestyle, but it is not my place to pass judgment, or anyone else's. It is up to each individual to choose to live their lives the way they wish.

I am deeply opposed to hate of all kinds and making people feel uncomfortable simply because they are different. We are all made up of the same energies from the Universe and we should all be treated equally and fairly. (I guess I have always known my purpose was to try to eliminate all forms of discrimination and rebel against the current powers for they are more corrupt than the Roman Senate was centuries ago.)

I have always been the one to ask, "why not?" when everyone else was asking why. More crimes are committed in this country on the other side of the bench in a court than on all of the streets of the entire world. I see what's happening to this world and it sickens me. The "powers that be" control technological breakthroughs, lie to the people to keep them ignorant, poison us and dictate acceptable behaviors and force us into this paid form of slavery called a job. Those who don't do well in the job market are rewarded with slavery and those who succeed are taxed into poverty when the law clearly makes no American liable for an income tax. (This was one of my obsessions and I will share this information with you if you wish, and it isn't immoral if you aren't liable for the tax in the first place!)

I don't know what color my aura is, but I can take a wild guess. All this time I thought I was crazy but now I realize it's the rest of the world that's messed up. I am interested in meeting people that are different like I am and will probably appear in your chat room soon under the handle portal_of_winds.

My other deep interests include anything paranormal from ghosts to UFO's (which I know both to exist, although I have never seen either). I can sense energy as well as emotion, so although I've never seen ghosts, I do feel them. I'm also interested in government conspiracies and liberation of people whose rights have been deprived illegally. I'm deeply involved in lucid dreaming and remembering my dreams. I still have a ways to go before mastering the lucid dreaming techniques, but I am progressing quickly. I'm very interested in electromagnetic fields and learning how they affect people. I believe it's possible to download information via electromagnetic fields to learn things quickly. I also believe this technology exists, but is being suppressed as well as many other technologies that would benefit mankind. If we were all put on level ground with modern knowledge, the privileged few would be overcome by imagination breakthroughs of the masses and the schools would no longer be needed. I believe extraterrestrial life is being hidden because the government would lose its tight gripping control on the people. I believe other technologies are being repressed to keep us enslaved in this oil-powered Hell of a miniscule existence. I believe in self-medication and the free use of any nature based substances including marijuana. I believe marijuana is illegal because the plant is capable of healing the planet and producing over 25,000 different products from clean fuel to rope, and would rejuvenate the soil, as well as allow people to find free relief to many common ailments that the pharmaceutical companies depend on us having for profit. In addition, it is a renewable resource that is free or very cheap and the world cannot tolerate free clean unlimited energy.

Well, I have provided an elaborate background on myself and my beliefs. I hope this will shed some light on what I may or may not be. I just consider myself different as I am not privy to deluding myself into thinking I am God-like, as some megalomaniacal stage healer. I believe I am, in fact, of the First Wave Indigo Children/Adults. This label is the only damned thing that has made sense to me in these 23 years of not knowing who I am or why I am here and what to do. I am pretty much against labels of all kinds but this one seems to fit so I'm ok with it.

Well, I'm pretty beat after this long day of "edumacation" lol. I hope to hear from you soon and very much wish to maintain contact with you, as you seem to have answers to a lot of the questions that I have been asking myself all these years. If you have any questions of me, feel free to ask anything no matter how personal it may seem. I'm always open and completely honest, and I don't take offense easily. It takes quite a bit to piss me off. Not many people are capable of this at all. The few who did, wished they hadn't. I wasn't always so mentally disciplined as I am now and used to seek revenge when I was wronged. Not in physical fights but in subtle ways more defeating than a right hook and often less explainable. Now I just chalk it up to other people's ignorance and don't let it phase me. Oh, I should mention, I have no idea what my IQ is, but I don't really care. I don't believe science can determine a person's intelligence, or capabilities. If they could, all of our poets would be writing, all of our musicians would be performing and all of our scholars would be asking questions that many cannot even imagine. No one would be poor and everyone would have their place in this world. As it is, however, our prodigies are living in slums, retarding themselves with television, and our real athletes are getting fat in suburban wet dream homes with parents that pay no attention to them leaving them to their own devices.

Ok, I'm going now, I'm sorry. It's just that every time I think I'm done, I see something else wrong with the world. Good night for now. Peace and happiness in all your endeavors and may the warm joyous light fill you for the work you are doing.

You can contact me at this email address anytime. Unfortunately, I am not working at this time, so I can be reached anytime by phone. My entire department was downsized, so I am collecting unemployment and trying to better myself, and further my education.

Thanks for taking the time to read this.

Sincerely,

**Robert D. Johnson**

Sun. 4-11-04 12:43 A.M.

Dear Robert,

Your letter was wonderful, like it could be titled, "Inside The Indigo Mind," or "Indigo 101...How an Indigo Operates."

I understand your dilemmas. I was just talking to one of what I call my "Power Indigos" tonight about some of these same things. We were discussing the "monetary system" and how it operates to keep everyone in chaos, with their backs bent and their mind mush, and no time for spirituality after they go to work, take the kids to soccer, and get dinner ready, help the kids with homework...there is nothing left for themselves. It is despicable that a family has to have 2-4 incomes to make life comfortable. We were brainstorming to see how we can step out of their carefully guarded "hologram of tyranny" without them noticing.

I hear you on the illegal tax "invasion." I know that taxes are illegal and don't want to support their illegal system.

I hope you do venture into my chat room, last week was incredible and it just keeps getting better. New people show up each week and we have a blast.

Blessed Be....

**Laura Lee Mistycah**

Sun. 04-11-04 12:52 A.M.

Dear Laura Lee,

I am deeply grateful that you responded to me so soon. There is one thing that I would like to clear up about the tax system however. The way the laws are written they are 100% legal and constitutional. It's the application of those laws that are illegal and unconstitutional. I'm sure you already know that, I just don't like misconceptions of any kind. I could write a whole extra letter simply on the way the government has swindled America into thinking they have to pay a tax when it is voluntary, as it cannot be mandatory and legal at the same time.

Most people are threatened over other people's ideas, but I find a second viewpoint can often be a breath of fresh air. There are people out there that are better thinkers than the "powers that be" and if we are to make a difference we have to unite. Changing the world won't begin in Iraq. Stopping terrorism didn't start in Afghanistan. It all begins right here at home with those of us courageous enough to stand up and scream, "I've had enough, and I'm not going to take it anymore." It seems from my viewpoint that most people simply don't care about what's going on as long as they have this illusion of security. One day soon, (sooner than they know) that security blanket will disappear and it is going to be up to us to take care of it. If we didn't have these sanctions against these other nations, impoverishing their lands, there would be no reason for them to hate us and terrorize us. Like I said before, I don't believe it was the Muslims behind the 9/11 attacks at all. I think they were an all too convenient scapegoat. Think about it. How can we have no clue to the specifics of the attacks, then release a list of the people behind it so soon after. There would be no reason for us to be on the brink of nuclear (not nucular lol) war with North Korea. Current events have been another one of my obsessions, and writing as well as verbal skills have always come to me very easily. I think I could help those by sensing their emotions and articulating them for them.

As for stepping out of the tyranny, the only thought I have been feeling recently, is that of moving into some remote part of the forest somewhere and living for myself without the rule of the oppressive doctorial intellectually inferior. But this wouldn't help the rest of the people that feel the same way I do. We have to find a way to take back our country before there's nothing left to take back but radioactive wastelands. What we need to do is find a way to get the complacent public involved and make them see what's really going on. It's too easy to turn a blind eye when you can't see what's really happening and have talking heads (politicians) telling you everything is ok. It's like the government has somehow got everyone looking through a Sesame Street candy coated stained glass window of lies. Our government has become oppressive and immoral. It is not only our right, but also our duty to do something about it. The authors of the Declaration of Independence agree, as they state this right in it. I never thought I would be ashamed to be an American, and I am not. It is not the American people doing these horrible atrocities against mankind...it is the American government.

The only thing I see that can be done at this point is to wait until this house of cards crashes. And then we pick up the pieces and advance our people into a new enlightenment, a new era of technological and spiritual fulfillment. The only difference being we put the technology to work for us, not against us, and we don't suppress ingenious breakthroughs. With all the derivative scams floating around out there, it's only a matter of time before the economy crashes. If J.P. Morgan falls, the rest will go like dominos. They are at the top with the most red ink on their books, a financial casino if you will, and someone will come along to break the bank soon.

This may be public knowledge already, but I feel it's important to mention that the combustion engine has been obsolete for over 50 years. The technology to replace it has been suppressed to keep us under the rule of oil. Oil has turned thugs into presidents and given corporations more money than God. It isn't just America that has been corrupted. I feel all of this bloodshed with Iraq and word wars with North Korea are nothing more than a charade at the expense of the citizens. The governments of the world have already decided the course and are acting out the future like some poorly written horror movie. We have ousted a brutal dictator in Iraq. Sure I agree Saddam needed to be taken out, but the war should have ended there and should not have been brought to us under false pretenses. Instead we were lied to about the motivations of war and have continued our occupation of Iraq, murdering innocent women and children. The Iraqi people aren't picking fights with our troops; they are simply starting to shoot back. They want democracy, but on their own terms and they have a God-given right to that. I think this was planned from the beginning to give us an excuse to occupy the territory indefinitely. I can see through the lies to the bigger picture. It is about control...control of key strategic lands to help facilitate the enactment of World Government. Now that my eyes have been opened to the truth, it is impossible to close the lids again. It would be un-American to turn a blind eye when I know what's really happening.

I don't know if I'm clairvoyant or not, but I can see the future. If the world stays on the same track, here is the outcome: All citizens' rights will be removed from every person throughout the world. Financial freedom will become slavery for survival and nuclear war to facilitate population control will become a fact of life. All former rights will be turned into privileges for the few who conform and be "good citizens." All country borders will be eliminated, but if you want to go somewhere you will have to ask Big Daddy Government first. Anyone who shows the slightest amount of dissent will be shot on sight, all original thoughts will be made illegal. There will be a cashless society where everyone is inventoried and controlled through some sort of ID tracking. There is a great quote I have heard that is not mine but I do not know who said it. It goes like this:

"With the first link the chain is forged, the first speech censured, the first thought forbidden, the first freedom denied, chains us all irrevocably."

These are not only words of wisdom, but also of warning. The first time any man's freedom is trodden upon we are all damaged. We think we've come so far, the torture of heretics, the burning of witches, all ancient history, and then before you can blink an eye it threatens to start all over again. Villains who twirl their mustaches are easy to spot, but those who clothe themselves in good deeds are well camouflaged. There will always be people like this amongst us waiting for the right climate in which to flourish, spreading fear in the name of righteousness. Vigilance is the price we have to continually pay for our freedoms if we are to keep the freedoms that we hold most dear.

Here are my thoughts about life and the Universe. They are controversial in the mainstream I'm sure, but they are my thoughts. Here they go:

The Universe is said to be expanding. I believe the Universe expands in direct proportion to our perception of it. Nothing can exist that cannot be thought of, and anything that can be thought of, can exist. As we evolve and open ourselves to possibility and new thought, our Universe and reality will slowly change to integrate the new thoughts into our new reality. Until the fear of change is overcome, we will be limited as a species. Knowledge and new ideas as well as original thought that defies current common truths such as I have stated, are very dangerous as those who fear change are capable of anything to protect the reality they know. Some of the most brilliant minds in existence are locked up in mental institutions because they think without the limitation of reality. Even though these prodigies are capable of distinguishing between what is real and their ideas, they are nonetheless locked up and deemed dangerous. This happens every day. A person can be completely aware of right and wrong, be of no harm to anyone, and have committed no crime, but may still be imprisoned simply for having a new idea. The things that make the least sense and sound like non-sense, or utter gibberish, are often the most truthful perceptions of reality. To perceive reality differently is not insanity.  However, to do so without extreme self-control is true insanity and also dangerous.  Extreme mental discipline is something that those who are truly insane lack.  Life is a paradox, a fractal at the subatomic and even interstellar levels.  If the sun of our solar system were to be split like the nucleus of an atom in an atomic bomb, the result would be similar to scale.  Our solar system is equivalent to an atom.  Both have orbital paths, "planets", if you will, traveling in those orbits and a center that all of these "planets" revolve around.  It wouldn't be surprising to find forms of life similar to our own living on the surfaces of the rotating spheres of an atom.  If we were able to magnify to a level that would make atoms visible as earth is to us we would most likely find life on these atoms.  We would be able to explore space by simply taking a closer look at what we find on our own planet.  I would also suspect that traveling between rotating spheres on an atom for a subatomic life form would be similar to humans traveling to Mars.  To scale the distance would be similar.

Talk to you soon.

**Sincerely,**
**Robert D. Johnson**


**AUTHORS NOTE:**  *At this point I asked Robert's permission to print his letters in this book.  He consented and wrote this letter afterwards.*

Sun 4-11-04 8:57 P.M.

Dear Laura Lee,

This message is for all of us.  Everyone on Earth not just those of our kind [Indigos].  We are here in one way or another, to break the traditional conformities and usher in a new era of enlightenment to all of mankind.  Most people will resist this because they feel fear of things they do not understand.  Do not conform to these people's wishes.  We are all unique in our own ways and are more intelligent than the average person.  We are not better or worse, we are just different with new ideas that frighten the masses, as our information contradicts their programming.  We write our own programming and individually control our destinies.  We have a purpose, a mission if you will, and that is to save this planet and all forms of life on it from their own ignorance. It's a big concept but we are all up to the challenge. Like many Indigos, I was a social outcast because this is not a society. This is a pseudo-society, based on flawed principles and egomaniacal pretenses.

We are how we are because some form of this Universal nature needs us to be the way we are. We all feel this, but most don't recognize it because the programming of the masses is beginning to infiltrate our own ideas.

To make it simple we are feared.

The "powers that be" can recognize us by our actions and are trying to shove us into a corner to keep us from accomplishing our goals. I myself was forced out of high school when I was 16. It was deemed in my best interest for me to leave school and get a G.E.D., which of course I did and now regret. I thought that they knew what was best for me, but I am the only one who really knows what is best for me, and the planet. We have to be ourselves. The equilibrium of variety has been disrupted by conformance of the masses and we are here as nature's way of balancing out this disruption. In all of nature there exists equilibrium. When you leave a hot cup of coffee out it gets cold, when you leave a cold soda out it gets warm. This is the same situation. People have become too alike to distinguish one from another, so here we are. Our purpose is clear although the task will be difficult. We however, are born problem solvers and will find a way to expose the corruption of the world and bring it back into harmony with the Universe.

I know many of us contemplate suicide but this is not the answer and before any of you consider it, I suggest you take a long deep look at this option as a non-option. This is exactly what they want. I have made a conscious decision not to die because I will not let them win without a fight. I may be killed by the hands of the very people I am trying to rescue, but it will not be by my own hand. I live each day simply to be able to see the newest ridiculous ideas thrown out into the world by people who are a dangerous savage child race. We are here to save humanity from itself. The Universe has commissioned us to bring new thoughts into the world and to expose the technologies and ideas that have been repressed, all to benefit us, not as a single separate race but as one of the many facets of all humanity uniting the world in the common good of all people, Indigo or not. Would any of us dare tell the Universe no? While there would be no punishment for telling the Universe no, there would also be no fulfillment or pride for accomplishing our task. Our mission is not one of a demand or order made through the threat of negative repercussion, but is a dying request of a planet wishing to survive.

I have sent Laura Lee Mistycah several messages recently. She is dedicated to helping us find our purpose. She requested to include my letters in her new book. I agreed whole-heartedly to that and wish her to include this message as well should she come across it. The planet is struggling for survival and has asked us to help it back into harmony. I for one am willing to face the worst hardships to help. I don't care about what other people think of me; I don't mind ridicule, hardship, or even facing certain death to do my part. We are all of free will and spirit, and must make our own decisions. This message is not meant to influence your decision but simply to show you some of the options available. We can either:

A. Give up now, or
B. Fight with our last ounce of breath to accomplish what we set out to do.

I choose B. If death is the worst consequence for my actions then I choose to act, for even death is not finality. We all have some sense that there is something more to life than this even without proof or faith. We just know it. Energy is forever it never dies. It only changes form and is usually not visible. Many of us have never heard of the ether. This is where energy exists in a form not visible, but none the less detectable. I encourage everyone to research this phenomenon for it holds the very keys to our existence, all forms of that existence.

I know the world makes a lot of you sick to your stomach. It does the same thing to me. But we can do only two things:
A. Suck it up and accept it, or
B. Do something about it.

We were put here to do something about it, so even if I am alone in this quest, that's damn sure what I am going to do. I don't welcome death but I don't fear it either. So what I am going to do is buckle my seatbelt and drive, not just simply enjoy the ride. We have to unite to accomplish our goals. None of us can accomplish this huge task by ourselves.

Think about this for a moment. You feel rebellious and you get ill at what you see happening around you. This is because there has to be a rebellion and something is gravely wrong within the minds of the "powers that be." Paranoia is associated with conspiracy theorists and they are mocked. I say paranoia is a sense we were given to help us see clearly when something is wrong. It is a feeling we get even without certain proof of wrong doing. I say many, if not all of the conspiracy theories out there today are largely based on some degree of truth and are well founded. The truth is, "the powers that be" act in secret more often than they act publicly. Every secret action is a conspiracy: The Manhattan Project, Project Blue Book, Project Sign, the Majestic Twelve, The Kennedy assassination, the 9/11 attacks, the Federal Reserve Act, the Internal Revenue Service, I could go on and on. Every one of these things began in secrecy and the truths of the matters are not disclosed. This is a conspiracy. When a nation's rulers choose to operate with impunity under the guise of national security there is reason to be suspicious. These people circumvent all the checks and balances of our constitutional republic. The truth is, there are many black ops programs out there from anti gravity, to E.M. field experimentation to bio-warfare engineering. I have no proof but like many of you, I just know these things to exist.

What these people don't say is far more important than what they do say. Their silence speaks louder than their words, but most people are too deafened by media spin to hear it.

So now you know why we are here, and what we have to do. The only question now is how do we go about it without using violence. Violent conflict solves nothing; only educated debate can prevail. We just have to find a way to be heard. And this is the reason many of you feel isolated and frustrated. You are isolated, and the "powers that be" would rather you kill yourself than open your mouth. Your ideas are a threat to *reality* as they know it and they consider you a threat to National Security. I know there is a draft coming soon to prolong the battle in Iraq and force the people into oppression. I for one will not kill for oil, or any other reason. I cherish the sacerdotal right to life of all forms. I will not be a part of enslaving a people to preserve their illusion of freedom. I know I am not free in this country. At least under the rule of the pharaohs, people knew they were slaves. To be a slave and think you are free is the greatest crime against all humanity.

I leave you now to contemplate the thoughts I entrust to you and if this is my only contribution to mankind, it is far more valuable than the creation of the atomic bomb. My words are meant to inspire people to think and create; the A-bomb is meant only for destruction and oppression. True future breakthroughs will not be of technology, but of the mind. Deep inside all of us lies a power far greater than the fastest super computer, and faster than the most technological craft. The power of our imagination traveling at the speed of thought is the greatest power in all of the Universe, and if we are to survive our own differences, then we are going to have to push this power to its limits. To all of you who read this message I wish you joy and happiness, as well as the freedom and spiritual enlightenment that you deserve. You'll be hearing from me in the future.

Until next time.

Rev. Robert D. Johnson (24)
Fairfax, Virginia
portal_of_winds_69@yahoo.com

## The Universal Heart

You know you're an Indigo when you're on your 3rd career choice by the age of 25, starting from highest-paying career to the lowest, but in the end definitely has the best livelihood. I am already 36 years old and I love being a chef. Have I ever wondered if I could "supercharge" my food with powerful, healing nutrition just by savoring it, meditating on it, and being grateful for it? Well yeah, I can do it while preparing or eating a meal, and anyone who eats it will have the potential to heal something inside of them. What is YOUR special way of amplifying the positive and "discharging" the negative? Perhaps you have many.

Most of my life, I have had this familiar feeling that I was about to come home. I don't belong here, not only on this planet, but also not in this particular three-dimensional fun-house. Home is kind of far away, but only a couple of steps out of reach, and you need to remember the magic key or code to get there. It seems so long and horrible a journey,

168

including the pain and misery. There is not enough love here. Then finally, it all made more sense to me when I realized all I had to do was change my Heart...some say that is where our mind really lives. Can you get into a state of mind, or better yet, a "state of Heart" in which you can make your pain malleable and flow into Love energy instead of that hard-nosed, thick and murky energy that resides in you and reminds you that it's there with dis-ease, aches and pains? When you show that Love to others, they can feel it and it goes to work on them.

When your power starts to turn on, your Heart opens up really wide and after a while you give birth to your dreams through your Heart. Everything starts to inspire you. Your velocity increases exponentially. People and things you need show up to help. The channel widens and strengthens. The coincidences and the synchronicities tell you stories and teach you about the Universe. Keep a journal so you don't forget about these important messages which you may need to decipher many months later

After having the pleasure of consulting with Laura Lee, I realized I have many contracts to fulfill. 16 in fact. Many of these contracts have to do with healing. I discovered that I can intentionally send energy from the Universe via me out through my fingers. As a Compassion Teacher, Tone Healer, Geometry Healer, Chemistry Creator, Harmonizer, and Humor Healer, this reinforcement helped me realize I really can help to heal the planet. What if I could intentionally put my vibrations into the food I cook via laughter, music, meditation, color and shape? I thought it seemed pretty science fiction at first too, but I have dreamt of this and I absolutely know deep in the pit of my heart and my gut, that this is possible not only by me but anyone should be able to do this if they put their mind to it, because we all vibrate. And, this ability I do not believe to be limited to food. I feel I was blessed with "magic hands." I like to play piano, my second (future) dream job, and one day I hope to be performing. Many people have noticed my "green thumb:" I have an avocado tree forest in my apartment. Because I like to meditate in nature, perhaps I brought the forest to my home, one of my contracts being that of a Fairy Kingdom Assistant, or guardian of plants. Other activities such as knitting, calligraphy, typing, painting, and massage, I feel I do my best work when there is the intent of transfer of unconditional love energy.

Music is such a beautiful mysterious avenue for me. It is my second language. It invokes incredible power and some of the most passionate of energies possible to be experienced in the human realm. I have an "audiographic memory" for music. I can remember every note of the most complicated song playing exactly as heard. Fortunately I cook in a jazz restaurant. I am lucky to hear live and very healing jazz performances every night that I work. To be a customer would be an incredible experience. The musicians and the chef are pouring their hearts out to you.

My parting advice would be that when you have agreed to take on triple the amount of responsibilities for healing this planet, you may run into approximately triple the amount of obstacles to overcome, perhaps more. By age 4, I had already experienced being in a traumatic earthquake, a fatal car accident and kidnapped by a child molester. Embrace each obstacle with your powerful energy and learn all you can. Perhaps your lessons are intended to teach you the way not to run a business, the way not to treat people, or seeing those critical points where you need to change your pattern or your hue a little in order to grow and succeed. Be diligent and learn your lessons and move on with initiative. After all, we are all "Knights in Shining Armour" or "Ladies of the Lake." We are here to recreate "Camelot" because we know it really exists—isn't that where we come from? We are the incubators, the infiltrators, the instigators of Unconditional Love and we need to teach others how to love without judgment, without favoritism. Don't give up. We are making a difference. And, don't forget to breathe. May you be healthy, wealthy with love, and wise. The Castle awaits!

Cheers fellow Indigos!! May we work together soon.

**Liz C. (37)**
**Vancouver, British Columbia**
*elizajayn@telus.net*

# Earth Child

As a child, I was always dreaming about distant planets and galaxies, associating myself with living somewhere other than Earth—not because it was out of distraction from my daily life of living, but because it seemed natural. These daydreams became the blueprint of my soul as I grew older, never feeling like I totally belonged to the Earth or its people. It was like I was yearning to be back home on a distant planet that I had originally come from...kinda like in the movie Superman. Growing up as a teen, I was harassed a lot by others about the way I dressed and walked. Not only did I not meet social standards, but also coming from poverty, it seemed I wasn't good enough for the public. I grew up with both fear of achieving and fear of persecution. I knew that I was much more than what people expected of me.

I knew I was good in my academics. I went from doing good to doing poorly and back to doing better in my classes.

I had another emotional front that was very limiting at times—my family and extended families. I didn't like my childhood a lot of the time. I grew up the oldest of seven children. I was forced to be much more mature than others, and I gladly accepted being more mature in my assumed nature by not showing emotion while growing up. I am Native American Indian as well and was brought up with customs of my ancestors, which helped me to ground myself in my spirituality later in life. I was very much connected to the Earth, the elements and its Spirit growing up. At times, it was another form of release from the emotional pain of growing up. My mother raised me to be a Catholic, but I chose the Native path. The instillation of praying to something greater than myself and ever-knowing, was what I connected to the most. I carried prayers in my heart ever since I was young.

Gently releasing these prayers, having contact to a higher power, and pursuing a better life from that in which I currently lived, led me to the occult, to the New Agers, and back to myself. I began a life of emancipation from restrictions that weighed on me spiritually and physically. I found drugs and alcohol along the way and benefited from their false security for a while. I was pushing myself closer and closer to life threatening dangers. In my late teens, I lived apart from my parents and found that I needed to find my own answers to who I was and who I was becoming after I found that a lot of the things I built in my life for myself were falling through the cracks. I was doing a lot of drugs and alcohol, more than what I was used to. I had a well-paying job and proceeded to get another that was much more risky. I owed people money, including my roommate and friend. I really didn't like me at this time. I decided to look within to get some of the answers I needed. I started with my genetic make-up and the codes imbedded in my make-up. I love science and I did in high school as well. So, I headed out to find more about my Native American ancestry and recover my walk in life.

Well, this set a foundation in my life of exploring who I was until now. Along the way, I managed to repeat old behaviors and patterns trying to make it all right and smooth. But it just wasn't perfect. Emotionally and physically I was tired and down to my last wits. Nothing was working out for me. My family was growing up and still the same. They didn't respond well to the new spiritual side of life I found, except for the younger ones. I succeeded through my trials and tribulations in finding out more about my Native ancestry and was reconnected to a tribe that still practices our ancestors' traditional ways of living. The connection started to make me feel much more complete, and the answers I sought started to come a lot faster, especially when I took their advice about seeking help with my problem with addictions to alcohol and drugs. Since then, I have been able to stay in the present long enough to tolerate my emotional past of verbal and physical abuse, but most of all spiritual abuse. As I stay sober I become much more aware and clear of who I am. The answers I seek come to me without even seeking them. Working to get better and centered in the present has allowed me to come into contact with people who can tell me more about myself, like the Indigos. Friends among me now share much more about themselves with me and the path of the Indigo people.

At first I thought this all had to do with the new wave of children that Native folks regard as the Rainbow Children. I was not included among them...so I thought. During my search and work with developing my spiritual self, a friend in a Reiki class I was taking, suggested I look at Laura Lee Mistycah's page on her website about the first wave of Indigos. At the time, I was well aware of the Indigo children and up until then was not aware of the adults. I read the material on her page and started to associate much more with her information and the experiences of others that she had helped. I identify with a lot of the things she mentions on her Indigo checklist. Besides being born in the year of 1973, I, too, thought of solutions in my head for very difficult problems with no paperwork to prove them. I came from a very (mentally and spiritually) abusive upbringing, became cast as a misfit, associated myself and life to comic book titles such as the X-Men (big fan)...my life took on new meaning, and I knew that I was much more and beyond than what people tell me I am. The metaphysical and paranormal aspects are very evident too in my Indigo life. Being touched by spirits, visited in the dream time, super empathic, a lot of healing energy, a tremendous amount of compassion, psychic and telepathic abilities, and know I am capable of much more that I have not yet tapped into.

As my life unfolds and evolves, I learn that I need to take proper care of myself. Even if I don't do it immediately, I must stay on top of that thought pattern, making sure it is empowered. I've learned not to be dependent on others empowering me...I must do it for myself. I've learned that when all seems against me, I am distracting myself from the truth; that there are still things that are working for my benefit. I've learned that my emotions really count, that I am no less of a human than others and that I too have the right to love. Love is the key to holding ourselves in the present. Love of self and others...even inanimate objects.

Sometimes, we feel we don't belong to this timeline, that we belong to another because we feel so much more evolved than others. We can't comprehend the senselessness of hate and war. This is part of our journey. Honor yourself and gift yourself with the gift of life. I invite you to learn the path and the lessons of love. As a healer, I tend to overdo it and give too much of myself and then have nothing left in return. I get bitter or in a space of resentment. It's never easy but we must find ways to keep ourselves Number One and from being depleted of energy from others. The moment you start to get better, you will be challenged and tested. Hang in there and find a supportive group that reflects who you are in all that you want to accomplish in bettering yourself.

Better yourself for yourself, and not for others, no excuses, this is your time. As a friend of mine puts it "stop hitting that snooze button." We are the Rainbow People that my ancestors spoke of and still speak of today.

Be well and happy in the light of your journey!

Taino'ti (may the path before you be noble),

**Tonina Opia [Dolphin Spirit] (Age 32)**
**Orange County, New York**
**Toninaopia@verizon.net**

# The Curse

For as long as I can remember, my interactions with people have been very frustrating. I began to notice as early as kindergarten that it was really hard for me to make friends, and the friends that I did have, I never knew if I could really trust them. It was often the case that when other kids would pick on me (which was quite often), my friends would join them. This would happen a lot with the kids in my neighborhood too, so throughout most of my childhood I didn't feel like I had any true friends. This is a feeling that stayed with me for a long time. School was also the place where I learned to keep my mouth shut and never express my feelings or opinions. Whenever I did, I would be made fun of, be told to shut up, or just be ignored.

I grew up in a very loving family, but I also felt really out of place. Being the youngest in my family would be pretty frustrating sometimes. I have one sister who is ten years older than me. When we both lived at home, she was in high school while I was in grade school. The most memories I have of her when I was growing up are when we used to fight a lot over stupid stuff. This isn't anything unusual in a family with multiple kids, but it felt like I got in more trouble for it than my sister. For this reason, I felt a little bit of resentment for her until I was about 11 or 12. I was 9 or 10 when she got married and moved to California for a year or two. I always thought that these were the reasons that we never became too close. I love her very much and we actually have a good relationship at the moment, but we still aren't as close as I would like to be. Alcohol played somewhat of a big role when I was growing up too. I wouldn't go as far as to say that my mom was an alcoholic, but when she would drink, I had to be really careful of what I said to her and how I would word it because it was really easy to offend her. When she got offended, it would ruin her mood for the rest of the night, no matter how much one would apologize to her. This scenario rarely comes up now, but I've always felt that this was a big reason for my feelings toward alcohol; I HATE IT!!

As the years went by I became a shy person with social anxiety. This seemed to increase more throughout high school after having one bad romantic relationship after another. With the exception of three relationships (including the one I'm in right now), I kept getting boyfriends who were emotionally and psychologically abusive. Some would even have girls on the side here and there.

Two of these tyrants were the type to make me feel so guilty about hanging around my friends so that I would slowly but surely quit just to keep the peace. The relationship I had before my current one was by far the worst. I still believe to this day that the only reason we got together was because I was put under a love spell.

For the record, I'm not just saying this because I don't want to take responsibility, but he definitely had the means to do it. To begin with, I wasn't attracted to him whatsoever. I didn't even know if I really liked him when I first met him, but I figured since I didn't have many friends at the time, I better not appear stuck-up, so I would talk to him whenever I saw him at school.

After I got to know him a little he told me that his mother is Wiccan (and I found this out for sure after I met her) and she had a lot of spell books that she would let him look at. After a while he managed to acquire a picture of me and a piece of paper that I used to blot my lipstick. Then one day out of nowhere he started to appear more attractive and I had an easier time getting along with him. At first he seemed like a funny, likable, and very charismatic guy who was obsessed with vampires; which for some reason, I found kind of attractive. He had aspirations of becoming a stockbroker so he could be rich. He would always tell me that when he becomes successful, he would take care of me. I would always tell him that he could do that until I became a rock star (which is what I wanted do at the time) but he didn't seem too comfortable with the idea. He would also tell me about the fun times he had while living in Seattle.

For some reason, some of his stories sounded a little too movie like. About three months into our relationship I started to notice some things about him that didn't set well with me. He seemed to really take on the role of alpha male around me and our friends. By this I mean that he would try to dominate our male friends and treat them like crap while he would flirt with our female friends (in front of me) and treat me like the token girlfriend. He also started telling me about how he would practice being a psychic vampire.

For example, one night he was complaining about how he wasn't feeling well, like he might be coming down with a cold. Then he made a comment about taking some energy from his best friend so he could feel better. The next day at school his best friend threw up in class and went home sick, but my boyfriend on the other hand made a miraculous recovery. After being with this guy for a while, he pretty much had me convinced that our friends didn't really like me too much because I was cold and distant (I was actually kind of quiet and shy) and they liked him better because he was funny and charismatic. I often thought that the only reason he didn't get physically abusive with me was because I had a couple of male friends who would waste him if they ever found out about it. So instead, he would make subtle threats and mess with me emotionally, psychologically, and psychically. I didn't talk to anyone about this for a while, but one day I was brave enough to confide in one of my friends who happened to be his best friend. The very next day my boyfriend started talking about a dream of his that told him that a female in his life was undermining him, and if he ever found out who it was, he would beat her to a bloody pulp, and possibly kill her. Then he muttered under his breath that he hoped that it wasn't me. That was enough to shut me up.

One day his best friend called to tell me that my boyfriend was cheating on me, that he said a lot of nasty things about me, and that about half of what he told me about his life was a lie. His best friend also told me that the main reason he and our other friends would hang around and tolerate his rude behavior is so they could hang around me. After I found this out I confronted my boyfriend, but ended up still staying with him long enough to gather up the courage find a way to get him out. We actually parted ways peacefully and mutually. He told me that since we were parting ways he was going to use the freedom to practice dark magic, and I told him that I was going to go forth with the light.

From then on we lost all contact with each other, and in less than a year after we broke up, his best friend and I started seeing each other. We have been together ever since. As time went on, it seemed like most of my friends were slipping away, and the only friends I had (who happened to be male) didn't really take a liking to my new relationship with my current boyfriend. They accused me of controlling him, which is something that I really resented because I would never dream of doing such a thing after being in a controlling relationship myself. I felt really betrayed by people that I thought were my best friends. After a few months they started to come around again, but it always seemed like they were much closer to my boyfriend than me. I didn't have any female friends at the time because I lost trust in females after I had so many "friends" stab me in the back throughout my life. I also had this weird fear of showing affection to my boyfriend when there was anyone else in the room. I could never really explain it. This was also around the time that I stopped wearing make-up and gained weight.

Throughout the years my feelings of alienation got worse. It seemed like everything I did to try to come out of my shell would backfire. I tried focusing on the fact that everything is an illusion and that we can change our lives for the better anytime we wanted as long as we have love in our hearts. That didn't even work. I would even try some Wiccan spells here and there, but they only worked for a short period of time and I would be back to square one. It just seemed like no matter what I did, I would still end up being a dull and boring individual who would be overlooked by everyone. In spring of 2004, I started getting depressed more often, and it grew into full-blown depression by early summer. I was unemployed, my best friends and I drifted so far apart that I was starting to wonder if they were even my friends anymore, and the one friend who I knew was genuine got deployed to Iraq. I also found out that there is a new draft being worked on behind closed doors for this war. With all of this swimming in my mind, I would bawl my eyes out at least once a day and even started thinking about suicide; which is something I hadn't even considered since junior high and early high school.

My boyfriend is such a blessing. If he hadn't been there for me as much as he was, I probably would have gone through with it. He would even walk miles to my house at two in the morning to make sure that I didn't do anything stupid. He was (and still is) the most loving and supportive person that I know. I'm very lucky to have him. This depression eventually led to insomnia. No matter how tired I was, I wouldn't be able to sleep until between five and eight in the morning. Then I would wake up anywhere between three and five in the afternoon.

The last time I woke up at five in the afternoon I decided to put an end to my whacked out sleeping schedule. I stayed awake until nine the following evening so I could finally wake up early enough to look for a job. From this point on everything in my life started to turn around. At first, I found that being a reborn early bird was fascinating. I was finally able to do some things that I wasn't able to do before because of my sleeping schedule; such as go to the library. I went to the library one day with the intention of finding what I like to call "brain candy"; something that makes you think and could possibly be spiritually enhancing. I got just that when I stumbled upon Laura Lee Mistycah's book, Kryahgenetics. Just a few days after I started reading it, I realized that the things that bothered me a week before were all of a sudden not bothering me. Reading Kryahgenetics helped me push these newfound positive feelings to another level. I started to really feel that everything is just an illusion and that all we need is love. During this time my intuition was also starting to pick up speed and was telling me to become a recluse for a little while so I could make sure that all of my old feelings were really dealt with. At this point in time, I finally I found a job that I'm very happy with.

After reading Kryahgenetics for a second time, I decided to get a hold of the Aulmauracite rock and Aurauralite pendent. Before I called Laura Lee to see about getting those, I decided to give her website another look. This is when I found her section on Indigos and made the discovery that I was possibly one of them. When I called Laura Lee for the first time she started telling me about the Indigo book that she was working on and asked if I had a chance to look at the list of Indigo traits. I told her that I did and that I identified with most of them. She told me that she was definitely able to see that I am an Indigo, and that these rocks will really help me out. She also threw in 5 little grid rocks to set up at my house. Since we live in the same town, she decided to meet my boyfriend and I at a local restaurant parking lot. This is when things started to get really interesting. We agreed to meet at the parking lot at 1:15 in the afternoon. My boyfriend and I got there a few minutes early. Laura Lee told us that she would be arriving in a blue minivan, so we were keeping our eye out for one. I don't think I ever saw as many blue minivans as I did that day. None of them were driven by Laura Lee. When she arrived (about 45 minutes later), she was actually in a small car that wasn't blue. There were a lot of people in the parking lot that day, but she knew who we were right away. When she approached us, she told us that she was having car trouble, and had to use her son's car...which left her with the impression that it was really important for her to get to us. As soon as my boyfriend and I put the pendants on we felt an extreme peace that we never felt before. When Laura Lee talked to my boyfriend for a few minutes, she realized that he's an Indigo as well!

After we parted ways, my boyfriend and I went back to my house to see about getting the grid set up in my room. (I felt that my room was the best place to put them for now until I move out of my parents' house). We were encountering difficulties, so I decided to email Laura Lee some questions. It took her a little while to respond. When she did, she told me that her computer locked up when she tried to reply to my email. Almost every time we communicated through email this would happen. I put off setting up my grid for a couple of weeks because the way my room was set up made it difficult. During this time my positive feelings of being a walking beam of light started to dwindle a little, and the communication between my rocks and I became a little more difficult. After being interrupted for the hundredth time during my rock meditation, I decided to rearrange my whole room so I could get the grid up, and every possible roadblock seemed to surface. For instance, when I tried to move my bed, it wouldn't budge for anything. I got frustrated enough to stop what I was doing and confront whatever was trying to keep me from setting the grid up. I told it flat out that no matter what obstacle it tried to throw at me, I will always find a way around it and it had a choice to either leave me alone or get defeated. At the time I had no idea who or what I was talking to, but after I said that I had no problem moving my bed; but that wasn't the end of it. Just for safe measure I gave my boyfriend a call to see if he would mind helping me rearrange my room after we both got off work. He agreed to do so after I told him what happened before I called him. After that I decided to knit little squares for the rocks to sit on at their corners. As I was doing this, I was finding a lot of breaks in the yarn, which was something I never had a problem with before. Because of that, it took me a lot longer to finish them than it should have. That night I only worked three and a half hours, but for some reason I was feeling really drained of energy. After my boyfriend and I got off work we had a little bit of coffee and got right to work on my room. We encountered little distractions here and there, but finally got done arranging my room perfectly to set up the grid rocks around two thirty in the morning. Immediately, my room seemed to let out a sigh of relief, and I was extremely happy to overcome such annoying odds.

A few weeks after that incident, I decided to have an Indigo reading with Laura Lee, hoping that it could help me get to the bottom of this resistance. I was ready to get going with what I was put here to do. At Hal's request, Laura Lee cleared her schedule so she could do the reading that day, and asked me to reply to the Indigo profiles and how they do or do not apply when I came. During the reading I found out that I had two very powerful implants. One was telling me that I don't deserve to live, and the other was telling me, "We're watching you." Laura Lee was told to help me get rid of them right then and there. After my session I felt great, and my interactions with people were starting to look better. This energy lasted several weeks, but then work and school got extremely busy and I was left with very little time, if any, to work on my Indigo contracts. Because of this, I started to feel a lot of stress, and I started to notice that my old negative feelings were trying to make their way back into my life. I was beginning to believe that since I got rid of the two implants during my Indigo session, all of my remaining implants were working overtime. The only thing that kept me from letting the implants take over full swing was keeping in mind that I am here for a darn good reason! I also kept reflecting back to the last half of summer when I was feeling really good about everything. Keeping those two things in mind made me a very stubborn person. I decided that I was going to get to the bottom of this and find out why these feelings and circumstances were popping up.

When work finally slowed down, I took the opportunity to spend more time with my power rocks to see if they could give me some information about my implants. The rocks were able to tell me the functions of the implants, but I couldn't get any information about where the implants were coming from; and when I would try to get rid of them, they wouldn't go away. The idea about getting Laura Lee's help with this kept coming to mind, but I didn't act on it at first because she already showed me how to get rid of implants once before, and I didn't want to come off as lazy or dependent. After the last time I tried to get rid of the implants myself with no success, I finally decided to get Laura Lee's help again. When I contacted her with my problem, she assured me that there's nothing wrong with getting help. She told me to make a list of the implants, and she was able to schedule an implant removal session just a few days after I contacted her.

When we began the session she asked me to read the list of implants to her, which included: "I'm a dull and boring person," "keep your heart closed," "no one will notice you," "you always screw up - you're always to blame," and that I felt invisible. When Laura Lee started tuning into the implants, she was being told that everything on the list tied into one source...a curse! It turns out that in my life right before my present one I had a curse put on me.

Sometime in the late 1950's or early 1960's I was a woman who married a tyrannical jerk because he got me pregnant. When this happened I was about 21 years old and he was about 38 or 39. He was a total control freak who didn't like anyone (particularly other men) looking at me, so he would make me dress up as plain as possible. Of course he was also the type to have plenty of women on the side. He was violent and an alcoholic. I especially didn't like being around him when he drank because I never knew what he was going to be like. He was also a wealthy businessman who would like to host little parties for his rich buddies. He wouldn't let me speak unless I was spoken to, or to offer our guests more servings for their meal. He would only let me dress up for these parties every once in a while, just to make sure that no one paid attention to me any more than he wanted them to. He also kept me away from my friends and family. This included my sister, who I was really close to. He was also the type of person to exaggerate and lie. Whenever I would point out the faults in what he was saying, he would get furious and tell me to shut up, and even get violent with me. Even though he was rich and we had a big house with nice furniture, none of it mattered to me, because I felt like a servant and prisoner more than anything. Most of the time he wouldn't even let me leave the house, but sometimes he gave me money to shop for clothes. I tried sometimes to save up money so I can get a bus or train ticket to escape from him. I would take some of the expensive clothes that I bought back since I couldn't wear them most of the time anyway, or save the change from my purchases and stash it away, but he would find my stashes and get furious. There have even been times when I thought I had enough saved up for a ticket, but I would be short a few cents, so no one would sell me a ticket. My husband was also into black magic and learned Voodoo in the southern states. He would put spells on me here and there, but I would be able to break them by keeping my mind focused. This wouldn't make him happy either.

Shortly before my death (I died when I was 25), I witnessed him murder someone. Laura Lee said the person he murdered was his most trusted servant; possibly his butler. This servant and I were secretly friends. We didn't have an affair or anything, but this man would have done anything for me. He wanted to see me escape from my husband so I could go back to my family and friends and be happy again. The reason my husband killed him was because he saw the two of us talking. I don't even know if he overheard anything we said, but just seeing the two of us talking like we were friends was enough to get his imagination going and put him in a rage. He killed him right in front of me. Then he let me know that I would be next if I told anyone. Shortly after this incident is when he put the curse on me. The curse involved a combination of dark Wicca and Voodoo. He had a Voodoo doll with a gag taped to its mouth on his alter; accompanied with black candles. The purpose of the curse had three main qualities:

Keep Quiet- don't say what you know, think, or feel.
Stay Invisible- mousy (don't stand out in any way).
Friends are patronizing you, they don't really like you.

He put the curse on me not only because he wanted me to keep quiet about what he did, but he also had a feeling that I was going to reincarnate and come back as someone more spiritual and powerful then him. He knew that I had talents in that life because I could overcome some of his mind games, so, to say the least, he wanted me to stay silent, invisible and friendless for eternity.

After he put the curse on me, I mustered up enough courage to go to the authorities and tell them what he did. Because of his position in the community, the authorities decided to do an investigation rather than arresting him right away, even though they HAD an eye witness. Because of their lack of appropriate action, he knew that I sold him out. This also gave him the opportunity to kill me by beating me in the head to death. Of course, he had a real difficult time trying to cover up my death. He tried telling the authorities that it was an accident, but they didn't buy his story this time.

It was time to set things straight. Laura Lee guided me through the curse removal. We had to do a ritual similar to his, but modified it to fit the occasion. Laura Lee set up an alter on a table with a black tablecloth, put a power rock at each corner, and a black candle at the center. To begin with, I had to visualize myself removing the gag from the Voodoo doll, light the candle, and recite each line three times with passion:

I know who you are and I saw what you did,
From this point on your curse I do rid.
I free my mouth,
East, West, North and South.
I remove the gag,
And the stuffing's of a rag.
I blast the shield of invisibility,
And I set myself free.
My circle includes only true friends,
Who will stick by me till this world ends.
I AM FREE..... TO BE ME
What prevails now is my freedom,
From this moment, through the rest of the time continuum.
I AM FREE, I AM FREE, I AM FREE.
Through all eternity...
BLESSED BE

I did this and some other thing to lift the curse, and it worked! So, not only did he go down for two murders, but I came back in this life, got rid of the curse, and now I'm telling the whole world what he did. So much for eternity, HAHAHAHA!!!!!!!!!

After the curse removal, I noticed a difference right away. I communicated with people a little easier. Animals and children noticed me more, and I wasn't as afraid to speak my mind as I used to be. I even started to dress up a little more. The change hasn't come into full swing yet due to some lingering implants, but thanks to the curse removal, I'm now able to get more information about them and know how to get rid of them.

I also want to say for the record that I couldn't have asked for a better family to be born into. In spite of how I felt about some things from time to time while growing up, they are truly loving, supportive, and encouraging beings to be brought up by. I wouldn't trade them for the world. I also feel truly blessed to be with the boyfriend I have right now. He has shown more love and patience than anyone could ever think of asking. As for my best friends, I am so happy and grateful that we are still in each other's lives. I believe that our paths may have moved away from each other for a small time, but I believe that our paths may once again come fully together because we may have a lot of work to do together (they're Indigo's too). Even if we continue to part ways, I will always be grateful for our friendship. I love them dearly. And for Laura Lee, I can never thank her enough. I feel so lucky to have stumbled across Kryahgenetics, because it would have taken me a lot longer to find out about my life's purpose and especially about the curse. For all I know, I may have never even found out.

May the light be with everyone!!!


Lynn. G. (Age 23)
Spokane, Washington
smokeyantonwilson@yahoo.com

# To all the Indigos reading this...

**I**t's been a rough ride until now, many dark times, many times when you wondered how you keep going in this topsy-turvy world. I've thought to myself many times that this world isn't worth saving, that there's too much darkness and misery, yet somehow every time I had those thoughts, I'd take a stroll and be surrounded by people. I'd see loving couples, parents with innocent children, and babies in carriages with not a single worry. I'd feel the better half of all humans around me and realize that it's all worth the dark times I've been through if my presence as an Indigo on this planet will help provide a much needed brighter future for all.

A lot of us live in two worlds. The "real," "normal" everyday human world and the world we touch in our dreams, the places we feel we've been to, where everything is just so right. There is a delicate balance which must be maintained. Trying to live only in the "real" world will have the other one haunting you subtly, while trying to live in the other one will make those around you think you're losing touch with "reality" (their version of it).

There will always be forces in this world that will try to convince you that you are "less" than you are. Family, friends, strangers, teachers at school, colleagues at work as well as "unseen" mind demons and foreign consciousnesses, a lot of these will all try to make you believe as much as they can that you CAN"T do something...but if you believe it, then so will it be.

Really, it's that simple. You come across a situation, you FEEL you can do something about it but something holds you back. I say to you: Don't Hold Back. It's what we're here for. You feel it, you can do it, even if you don't understand how, your Higher Self is your ally and will do the things you can't comprehend, but feel. You just have to give the signal and stand firm.

True Love is something every Indigo on this planet will seek out at one time. It will be a difficult and long journey. Many times you will think you've found that special person only to find that it wasn't, that the magic faded. All these are precious, important experiences. Harbor no hate in your heart, leave behind friendships, not enemies, or else you'll hurt inside.

I say to all of you that as you become more and more who you are, you will inevitably attract other Indigos into your life, you will become like polarized magnets, it is inevitable. Many years of loneliness you will have to endure, but they Will end and you Will find other Indigos, as well as that special person, most dear to your heart.

I am very sure that, if we wanted to, we could have led rich luxurious lives with everything a selfish heart could ever desire. We could have chosen lives without a care in the world, looking the other way when someone would need our help. But that is not our nature, we cannot, shouldn't, don't even want to change it.

To us it doesn't seem more difficult to do good than harm, to love rather than to hate (although on this planet we will sometimes succumb to darker moments). For us everything is the other way around. Why not help a fellow human being? Why not be there for someone in their time of need? Really, I've seen how even the smallest effort can be of Great help to someone, so always try to do what you can.

We are made of sterner stuff. It's up to us to keep on living our lives here, walking against the wind, holding true to our nature. And I tell you all we are making a big difference, I've seen for myself how our presence brings out the good in people, uniting them and helping them put aside their differences.

A task has been given to us that only we can do, so... **Stand tall and shake the Heavens!**

**Lother Dimitreu, (Age 23)**
**Bucharest Romania**
**lother555@hotmail.com**

185

# Shove-In Removal... (How Long Was I Out?)

**M**y name is Kim. I was born in Toronto and after graduating from York University where I studied music, I took a road trip that landed me in Arizona for a year, then took me to Minnesota where I now reside.

Recently my sister had a reading with Laura Lee, and she immediately knew I was an Indigo also. After seeing how important it was for Indigos to have Aurauralite, she sent me a necklace and grid stones. As I spent more time with the pendant, I was compelled to do the same thing and have a session too. My sister also sent me Kryahgenetics and I loved it, but didn't finish it.

I was in a rut, not in the highest of spirits and was sick of being that way. I felt like I had been in a depression for so long. I just didn't want to do anything and nothing seemed to work to get me out of it.

I e-mailed Laura Lee with my list of Indigo Traits, which is a requirement for an Indigo reading, and she immediately sensed a couple of shove-ins in me. A ding went off in my head - is this for real? A few weeks earlier I had a dream, the kind where I am lying in my body but I can hear myself talking to other people. This time, I was telling someone that I "didn't like the decisions she was making." Someone was running their hands through my hair, and I could feel the tugging and the feel of the hair. I didn't know what the dream really meant until I had the reading. (It was sort of like the voices were talking about me!) That was only one of the handful of weird dreams I had during that week or so.

On 07/28/2004, the day before the reading, I placed the grid rocks at four corners of my apartment and the center. The day of the reading I called at 6:30 p.m. I had lit candles, incense and put some salt in water on my altar. I then took some deep breaths. I wasn't sure what to expect. I have had my altar for a number of years, but only used it a few times, because I know it has power and protection that I don't want to use foolishly. We went through a meditation and I did the best I could. I tried to visualize the Egg as she asked. I stared at my candle a lot, because I found that had worked for me in the past.

Laura Lee said that she sensed there was one female and one male shove-in in me. Here is the story.

Eleven years ago, a female ghost named Sarah Jane latched onto me after I was hit in the head. I found that my life had many similarities as Sarah Jane's. I don't think I can pinpoint a time when I felt a difference in myself, but I definitely remember hitting my head quite a few times, which is how shove-ins usually enter....by getting knocked out or rendered unconscious in some way.

When I was younger, I didn't deal well with anger and used to bang my head against things a lot. Also, I didn't like eating much so my circulation was bad. Maybe I was anemic. A few times I would get dizzy and faint, banging my head on things like dressers. I have also had dreams of being wounded in the back of the head, but nobody would help me because they couldn't see that I was wounded. Looking back, I see the gradual build-up of energy and the need to purge it. I felt like I was writhing in my own skin!

Eleven years ago in 1993, I was 15 years old. I had a broken heart from a one-night stand and was very depressed with low self-esteem and a dreary outlook. I didn't really confide in anybody about this so I felt very alone and isolated. I had a lot of sexual issues going on at the time and was not receiving the kind of love and attention that I craved and didn't understand why. I started to get testy and very obnoxious at times. I also began to drink and felt like nothing really mattered other than finding someone who would love me.

Sarah Jane was a prostitute who died in the 1920's when she was 31 years old. She had been brought up a Christian and after being raped she thought a decent man would never want her, nor that she would get into heaven. This sent another ding off inside me as I had some similar beliefs. Although I never was a Christian, my parents belonged to a Christian church before I was born. I always felt bombarded by that religion from all angles in my life, but I refused to follow it. Deep down there was something telling me that I was going to hell too! There was always this voice in my head that wanted to prove the Bible wrong. Deep down I really believed that all religions were the same.

Also, within the next year, when I was 16, I was raped and stalked by someone who called himself my friend, which was devastating and filled me with anger and also despair. During that time I also started to have dreams where I would be touched sexually, which continued over many years. A part of me wanted it to happen because I was so lonely, and another part was deathly afraid of it. One night a few years ago, I got fed up with this happening and I laid in my body, half asleep, and jumped up and told whatever it was that was doing these things to "get the fuck away from me." I saw a few columns of black smoke wisp across my apartment floor and hide behind the walls of my balcony. I couldn't sleep for a week!

Sarah Jane was quite attractive and used her body to get things. I have always been attractive: Enough to always get gawked at by passing cars and old stinky men. It wasn't pleasant. I didn't intentionally use my body to get things though, but sometimes I didn't have to try! There are so many perverts around. Sarah Jane had an alcohol and drug problem and died of a drug overdose. Some of her characteristics were that she was bitter, rude and testy with low self-esteem and lots of anger.

By my second year of high school no one wanted to be my friend, like I was a disease. I never understood that either because I was never not nice to anybody. In fact the people who really knew me, mostly adults, called me an angel. I started to hang around guys because they were the only ones who would talk to me. I found only a few good friends in school, and they were all guys! They nicknamed me the Queen of Darkness. I became very bawdy and mouthy, but never wanted to date anybody because I was in love with the past.

So many things make sense now because my life had taken on the energies of Sarah Jane. I finally realized why I lived with certain people and in certain neighborhoods. I never understood why there were always people with drugs around....and hookers and strippers! Also, why men were so sexually attracted to me. One neighborhood I lived in I didn't know anyone, but everyone knew me by the way I walked (how weird is that?). I was giving off an energy that wasn't what I wanted to give off, but emanated it anyway. I had a stripper for a roommate and I hung out with her at her job a couple of times — I was 18! She even wanted to be my girlfriend! I've been grabbed and kissed by strangers, and once I was slapped in the ass by the landlord I had, whose wife believed he looked upon me like a daughter! I couldn't believe the way some humans acted or why this was happening to me, which made me more and more depressed.

The second shove-in was a man named John. Laura Lee said that he shoved in about 10 years ago. She saw that I was knocked-out in someone's house or somewhere other than my home. By then I was drinking some more and had a few times where I didn't remember anything at other peoples' places.

188

John died about 40 years ago, in the 1960's and was 40 years old at the time of his death. He died confused, beaten down, lonely and destitute. Looking back, I can see that John shoved in at a time when I had given up on everything and became very bitter and sarcastic. I liked to wear black and listen to really heavy music, and also Romantic piano music and let the melodies make me cry. I liked to cry and I always felt like I needed to.

I met someone, when I was 18, whom I dated for a year or two and lived with. It turned out to be a very destructive relationship, which started out in a taxicab after a night out at the bar! One day he slapped me in the face and I turned in a different direction. After that, I woke up and started to look for GOD, and made myself my number one priority. I ended up taking a religion class in university that I learned a lot from and experimented with a few different things like Hinduism, Witchcraft but mostly Norse mythology. I have always felt a strong tie to Freya, Sky Mother and bearer of the knowledge of magick. I have always felt magick, but also felt that something was holding me back against my will.

Laura Lee asked me if there was anything that I wanted to tell her before we got off of the phone and she went to work. I was looking at the print-out of the Kryahgenetics Egg on my wall and I thought of something. In 2000, I met a friend who had a dream where he was told by the gods (he worked with Norse gods) to go to a certain place. There he was guided to take an Egg, which was purple and covered with all different kinds of jewels, and remove it from a pit full of snakes and take it to another location. My life had taken a big turn after I met him and a few months later I met my present love who I think is just right for me.

Laura Lee told me about the time when she and Ronnie were trying to help with the Twin Towers. Some exterior force put a "net" over them so no one could leave and no angels could get in. They used Eggs to put the people in so they would be able to pass through the "net" and go to the angels. She thought that my friend was using the Egg, maybe without knowing what it meant. He was a bit perplexed by the dream he had. He told me that the reason they had him take the Egg was because they couldn't touch it. This made me feel like I had hit a home run, like I was connected to the right circuit, which would lead me back home.

Then, we got off the phone and Laura Lee went to work. I was sitting on the floor with my eyes closed and within a few minutes I felt something come up from out of my stomach into my head and all of a sudden I burst out crying and could feel sadness and sorrow, very

189

cathartic. I wasn't sure what it was, a whole bunch of emotions wrapped into one. Also, I saw a few flashes from dreams that I had had before, ones that seem like Sarah Jane using my body for whatever! I didn't really feel anything except that and then I calmed down. The next 10 minutes I didn't feel much, but I think I was trying too hard or was shaken.

We got back on the phone and Laura Lee started explaining what she did. I was crying and I felt shivers all over the whole time she told me what she had done. She worked with Sarah Jane first, not surprising to me, and Laura Lee described how the Kryahgenetics Egg she quarantined her in became transparent when she brought her to the Angels portal and she could see the truth of what was going on. Laura Lee also said that she kept looking back and forth from the Angels to me, totally confused and started to feel bad. Laura Lee said to her that she was going to heaven and to a place in heaven that helps you see the good in everyone, including yourself!

Laura Lee said it seemed like she had connected to her higher self and when she realized the truth of things she would say things like, "Tell Kim I'm sorry, I'm so sorry, she didn't deserve to have me control her, and I don't expect her to forgive me, but please tell her I'm sorry for what I did. I wish I could make it up to her." Laura Lee said she was very repentant and knew she made my life a living hell. When she was going toward the Angels she kept turning back to me until she was gone. All of these words hit me and I felt like crying more. All this time I thought I was responsible for creating my own little hell, and it all made sense now.

She worked with John second. When he died he wandered and when he felt my energy of depression he sort of latched on unknowingly. When his Egg was placed in the portal, all he could say was, "I'm in heaven, I'm finally in heaven. I can see angels!" I felt an immediate relief of depression and renewal. Like every attempt that I had made to get rid of it worked all at once!

Then Laura Lee said that Archangel Michael had a message for me, that my life is about to make a grand change, a total revolution, turning around for the better... on a higher plane and to tell me that I am dearly loved and cherished.

I have been waiting for this. I read a few books by Stuart Wilde and he talked about how when you decide to embark on a spiritual journey once you raise your energy you have to settle on a plateau.  I felt like I was on that plateau from the time I was 21 when I decided to find out how things really work.  The next level is achieved after energies have been stabilized and this is what I've been waiting for.  I knew someday I would get some kind of message from this Archangel that would change my life!  I have tried only a few magical things in my life and I always felt a strong connection to Michael.  I have a book called Messages From Michael by Chelsea Quinn Yarbro that really changed the way I look at things.

After the reading, I sat down and absorbed all of this information with the help of my boyfriend.  Even he was surprised at what had happened.  This had explained a lot of my behavior, but I immediately saw how this has been affecting my life for so long.  I remember when I was a teenager, I was so depressed and suicidal that I would say to myself, "If this is the way it is, I don't want to live past 25."  It's amazing how your own words can come true, I just turned 26 and things did change!

Later on that night I had to work on my computer typing out a conference call.  I was feeling the effects very much.  I stepped away from my work and when I came back, I looked at the screen and as I read I felt that the words were directed at me:

"When you look down the road, the next couple of years, where do you think the most opportunities are for acquisitions or for internal growth?  Obviously you've got a lot of things firing really well right now.  Are there any particular areas you get especially excited about when you think about growing, either internally or externally?"

I immediately started talking back in my head and then started typing back in a different document on my computer.  It helped me direct myself, to tell myself what I wanted.

My answer (part of it anyway):

"...I want my memory back, to fully explore my talents, and blend them together into a great big web that surrounds the world with joy - a wall of sound that everyone can understand and enjoy even if they don't know why..."

As I was finishing up my work, I got stiff and decided to stretch.  I closed my eyes and stretched my arms behind my back and in my mind I saw an image of myself.  I could see that image connected to my body by rays of dark light and it was moving the way I was and I felt release from the stretching. It was glowing, kind of like a sheet of sparkles. I could feel it too. It reminded me of sunrays through the clouds, how they are angled (Jacob's ladder), but covered with stars.

After that, I started to hear music. It sounded like it was coming from behind me. There was a very soothing male voice singing (probably baritone), and it was the most beautiful music I have heard in a while. Also, I could feel laughter and it made me want to laugh. Like someone was very happy about what had just happened! Throughout the rest of the time I was working, I could hear faint sounds of music here and there. I hear a lot of music in my dreams, but could never connect to it very often while I was awake. Now it was flowing out!

I saw a lot of stuff in my head when I went to bed and it was in full color! I didn't remember my dream, but I woke up feeling totally different. I was very tired the next few days, but a different kind of tired, and very thirsty. I have started to drink a lot more water, which I have wanted to do for a long time. I usually drank a lot of pop just to keep me awake because I was so lethargic and grumpy at times, hoping it would perk me up.

The next day, I felt that this was the strangest thing that had happened to me. My neck loosened up and I felt lighter.

One morning I sang for a couple of hours and it was the most cleansing thing. Before, when I sang, I felt blocked in my throat. It didn't feel physical. It made me depressed and I didn't know what was wrong with me, so I gave up on it. Now I can sing and don't feel the blockage anymore. And, I don't care if anyone can hear me like I did before. What a change!

It feels like I don't remember anything I learned in university, but I can figure out music with no problem, subconsciously maybe. It feels like my subconscious has taken over and I don't have to worry about anything anymore. It's odd, hard to explain.

When I am awake I am more alert. My physical perspective has changed, like I have gotten my own eyes back. Also, so many things about my body have changed. I noticed the ability to smell has changed and my hearing is more balanced out. Now I hear well in both ears! And, I can visualize more easily. I can tell though, that it is just the beginning of things. It is like a very soft hum in my head that I know will get louder one day.

It feels like certain parts of my body are healing. The first night when I had the reading, before I went to bed, I asked for healing of my body. I felt my abdomen tickling, something in my reproductive organs. Later on I found out that what I had was ovarian cysts, which I think are a manifestation of this whole episode. I work in the medical field and I am convinced that all disease roots in the mind.

I always wanted to become vegetarian or do this or that, but never did. I feel like I can now. I'm not afraid to go out in public or be around a lot of people now. It's a piece of cake. Before, I was always paranoid.

I feel like my subconscious has to do a cleanup on my mind. I definitely felt the residue. Until all the garbage in there that isn't mine is removed, I can't use it or fully go into my dreams.

It's strange having control over myself, sometimes habit wants to take control, but I realize what I'm doing and try to change it. Now when I think about changing things, I feel myself projecting that energy, where as before, it didn't feel like it was going anywhere, but back inside myself to be tormented. I have always been sort of a thinker and a philosopher and I was starting to drive myself insane. I thought everybody thought I was insane!

My inner vision is getting lighter. The darkness is slowly being removed. But, on the other hand, I can see much better in the dark...like, it's tinted blue and everything has blue in it, and I measure the blue. So, I'm not sure which is which. But I feel some places I've been to in the past few days have been really light, brighter than the sun. Very warm and happy.

I had a dream where I was taken to a property with two houses. On the right was a house that I have been to before in my dreams, and on the left was a house that was half built. I think there are two meanings for this dream to me. The first that there is a new part of me that is being built in my subconscious, and second, a foretelling of events to come.

Within a month of having this dream I decided to buy a house. I found a house that was close to my friends and seemed absolutely perfect. I had someone show it to me, but I had no experience in the house buying process. It turns out that I was inappropriately talked into buying this house which turned out to be a "handyman's nightmare" as my brother in law called it. I took a few digital pictures of it and there were a handful of orbs, and I started to have big doubts about it. After consulting a lawyer I got out of buying this house. Within a week we found a house that is perfect, it is even blue! It is everything that I would have ever hoped to have.

I went to a friend's birthday party in July and stood out in a field to watch the Blue Moon while it stormed outside. I definitely think it was a significant Blue Moon for me! Especially since both full Moons in July (I am a Cancer) were in Capricorn, which is my Rising Sign.

The following week I decided to also get the Indigo Reading. In the reading Laura Lee helped me remember exactly what I'm here for, and making music is one of those. It was great because I didn't feel like I wasted my years in school learning about music for nothing! I know what I'm supposed to do now and I feel good about it. I feel like I have a fresh start to do it with — without resentment and with a lot of understanding.

I have been unsure what to do with myself, but I am able to hear the hints from my intuition louder. I am starting to work at home in the month or two, which I have been waiting for. I can definitely see a change spinning for my near future with limitless possibilities, and the changes are coming faster than I had expected. I also feel the warm presence of so many things around me.

I never thought about not forgiving Sarah Jane. It was more like, "Finally!" Like I'd been waiting and waiting for it to happen.

I finally feel connected again.

**Kim R. (Age 27)**
**Minneapolis, Minnesota**
**kimmy@mnrad.com**

# A Love/Hate Relationship

## "We must create support systems. We must start networking so that we can prevail in this world that we don't fit in."

Being Indigo has been both rough and humbling at the same time. I fit the typical Indigo list: Difficult childhood, feeling left out in social situations, being ultra-sensitive, intuitive/psychic, etc. Lately, however, I am beginning to think that part of the experiences I had while growing up were meant for me to experience in order to be prepared for a life of making the world a better place. Maybe this is true of all Indigos?

I am grateful that I know now that I am an Indigo. ("So, that's what's wrong/right with me!") I finally feel somewhat "normal," or at least I know that I'm not alone. There are numerous Indigos that have/will/are experiencing the same experiences. The more I explore being an Indigo, the more Indigos I find that are similar to me.

I have a love/hate relationship, however, with being Indigo. I am grateful that I am not alone in this world with who and what I am, but I hate that I have been thrown in this role that does not fit in this world.

Being Indigo, I have these thought processes and beliefs that do not fit in this world. For instance, I don't believe in work! I hate that we have to work to live! I believe that it is counterproductive to the human condition. Humans need certain things and they are not being met because we spend too much time at work, or we are unhappy with our jobs. I would love to live in a world where we only lived and worked for what we need. And what we need is food, shelter, laughter, meditation, etc.

Another thing I hate is how people are ranked and categorized throughout almost every group setting. Why can't everyone be equal?! Why does one person have to be better than another person?!

So, obviously, you can see how my beliefs do not fit in this world. And as much as I hate how things are, I do the best I can to live harmoniously. I'm not lazy; I understand that I have to work to live. In fact I actually have a good job that I love. And I rank and categorize just as much as everyone else does, if not more. I do, however, live with the knowledge of how the world should be and try to change what I can to fit my beliefs.

Sometimes being Indigo is difficult and at those rock bottom times I desperately do not want to be anything but an Indigo. I try my hardest, however, to embrace being Indigo and live on. This is important...in other words, I choose to live not die...life not suicide.

My advice to other Indigos is to embrace being Indigo, as amazing and mysterious as it is, and choose life over death...life over death...life after death. You will realize your choice of living will be well worth it over time...

Blessings and live on my sisters and brothers,

**Cricket, (Age 28)**
**Pullman, Washington**
**dreamycricket@hotmail.com**

*1.Love...*
*2.Live....*
*3.Repeat as*
*necessary!*

On Thursday morning, February 14, 1968, I was rushed to the hospital with what my mother said was appendicitis. There was a mini pandemic of Hong Kong or Asian flu that year. My brothers and sisters got it and got to stay home from school. So on the Sunday night before, I decided to feign illness to get out of school. Ha, it worked, yeah. I must have been running a fever on Monday because I got to stay home on Tuesday also, plus, I did get a "stomach ache." By Wednesday night I could not hold down solid food and felt miserable. It hurt to laugh and my oldest brother spent most of his waking hours trying to make me laugh. He enjoyed seeing me miserable I suppose. It was the first week of Lent in the Roman Catholic Church calendar, so it was time to concentrate on the Bible story of the passion of Jesus. I was raised Catholic and Lent lasts forty days and ends on Easter Sunday. Mom let me sleep in her room whilst "sick" because my room was too noisy and boisterous with two other brothers sharing one space, plus I could get my television time in her room. That night I was in too much pain and went to the couch so I would not wake Mom. (Dad worked and rented a room in Cleveland and came home on the weekends.) I sniffled in pain and realized that maybe I was being selfish. Other important things may be being ignored. I missed Ash Wednesday in the church a day and half ago. I felt guilty because I lied to get out of going to school! This wasn't working right, but whenever I tried to do something that's not right I always got caught. I thought about my catechism they taught me and embraced it. I started to think about the passion of Jesus as told in the New Testament. After all, it was the season to meditate on those things. I started to feel guilty for crying about my own pain when it's written in the Bible about the horrible things they did to their Christ. Ouch. I started to weep. Mom heard me and got up to see what was going on. It came down to showing her where it hurt, and it was over to my right side, lower than my stomach. She quickly got dressed and rushed me to hospital telling me that that is where my appendix was, not my stomach! I never heard of an appendix, except the appendix at the end of a book. Grade school didn't teach anatomy by the fourth grade, which is where I was. She said I might need an operation. Ugh. I thought I didn't want one; I wanted to die instead. I prayed to God to take my life. I was offering it to Him just like the Old Testament story of Abraham having to burn his son in an offering to God, only I accepted it as a fact - no miracle showing up in the nick of time for me. Plus it was Valentine's Day, so what a lovely gift of love. I passed out from the pain in the emergency room. A nurse woke me up a bit later. She had to prep me for surgery, which meant more pain for me; She was very kind and gentle, though. What someone ordered probably caused my appendix to burst in a few minutes; I begged her not to give me an enema, and she said it was part of the procedure so I would be clean when they operated on me. I passed out shortly after that. I woke up to count from one hundred backwards for the anesthesiologist and passed out on him, but the pain was finally wilting away. I woke up floating on the ceiling.....they were stitching me up. I got fourteen stitches. They had to clean my insides out because my appendix burst as they were slicing me with the scalpel to open me up. I found out later I was filled with poison and it went all over my body. They were talking about the operation and I didn't understand their words. So I went thru the swinging doors, but I was a ghost and they didn't swing! I went looking for my mother. She sat right outside having a cigarette. I did not try to talk to her. I believed I had died and was pretty happy about it; it felt great and I could fly. I could sense her love for me and I loved her back. The family doctor came thru the doors. He assisted the surgeon and he told my mother that I had a long hard night. He said I was a strong boy and it was up to me if I made it or not. "Cool," I thought. "I give up. Let's go to heaven." They wheeled my body out of the doors a while later. It was a bumpy ride and I kept going back into my body and out into my astral body. Talk about pleasure and pain; pleasure floating and being free, and pain back inside my newly stitched body.  Back and forth between the two as the gurney went over the bumps in the tiles.  They wheeled my body down a hall and let me sit.  They told my mother there was no room left to put me in; the hospital was full of flu patients.  My doctor came by to check on me after he cleaned up and got dressed, and got mad about me being in a cold hallway.  He got ruffled and told a nurse to get me in a room pronto or else.  "The flu patients can wait in the hallway; this boy gets a warm room.  He just had major surgery," the doctor said.  I didn't want a sick person to get kicked out of their room, so I thought if I just floated away that my body would die on its own and then they wouldn't have to disturb anyone at all, so off I went.  It was still dark outside.  I floated outside around the hospital about four times and I was very comfortable: Dressed in a surgery gown, floating above the cold snow of February.  I wondered when something would happen, because I did not know the directions to Heaven, and floating around was getting boring.  I blacked out, then awoke in a very dark, chilly place.  So dark, it was black as black could be.  I thought my eyes were glued shut, so I put my hands to my eyes, and no, they weren't glued shut.  They were open, and yes, I couldn't see a thing, not even myself.  I started to cry, wondering what cruel joke I played on myself.  I chided myself to not be a baby; I got what I wanted, so I sorta calmed down.  Then...I...heard...the Light.....if you can hear Light, that is what I heard.  I looked far off and saw a beam.  I could not see anything between me and the Light.  I went straight for it, thru the darkness.  How wonderful it was: Radiant, warm and inviting.  I approached with hope, not yet knowing what faith really was.  Inside, the shaft of Light flowing upwards from the black base of wherever I was, stood an angel.  The angel beckoned me forward, warning me not yet to touch the Light.  He asked me questions: Who I was, what did I desire, and things like that.  I must have passed the test, because he beckoned me inside.  He put his hands on my shoulders and we floated together.  The angel was made of the same material that the Light was and he told me to look at myself.  I looked, and was amazed to see for the first time that, yes, I was also made of the same stuff.  He told me to follow him.  Off we went up into the shaft of Light.  We went a ways, and he told me that I was to know anything that I desired, and that was a gift of love.  I didn't know what to say, so I said nothing; I just kept looking at what I was inside.....the sparkly ever-changing shaft of Light.  He gave me an example "of knowing" what I did not understand.  So I got it in my head, and thought about things, and decided (to my great disappointment in myself in later years) to say I didn't need to know anything, I already knew all I needed to know.  HAHAHA.  The angel told me that I did not need to ask right then and there, but inside the Light, it would come to me if I did wish to know the Truth about anything at all. That was OK with me at the time. We came to an area of the Light where the angel told me not to touch the outer perimeters or I may become involved with those on the other side of the Light. I then wanted to know about the Truth of that. He told me I did not belong there and to not be enticed by what I may see. I started to see peoples' faces, hands and legs. They saw me in the Light and called to me, wanting to touch me, but I knew the angel was speaking truth, so I avoided their glances and their promises and some of their clutching hands trying to grab me. Whew, the Light had been so nice up until then. We got away from those planes of reality and planes of time. Finally I was allowed to go outside the Light and look from the other side. I could float inside and outside the shaft. What I saw was a giant, flowing, ebbing, live piece of Light sparkling all the way thru space, thru time. Outside the Light, I was still full of Light and sparkled the same as the angel did. What joy could anyone ever want other than this??? Finally the angel called me back in by his side, and asked what my final goal was, and I said, "Heaven." He told me he had to go elsewhere now and I would know the way. Inside the Light, I knew it was the end of the tunnel. I knew God was the source of the Light, so God lives in Heaven, right? Hahahaha. So we parted with love and danced, and off I went to the end of the tunnel, traveling faster than Light, and slowing down, almost stopping time. This was better than a roller coaster ride in summer. I ended up popping out the top and landing in front of a big stone block fortress. I could not see inside. I went to this giant wooden two-door gate that was encrusted with some of the biggest gemstones I have ever seen, probably larger than anything ever found in the Earth. I knocked on the gate with my hands and fists. From the other side, a voice called out, "Who is it?" "AH," I thought, "It's St. Peter! Yeah!" I told him it was me. The voice said again, "Who are you?" SO, besides my name, I told him my story and how I offered myself up to God on St. Valentine's Day. I said, "Open Sesame." I thought the gates would swing wide open, but no...not yet. The voice said again, "Who are you?" So I repeated my story with a lot more detail. Now, for sure, maybe the gates would open. No. The voice then said, "Don't you know who you are?" "Yes," I stammered, looking back at the Light, not wanting to go back there because the only road led back to a hospital bed and pain. As I looked back, I remembered an old Irish blessing, the one that says, "May you be in Heaven a half hour before the devil knows you're dead!" A chill ran up my spine; it must have been more than half an hour, oh no! "Please, let me in; the devil's coming!" The voice was calm and told me not to worry. The Universe heard my offering and it was pleasing and well thought out. A pleasure from one so young. Did I wish to go ahead with my pleasant offering? "Of course," I implored. "So be it," the voice said, "Now watch." Inside my mind my life zipped in front of me, from when I was born to this moment; good and bad, people loved and unloved in my life, my faults and my good points. I regretted nothing. "Here I am now. Let me in." "Not so fast," the voice was saying. I must answer one more question, and it was, "Do you regret your choice?" AH, an easy question. NO I didn't, and also in my heart I did not. The voice showed me my parents at my funeral, and all I could do was see that they loved me and I loved them, but I did not regret my choice. Then I saw all sorts of relatives who would miss me, and no, still I did not regret a thing, yet the door would not open yet. I jumped on the stones of the gate and started to climb. I wanted in, yet the farther up I climbed, the taller the gate got. I kept sliding down anyway, so that was not a way into Heaven. I didn't know why the gates would not open for me. Then I was shown my friends at school who would miss me, and yet no, they can live down there, I belong here. "Please let me in." The voice beckoned me to listen, so I did. I heard the school principal get on the intercom for Morning Prayer and the Pledge of Allegiance. She had a message to convey first though. She told the school a student had a bad night in surgery and asked if they could dedicate morning prayers in his offering to God. Holy smokes, I could hear what was happening on Earth..... cool. We always said four prayers and the Pledge of Allegiance before class started, so I had to listen to all that. I had shouted to them to stop. I was happy in heaven and probably dead. "Dedicate your prayers to the living." I tried to get them to hear me, but it didn't work that way. I could hear them; they couldn't hear me...I told the voice I still did not regret a thing. "OH? Not a thing? Nothing at all?" I thought the voice must not be St. Peter, but someone filling in who had a bad sense of humor and God was off playing golf with Peter. "NO, NO, NO," never once will I say yes to that question. "Listen," I was told, so I listened. By the third prayer, Sue B. from the other grade four class broke off from saying word for word written prayers, and she started to say a prayer from her heart. She was always the emotional girl and she started to shed tears. Her words were pulling at my heart and my emotions. "NO!" I shouted to Sue, though she couldn't hear. "Leave me alone." I wanted her to stop praying and do it the way everyone else was doing it. I had to break down and for the first time since finding the Light, I felt sorrow. The voice again, "Do you still not regret your choice?" But I was embarrassed to admit I lied. I really didn't want to come back, so I tried the scaling the wall trick. The voice said to listen and he was going to give me wisdom. Though I shut my ears and decided God would take care of the St. Peter fill-in when 18 holes were thru. I was coming over! But alas, things get taller when you force them and all I could do was slide back down. The voice was nearly finished; it was saying how pleasing my request was and that I was truly loved, and for sure to love me as such was testament to my final choice. All I heard then was Sue, still praying her own prayer, and zap in a flash back to Earth I came. It took what seemed like four or five hours with the angel getting to the end of the tunnel and a split second to get back. POP went my head and my eyes opened to a black and white canvas with no color, lying in a hospital bed. I looked at my hands and they still glowed sparkly Light, only they started to dim, and then went out and the room was all shades of gray. I saw no color, and I thought the experience blinded me in a way. I wept out loud, louder than I had thought possible. I awoke my mother who was sitting by my bed and she asked what I wanted. I said I wanted to die. I kept crying out, "NO, NO, NO!" She tried to calm me. I told her I just died. She said, "No way," and that she was there the whole time. I told her she was asleep, I died and that I want to go back now. She hugged me and said things would be ok later. I asked her where the color went, though I could not explain my blindness. Later that morning I started to finally see color, but the experience so dazzled my own physical eyes that all I saw was black and white for a while. I confessed to the parish priest that I must have committed a mortal sin because I died and went to heaven, and at a young age I interpreted the whole thing as "getting kicked out of heaven." He asked what I was talking about so I told him, and he laughed at me and explained that surgery had put powerful drugs in me and that I had hallucinated the whole thing. But reading other stories of near death experiences, which were not being talked about in 1968, I didn't trust that the priest was talking the truth. What happened to me was really the truth, no matter what an adult might have to say about it. I finally told Sue in 1979 or 1980 about what she did and how I felt about it. I made her tremble and she told me I was weird. So I tried to explain further. She got tears in her eyes, and she told me to stop it; I was scaring her. I laughed and assured her that scaring her was the last thing on my mind. But sure enough, she adamantly told me not to say anything further about it, because I was totally blowing her away and that was what was scaring her. So I know it happened. So I spent a lot of my life "homesick," home being where a person goes when they die and leave this plane, but I now think things happen because they are supposed to happen. When I was around twenty-four years of age I got so lonely. All of my friends had paired up and either married or had boyfriends or girl-friends and I was the only single guy: No one to love, no one to hold. I gave myself a deadline to find a honey for my own, and one night the deadline was approaching. I lived with my mother still, and she had a really sharp knife. I think it was a Washington Forge knife; the sharpest thing I ever laid my hands on. I took it up to my room for that night, and went out looking for my soul mate. I came home alone and got the knife and went to the bathroom to do the dirty deed. At least on the other side, in the Light, I would be happy. I took off my shirt, angled the knife into my gut and angled the handle of it into the flange of the sink and leaned my belly into it. I closed my eyes and leaned harder and harder. I put all my weight into it; the blade would not penetrate. I looked into the mirror with tears in my eyes. I could not even accomplish this? No love of my life, the knife will not go in? What a failure. I jumped into the knife. No go. Geez. I picked the knife up in my right hand and cut my left forefinger and thumb, and sure enough, it's a sharp piece of steel. I gave up and went to bed. In the morning I looked at my belly and there was a slight red scar of a cut, from where I looked it was a "V." I thought, "V?...V for victory." I wrongly thought at the time that something evil wanted me here to be miserable and the V was a mocking symbol to me, but not really. In my older years I became less dependant on wanting to be wanted, and I finally found a few soul mates (but I realized that for me, soul mates are not a brass ring you grab and win on a merry-go-round or something you show off to your friends). The V was the forces of the Light winning that battle of a dark night of my soul.

"Dance like no one is watching. Sing like no one is listening. Love like you've never been hurt and live like it's heaven on Earth."

**Jace C. (47)**
**Northwestern Ohio**
cool4you_98@yahoo.com

# *Update*

AUTHORS NOTE: This is part of some correspondence I had with Jonathan.

I just wanted to give you an update of what has been happening in my life in the last week. In a time when I have felt lost and not sure of what the next step should be, I have finally come to a clearing in my travels. As of last week I was fearful of my future, not knowing which path was the best for me. However, in the past week I have come to realize that which ever path that "I" choose will be the correct path and therefore have no reason to let fear enter my life.

In the past few years I have had more and more times when things have happened which had a message of more than mere coincidence, whether that be a song on the radio or a random commercial or meeting someone. While some messages were clearer than others, I have had two experiences in the last week that have been crystal clear to me. The first is in regards to a tree outside my bedroom window that is currently halfway between life and death. I wake up every morning and this tree is the first thing that I look at...a tree that should be fully alive and energize me every morning. So last Saturday at sunrise, I am staring at this sad tree when my first task was offered to me. "Save this tree and make it well again." This initial thought was good enough for me as a thought but as I lie awake continuing to stare out my bedroom window, a flood of connective thoughts came to me.

While I was growing up, my Mom made sure that my two brothers and I were always active and involved with nature, trees being a keystone to the entire involvement. At our house my older brother and I each had a tree planted in the front yard representing our presence in the house. My Mom also had two of her favorite books for us as well. The first one being, The Giving Tree, which is classic to all that have read it, and the second was, The Beautiful Christmas Tree by Charlotte Zolotow. This book's main message was that "growing things need love." This book was given to my brothers and I as a final Christmas present for us to read each year and pass on to our future family. My Mom died two months later of leukemia on the 13th of February 1990, holding on just long enough to make it past my 9th birthday and being selfless enough not to darken Valentine's Days for the future. My Mom's ashes were buried under a tree planted in the Portland Arboretum. There was no doubt in my mind that all of these connections had a meaning beyond face value. The presence of my

Mom has always been closely tied to trees and nature and I have, after all of these years, finally realized my continuing connection with her.

The tree outside my window is one of my projects now, as I focus my love onto it everyday. It is also the only place at my house that has birdhouses hanging from it. For me the connections were clear between what I have always felt inside and what spiritual contracts were revealed during my Indigo Reading, I feel that I am finally on the right track. Since I agreed to the spiritual contract of being an Animal Kingdom Steward and Animal Communicator, I knew that those old birdhouses were hanging on that tree for a reason. I can't wait until the birds finally come back to feed in my backyard. I am sure they have much to tell me. As for the tree and the connection to my Mom, I am more sure than ever that my contract as an Earth Tone Healer and Goddess Guardian are meant to be and this is my time to refine my skills. Thanks to the contract reading that I have been given, I feel that I finally have some direction in my life and I can't wait for the adventures that the future will bring.

My second flood of consciousness came last night. I have currently been using the 13-moon, Day out of Time calendar. Each day is set to different tones and tribes combining to form a daily affirmation. I have been meditating daily on these trying to live by the energies that are most active on each given day. Yesterday the daily affirmation was, "I organize in order to equalize balancing opportunity. I seal the store of death with the rhythmic tone of equality. I am guided by the power of death." When I read this in the morning I had no idea of what this really meant to me until later yesterday night. I was in my garage looking at all of the junk and stuff that I had brought back from college. Just as I started looking through my boxes to see what I could bring into my room and what could be left outside in the garage, I noticed that there was a gust of wind that made a plastic bag move. I continued looking through my boxes when the wind blew the bag once again. This time however, I realized that the bag that was rustling in the wind was hanging on the arm of a skeleton from Halloween decorations, only to look down and realize that I was holding a box that had "EUREKA" spelled across the top. I just started to laugh to myself and continued my new project of organizing the garage and making some space for myself so I could start working on my sculptures again. This was important to me because I am currently living with my dad and his girlfriend and have no space that I can call my own, but with the space cleared in the garage I have a little equality in the house. It's funny how things work out once you start doing what you are actually supposed to be doing in life.  I also found some extra camping equipment, as well as some mirrors with paintings of women on them representing each of the seasons in the bottom of a box with other random junk in it.  Needless to say I was very happy with the results of my evening and feel much more attuned with the Earth and Her energies.

Jonathan B. (Age 24)
Portland, Oregon
jbatley28@hotmail.com

# Our Connection To Each Other

I've been where you are now.....homicidal thoughts, suicidal thoughts.....so sensitive we are...yet we need to see it as the gift it is in helping not only ourselves but others as well.  That's what we're here for and I can see that now.  So many things in such a short period of time have been revealed to me.  And even though I don't ask for validation – nor am I concerned about receiving it from others – I've come across those things that have validated so much of what I just *know.*  I don't tell others, I don't want to be scolded and ridiculed.  I pick my battles and the way that I address them... and I have that right.

Yet in order for me to get to this point in my life, I had no choice but to transcend above all that I've experienced in my life...all the horrors and abuses as a young girl growing up in a very volatile home.  The kind of home where if you breathed wrong, you were in jeopardy of receiving a beating.  And I lost count after so many years of how often my brothers and I were awakened in the middle of the night to clean the house, all because our Dad was on one of his kicks.  And we knew that no matter what, we would always receive a beating afterwards.....for a reason of his own making.  What a horrible way to grow up as a child.  Yet now I can see that I needed to experience these things in order to help change the thinking of those who live this way and also of society as a whole.  And also to help those who are in the middle of this right now.....and I know there many who are.  I see them every day on the street.  I know the look - I've been there.  I know the pain - I've felt it...and it still has lingering effects in my life, always will to some degree.  I weep now for that little girl I can see in me who endured it all.

I can also see the woman I am today and the accomplishments that I've made in my life.  The talents I was blessed with while growing up in such a home were difficult to sort through and know why I had them.  Imagine, if you will, me as a child being able to sense immediately while around many people if they liked me or not.....even if they had a smile on their face.  Being able to know their thoughts and intentions directed at me and also towards others they were talking to.  I didn't understand why they could be that way when I had just met them.  Imagine hearing the words on a daily basis of how worthless you are.....you know what I'm talking about.  You.....the one that's reading this now with tears streaming down your face or swelling up in your eyes...that is what's happening to me as I am sharing this with you now.

I believe it's important that I do share this with you, so you won't consider taking your life or even the life of the one who's abused you or is abusing you now.  I want you to know that someone does care and knows what you're going through or what you've been through.  The details of anyone's story are always different from the other, yet the similarities can't be denied.  If you won't listen to anyone else, then listen to a stranger who's been there.....listen to me.

You're meant to rise above all you've experienced in this life.  If you have to go inside yourself...and keep to yourself in order to heal, then please do.  Do whatever it takes to begin to heal.....if screaming in a pillow or somewhere in the woods in the middle of nowhere helps, then do it!  Do what you have to...to get that first release you need in order to begin a new life that awaits you.

Ten years ago I was the same as you are now...you couldn't have convinced me of this...and even in my miserable state, if I had read something like this I know it would have spoken directly to my heart and my soul.....and that's what I'm doing now. If you don't want to accept these words in your mind.....then let your heart open just enough to let these words touch you in this way...and know that someone truly cares for you.  I don't have to know you personally, I just know you're out there...like me.....and in doing this I'm also continuing my healing.  This didn't take overnight in happening to me...so it won't take overnight in helping you to heal. Yet I have taken it one step at a time...and sometimes major leaps have been made, especially most recently in the last few months. This healing can begin for you too.....it's beginning now with you reading this book.....believe in that.

It doesn't matter to me how many times I have to share my story with others, if this just helped one person not to throw in the towel so to speak...then this is worth it. And I don't mind receiving email either. If you need encouragement, want to share, want to connect and have support.....a group.....a person.....whatever it takes.....someone, anyone to lean on.....please email me anytime. I always respond as soon as I possibly can in my emails.

When you read the list concerning First Wave Indigos that slipped through the cracks...don't worry if you don't believe what you read.....your soul and your heart knows and that's all that matters. And that's all it takes to trigger what's needed in your life at this time...no matter how stone cold you think your heart may be. If that's the case, then all the light needs is just that little crack and your healing will begin. May Love light your path as you begin a new walk on a new path in a new direction for your life...and know you have a support group larger than you could possibly imagine.....physical form and otherwise...no matter what your beliefs are.

We Love You! Very Much! Please Don't Ever Forget This – EVER!


Savannah J. (38)
**Shreveport Louisiana**
lovelightstheway@hotmail.com

207

# We Are Our Own Creators... We Are Gods!

**M**y experiences, to say the least have been like walking through life's path blindfolded, totally relying on trusting the senses beyond the physical. I have had some amazing guidance by some on this Earth. I found out also that there were others who I depended on to guide me that were up to no good.

As an Indigo, I have found that you can quickly show the true intent of your work without even realising it until reflection later. As someone who has lived their life learning and soaking up all the trials and tribulations, I have sensed that there is more to the normal pump and grind of this rigid plane of physical density than we have been conditioned to believe. I realized that the space and time vortex that we are in is rapidly shifting into a new gear. It is so exciting, but the path of self-unity and re-awakening is also a challenge, to say the very least.

For me, the journey has been a roller coaster ride for many of my elemental systems. Physical, emotional, mental and spiritual aspects are being so heavily tested at many a turn. Boy, this can be tiring no matter the age. Sometimes it literally has felt like a battle with a hidden contender and, often, that has been the case. As an Indigo I have been faced with so many sneaky, hidden elements to contend with it is not funny. You stand up, you get knocked down, you turn, they turn and you literally think at times, "Am I going crazy?"

I have learned that it is not real and merely another attempt to head us away from our true essential Self.

Only when I don't trust my gut feeling, my "intuition," do I get shucked back into the illusion and boy does it give me the super-sized meal-deal treatment! I cop it fair and square! But if I stand quietly to the side, I have found that I don't need to get on the freeway of the illusion and go through the morning rush hour. Instead, for me, it is about feeling the inner whisper, trust and then I can travel the freeway at my pace and reach my destination. If I stand quietly to the side, I have found that I don't need to get on the freeway of the illusion and go through the morning rush hour with Mr or Mrs Road Rage in my face. We all have different vehicles that we have chosen to travel in and they all go at different speeds, but ultimately we are all heading to the same place.

Like most of us on this journey of life, I must have been on that freeway in the fast lane a million times before I realized what was going on. The signposts were heading me away from my true destination. So many times, when I was on my travels, I kept coming to signs saying "STOP...Go back, wrong way" or "You must turn NOW or else!!" when that is not what I wanted to do. And by doing this, as Indigos, we tend to draw extra attention to us. My vehicle (body/mind/spirit) was getting so tired from all of the extra miles and jump-starting that it was in need of some attention.

For me the biggest stop sign in my life has been the last year (2004). At a fairly young age, I have achieved many things in business and in my life. I have gained a great deal of knowledge from all of these experiences. It truly fascinates me how, within every moment and every breath, we absorb so much learning. I thank God and my soul for being able to appreciate all that is. I have always believed and trusted my spiritual Self for as long as I can remember. This was all about to be tested to the limit.

From what seemed like out of nowhere, I become very ill with symptoms reflecting a viral/bacterial infection. I was away from my native Australian soil, in the middle-east (Dubai UAE), working on an amazing business opportunity. My day started like any other day. I woke up to the sounds of prayer being broadcast over the city; for me this is such a beautiful way to awaken from slumber. As usual, I meditated and then headed into the hotel gym for a light stretch and also a session on some cardio equipment to get me going for the day. I had breakfast and then headed off to morning business meetings and events. I left the hotel room with a spring in my step and felt particularly great that morning, as I was embarking on an extremely positive and exciting business venture. All was progressing wonderfully through the morning events and then we headed off for a lunch.

Then something started to happen over lunch.

I remember something jolted my system, like a voice that I could not understand or a sound that went into my right ear. At the time I thought it was something that had been said by the people at lunch with me, but when I looked up they weren't talking. What happened next is something that was very strange. As we left the restaurant to head back to the office, I could feel the right side of my body pulling downwards and sideways, like a weight was placed on my right shoulder. Also, at the same time, it felt like my etheric fields were being stretched. Then I started to feel what I can only describe as feeling like a current going through my shoulder and then down to the toe next to my big toe. The best way I can explain the feeling in my toe is that it felt like a cramp. No one else noticed anything different with me, so I just continued on my way. I thought that I was just having one of those energetic moments and that it would pass (I was so wrong!)

As we entered the office area, it felt like I was literally phasing in and out of my physical body. I also remember that it felt like my body was pulsing or vibrating. This was not however, apparent in a physical context. I then continued up to the office, located on another floor, via a lift (elevator). When I departed the lift, I was still feeling the pulsing and vibration, but then something very weird happened. I remember, as we came out of the lift and started walking out of the foyer towards the office, it felt like something had run through my body and grabbed my energy source or conscious reality. It is such a difficult experience for me to explain. In my past years I have experienced many energetic occurrences, such as medium clairvoyance and other energetic and healing modalities, but I had no point of reference for this sensation.

Normally I love the feeling of being in a physical vessel and feeling the energy flow through my being, but this just did not seem right. To the other people around me I looked like my normal physical self, but I was feeling awfully strange by this stage. As we returned to the office, I remember I had to sit down because I felt exhausted. Normally I am so charged with energy physically and vibrationally that these strange feelings were starting to scare me a little. While sitting down at a meeting table with several others standing up around me, I remember I had to pull all of what remained of my energy to concentrate and focus. By this stage, whatever was going on was playing havoc with my hearing as well. It was a feeling of vocal sounds ushering in and out. My hearing echoed in one ear, but not continuously. It felt like I was outside of the present moment with others in the room with me. My vision would become foggy and all of the objects around me would warp in character and shape. Strangely though, when I spoke it came back.

I thought to myself, if this is my spiritual awakening, right here, right now, they could have chosen a better moment! If I let myself absorb into the sensations, which I did try, I felt that I would fall on the floor and pass out, so I didn't go there again. I liken it to someone or something playing with my sensors to let me know I was not in control. This is all exciting in its own way, but not when you are in a boardroom with business executives. I had to focus and draw on all of my energy just to be in that room and seem present to the others. Believe me, while I sat there, I was calling in every guide, teacher, master and vibration I could think of to move this on.

I finally got through the meeting, but had some new challenges in the days, weeks and months that followed, as the fear of what was happening to me started to manifest, more physical symptoms really started to kick in. The clinical diagnoses being described as an unknown viral/bacterial infection. How many times have we heard this one???

Having a fear that I had never felt before in my entire life, I did what I would normally never do and went on "the medical merry-go-round"... I was scared and wanted to do what ever it took to be well again.

Normally, I am one to stay away from western medicine because my sensitivity in body just can't cope with the intrusive onslaught they impose. And guess what? You guessed it - no medical test could verify what was happening to me. I was given the gamut of tests that prodded, poked and x-rayed every inch and element of my system. Months and months of testing resulted in inconclusive findings. It left the doctors scratching their heads and sticking me on the "anti this" and "anti that" medication merry-go-round (anti-biotic, anti-inflammatory and even anti-depressants which I just could not take). It seems theses are the drug lines that they prescribe when they don't know what is going on. I was not getting any better and the fear was mounting in response to what was happening to me...the illusion had me good this time.

I later learned from Laura Lee that western prescription medicine can contain many types of organic and metallic implants. This explained a lot to me about why I was feeling so sick and had a sense of wasting away. From the outside I looked fine, but inside I was fighting a war. I guess if I was feeling this distressed, I was no longer perceived as threat to anyone or anything on "the other team."

I did however have a L.B.A. (Live Blood Analysis test) by an alternative practitioner. I found this form of testing fascinating to view. We are amazing beings and if you ever have the opportunity, it is well worth having it done just for your own interests.

I had exhausted many modalities of traditional and alternative therapies. My wallet and my hope was quickly depleted. I went from a healthy, energetic, independent businessman, to being nearly bedridden with barely any energy to move around without getting puffed and had to move back home. This was an additional psychological hardship.

### My Path to Recovery With Some Great Friends, and a Few Rocks...

Working with the Aurauralite rocks and Laura Lee has definitely helped me to clear my challenges and open elements of my inner-self that have been shut down recently due to these psychic attacks designed to slow me down or, worse still, to stop me from my true life's work.

Within hours of my first session with Laura Lee, I started to see and sense my damaged auric energies again. When we delved into the sacred contracts that I have, they rang so true. Laura Lee helped me identify and work with these amazing powers that we all have in some shape or form. I am sure this is part of the guidance system that gravitates us into tapping into the divinity of our true selves. I have always felt there is more and now it all makes sense. I am sure that this rings true with you too.

I found it amazing and often confronting to become aware of the "hooks," both hidden and visible, inserted in the past and present, that can be attached to keep me off of the path of my own evolution. This knowledge answers a lot of questions and confirms my gut instinct and had made me aware of my capabilities as an Indigo to remove these.

In my case, it was within hours that I was overcome with such remarkable feelings of exhilarating energy and inspiration. I just needed to be in my space and reconnect with myself once more.

My advice: If you have the opportunity to experience a healing with Laura Lee and the Aurauralite rocks, watch with amazement how interesting the domino effect can be when you remove a hook and shut out undesirables that have been latching on to you for a free ride. After the hook removal, inspiration was literally coming into me every time I was speaking to someone. I was so excited to feel it again I nearly burst! This was not a new experience to me as I had channelled when I was younger but this had stopped when I was under physic attack.

Since then, I had people I'd met only once come across my path again out of the blue. They were again feeling lost and sharing their heavy hearts and dismay over their life direction with me. Sometimes within a few humbling intuitive words they awaken and find their way. I feel truly blessed and very humbled by this. For me, it is the most precious thing and warms my soul every time it happens.

So today, 18 months later, although not completely back online, I am charged with a different knowledge and awareness that gives me the source to deal with the ebbs and flows of life. It is difficult being wired with more sensitivity than most people in these times of turbulence and change. Within each moment of feeling the weight of it all, lessons are learned and they enlighten my path with a little more peace and joy. Hopefully, I am also helping to enlighten those that are in my life.

We are all here to "feel" this plane. In feeling lies the wisdom of each one of us.

Remember.....We are our own creators. We are Gods!

Andrew R. (Age 30)
Melbourne, Australia
ozstar_7@yahoo.com

# Indigo Surprise

I recently discovered that I am an Indigo child. I read about it on Laura Lee's web site and we came to talking about it during a session. All these years, I never understood why life was so much harder for me than others. I always felt different than my siblings. My parents didn't know what to make of me. My friends would lovingly describe me as "a little nuts", but accepted my unique way of viewing the world. I read Tarot Cards, "knew things," and believed in many of the less than conventional beliefs that society tries to instill upon us. I was one of the most "spiritual" people out of everyone I knew most of my young life. I had encountered others like me along the way, but they were all adults. As a child, I heard them and their wisdom and took it in to some degree, but I still didn't fully get it. I knew I had spiritual journeys to take but I had no sense of how or why.

After learning more about the Indigo child phenomena, I found some peace and understanding of such things that had plagued me all my life. I am still learning more about this profound life awakening. I now know that I do have a higher purpose and people like Laura Lee to help guide me towards it, in fact, we did a Ghost Busting together during a session! I was concerned because I was going to be staying overnight in a family home upstate that had, what we believe to be, 2 lost souls. I had always been afraid to sleep there and felt it had a presence in it without any "tangible proof". I just got feelings of energies that made me uncomfortable and actually scared. I was absolutely terrified to do the busting, even though it was over the phone. I did it any way with Laura Lee, and as the events unfolded, I found myself tuning into the spirits, surprisingly. I could envision where they were, the names and even a significant issue they were having. I had no idea I was capable of such work!

After the busting I went to the house physically and as instructed by Laura Lee, cleared it out and filled it with positive energy. I felt more comfortable sleeping there than I had since 1979. As a result of this experience and opening my heart and mind to my true Indigo self, I have found my fears about spirits had lessened tremendously.

Authors Note: Susanne was terrified of what she might find when she went to stay on the house alone and I was concerned because she has had challenges with panic attacks. I knew we had to clear it before she slept there, because this place was out in the middle of nowhere. After clearing ghosts, and understanding the challenges of the ghosts, she realized her part in freeing them from their earth bound bondage. It was a grand metamorphosis, and I knew she would be ok to sleep there. Now, here is the rest of her story!

I was recently at a B&B in New England and had learned about a ghost that resided there. I took it upon myself to introduce myself to the spirit and find out as much as I could about him. His energy was pleasant and he gave me a few details of who he was, and I was not at all fearful.

As an Indigo I now recognize this has become part of my life's work, to help ghosts or lost souls on the earth find their way home. I had fought with all these fears for so long. Who would have thought I'd be a Ghost Buster in my lifetime and no longer fearful of it?

The bottom line for me is that in addition to my amazing spiritual awakenings, I have found that it's easier to get out of bed in the morning knowing I have an important role in the Universe, and it's great to know I am not alone in this undertaking.

Susanne B. (Age 35)
White Plains, New York
themporess@optonline.net

# Mechanics of the Mind

Laura Lee was kind enough to ask me to write a few pages for her newest book. However, those few pages turned into dozens and then hundreds. Instead of relaying to you all of the specifics of the many experiences which led me to where I am today, I am going to focus on sharing with you what I believe to be a grounding rod for like-minded Indigos out there that may or may not have shared some of the same experiences as I have. By grounding rod, I mean something that you can relate to and hopefully use to help bring your feet to the ground with a sureness that what has been happening is not only very real but is very controllable and powerful.

I'm 31 years old and grew up as an Air Force brat and have been blessed with many cultural experiences from around the world as well as having been blessed with many "paranormal" experiences, to state it simply. I've had everything happen to me from automatic turning dials on cable boxes, to dreams of the future, to moving objects and strange bodily experiences like kundalini risings, which happened spontaneously. I won't go into detail of the many experiences.  At this time the important thing is that something is calling you and that is why you are reading this book now.

Something has drawn you here and that is no coincidence.  Actually, my favorite word in the whole world is SYNCHRONICTY.  Maybe you feel as if the whole Universe is bending and flexing to suit your needs at any given moment.  It may be as if the entire Universe were at your mercy.  Maybe you realize that you are brought from point A to point B in the shortest period of time possible without having to go through the middle steps.

Whatever the case may be, let me just say that it is very real and you are not crazy in the slightest bit.  Have you thought you might be losing your mind because some of your experiences are so intensely wild that the best screenwriter could not have thought it up?  Truth is stranger than fiction.  Do you feel you know that experientially and not just as some worn-out old adage?  Listen brother and sister Indigos, let me share with you some secrets that I have been fortunate enough to have come in contact with.  These secrets will unfold the immense power within you and you will have fantastic control over THAT which you really are.

To start with, let's just say that you are in the process of waking up from a deep sleep that has overcome nearly the entire human race for eons.  Most people around you are sleepwalking in a trance and they are spiritually dead.  There will be a time that they will rise from their graves or bodies to be resurrected and you just happen to be ahead of schedule.  Life is being full of Spirit and our spirit is our WILL.  If we are awake enough, we will be able to will things into being very deliberately.  Then, we will know what life in these bodies truly is.

Ask yourself what you want.  Do you want to know what in the world is happening to you?  Do you want to cry and shed many tears over the fact that nobody understands you?  Get over it!  That might sound harsh and cruel, but the fact is we don't have time to mess around.  We have a lot to work to do, so wipe the tears from your eyes and realize with your REAL EYES that we have much to accomplish in a short period of time.

As my friend, Chris Bush, long ago asked me, "What is the difference between a MAN THINKING and THINKING MAN?"  When you solve that riddle, the key to the Universe will be yours and anything is possible.  You may believe you built a Time Machine.  Please don't think I'm kidding you, because I'm not.  In this young, hip world, you have probably

216

seen "The Matrix." What is written on the sign in the kitchen of the Oracle that she reads to Neo? "Know Thyself!"

Who in the world do you think you are? John Doe or Jane Doe? Whatever your name may be, you really think THAT is who you are don't you? Are you that voice talking in your head? Let me propose to you that you probably have no idea who you are.

We are born into this world innocent, but there is a moment when that all changes in an instant. Because we are occupying these bodies in this 3D world, we visually see things as being separated from us. This 3D world is allegorical of a world of duality: Here and there. When we are born, we are given a name and are called that name because we are taught that we need to identify with our SELF. A SELF is separate from everything else. We visually see that everything is away from us and there is distance. There are other SELFs that have their own names to identify with, like "Momma" and "Papa." We instantly believe that who we are is that SELF. We are led to believe that is really who we are.

We believe that because the voice in our head, which makes reason and meaning out of everything, tells us that. To make it worse, we think the voice even sounds like us too! Before we had language to describe things in our own minds, there was not one single thing that had meaning. Whatever our perception of the world is, it was created with the language that we use; it is the WORDS that we speak. "In the beginning was the WORD." This is how creation began. We created our own illusionary worlds with the WORDS that we speak in our minds and to others. We have been making up everything the entire time and we sometimes believe that we are not creative! Since our whole world as we know it is all made up anyway, we might as well make it into something that empowers us.

Here is a little insight into the mystery of the Garden of Eden. Almost everyone knows the story of Adam and Eve. To get straight to the point, in Genesis, the story tells us Adam is the first MAN; it does not tell us Adam is the first Homo Sapiens. Literally, Adam means MAN, which means THINKER. Therefore, Adam is the first THINKING Homo Sapien.

Before Adam had eaten from the Tree of Knowledge, he simply existed and was in a state of nothing but BEING. No different from an animal or a baby. Eve was tempted by the Serpent to eat the Apple. Eve IS the SOUL of man, which was tempted by the carnal mind of man or the reasoning mind of man to know things; especially to know the difference between good and bad. Basically, it is to know the difference between things. This is when the world of duality was created in our own minds. Before that, everything was ONE.

The Serpent or Satan/Ego IS the reasoning mind of man, which gives meaning to everything. As a result of that, we are deceived from what is. Nothing has an innate meaning. The only meaning in anything is the meaning that our own reasoning mind creates out of nothing. All meaning is totally imagined and is therefore illusionary. That is the great deceiver! This is the underlying concept of the story of Adam and Eve.

The EGO is very related to what Satan really means. The EGO, among other things, encompasses the following: MEMORY, REASON and the TEMPTATION TO REASON. The temptation is more specifically Satan, since that temptation causes us to give in to actually reason and to draw upon our memory. All that together collectively is the Ego. One could say it is the end result of what is produced from the blending of the temptation to reason, reasoning itself and memory.

This is a very incredible power that we Human Beings have. We can have our worlds created on autopilot by Satan/Ego yapping away in our minds, while we think that it is us doing the thinking (when we are really being thought for) OR we can create with deliberate intent and choice, actively by thinking and making choices. Which do you prefer?

Now, allow me to share with you something that will empower you beyond belief. Please drop your defenses and take into your hearts what our birthright is. For the sake of example, you may think you are John Doe for example. Replace John Doe with the name that you identify yourself with. Where is your center of awareness? It is inside your head. Your vision is what you see out of your two eyeballs, isn't it? You may be accustomed to having your center of awareness stuck inside your physical body's head.

Practice this: Visualize your awareness floating around your body and throughout your body into every small, little space. Can you feel your awareness inside of your big toe as easily as you can feel your awareness inside of your right elbow, etc...? You can close your eyes and basically picture your awareness inside any part of your body. Therefore, your awareness is not tied down to the space between your physical ears, right? You have just proven that to yourself.

Now practice this: Close your eyes and place your awareness outside of your body about 10 feet, and look back at your body. Walk circles around your physical body with your awareness. You find it is quite easy to do. Now, you have just proven that your awareness is not tied down to your physical body, right? Of course, you may think that it is only your imagination, but bear with me and let's continue.

No matter what spiritual outlook on life we have, we may have to admit that various ancient scriptures do have many truths in them no matter how much they have been distorted by those with less than honorable goals. What I am about to tell you is the same as what has been taught by Krishna and Buddha and other Masters throughout time. God came to Moses and told him that His name is I AM THAT I AM. That burning bush is the divine spark within every human being. God said He IS THAT I AM. Now, imagine that awareness of yours that has no physical boundaries. You could even imagine your awareness on the surface of the moon and you didn't even have to wait for any time to pass to visualize that, right? It was instantaneously there without having to go any distance, right?

Try this: You can obviously sit there and say, "I AM." You can say, "I exist." Why? Because you are thinking that, aren't you? You are thinking that you exist, therefore you think, "I exist." You can definitely state, "I AM." If you think about it, there is no way that you cannot say that and be honest. That "I AM", is the most fundamental existence that you have before you tack on any descriptions such as calling that "I AM" John Doe or whoever you think you are. The "I AM" was there before your SELF was, wasn't it? Think about it for a while.

The moment you identified your true SELF with a name or something separate from that Infinite "I AM," you have "sinned." You have, just at that moment, separated your SELF from that Infinite Presence, God. Your true nature IS God. As soon as you believe the illusion that you are something different and separate from that, you have sinned. It has nothing to do with sex or anything of that nature. Believing that we are individuals and separate from God is the Original Sin. That is the first judgment.

Now, let us get into something that many Christians love to talk about and proclaim to be knowledgeable about. (I don't call myself a Christian; I am just using it as an example.) What is being born again all about? Going to a building where some other SELF dunks your head or body under water while mumbling some words. You then come up and are "born again?"

According to the Christian's book, we must be born again to get into heaven. We must be born again if we are to be saved. What are they talking about? Or at least, what do they think they are talking about? I understand the lip-service but appreciate it very little.

We are innocent and then are immediately "born into sin." We believe we are that flesh-body and we believe that we are separate from everything else. We are, literally, born of flesh because of that. We know from the "Good Book" that being born of flesh is sinful. I use these examples because a different understanding is being applied (apple lied) than what is taught to the masses. So, we are born into flesh. We must be born into Spirit if we are to be saved and considered "born again."

The moment that we cast aside the illusion that we are that SELF we have identified with, our SELF dies. Then, we have the awareness without that illusionary self and we see our true essence as being that "I AM" presence. Then we are naked as a newborn babe and are innocent as well. We have just been born into Spirit at that moment. Now, we are truly born again. We of course will still have the SELF at our disposal, which is necessary for survival in this illusionary world.

After that, we can take back different pieces of our personality and use them as we see fit. However, we are now a master instead of a slave. Before, we were a slave to our illusionary SELF, which arose from the voice of reason that talks in our mind. Now, we know who we really are and become masters of that illusionary SELF. That, my Indigo friends, is what being born again is about. Compare that to the dogma being spread like hot melted butter all over the place and ask yourself, "What makes sense?"

*We are born as naked as a babe can be.
*We immediately realize from our center of awareness, there is an outer world.
*Our communication with the outside world teaches us the concept that we are separate from it.
*Any communication from another body to our SELF, shows us a separation no matter how faint it is, since we are using 5 senses of the flesh.
* We begin to believe that we are separate from everything else.
* We begin to believe that our birth in flesh is all that we are.
* We are given an Earthly name to identify our SELF with.
* We believe we are that SELF.

* Fleshly life gives us apparent evidence that we are that SELF.
* We have just separated our SELF from HIM.

THAT is the Original Sin and we are born into it.  We have just eaten the apple.

**How are we SAVED? The Bible tells us how.**
 * We ARE created LIKE GOD: Genesis 1:26-27
 * GOD tells us how we are created LIKE HIM by telling us that HE is the "I AM THAT I AM": Exodus 3:14
 * GOD tells us that our SELFS do NOT exist, because besides HIM, there is NONE else: Deuteronomy 4:39
 * To return to HIS KINGDOM, we MUST be born again: John 3:3, 3:5, 3:7
 * The WAY to be born again is through I AM: John 10:7, 10:9
 * I AM leads the WAY: John 10:11, 10:14
 * The MASTER TEACHER YASHUA did works from I AM's perspective and NOT YASHUA's: John 10:25
 * The FATHER IS I AM and I is identical to I AM: John 10:30
 * YASHUA said that GOD said that we ARE gods: John 10:34
 * I AM IS the WAY, so therefore YASHUA is NOT: John 14:6
 * YASHUA said, when saying "me" he is speaking from GOD or I AM's point of view and NOT Yashua's: John 14:10
 * YASHUA said if we believed what he said about I AM, we would also do these works and more: John 14:12
 * YASHUA said to those who hear that asking in "MY NAME" is the name of GOD speaking through YAHSUA saying, "MY NAME," which IS I AM and NOT the "my name" of YASHUA: John 14:13-14
 * YASHUA is a CHRIST since he IS a SON of GOD; since he was led by the SPIRIT OF I AM and anyone else will be a SON of GOD, which is a CHRIST, if they are led by the SPIRIT of I AM: Romans 8:14
 * There WILL be many CHRISTS manifesting in this world: Romans 8:19
 * We ALL have access to the SPIRIT of I AM: Ephesians 4:6
 * Those of us who ARE led by the SPIRIT of I AM will be CHRISTS: 1John 3:1

\* If we lose our SELF, only the I AM remains because that is all there really is and therefore, the I AM appears and we are just like HIM. What WILL we be? We will see: 1John 3:2

Remember, I am NOT a Christian, I only use the Christian Bible for convenience and because of its popularity.

We are gods and we are currently in GODSCHOOL. Indigos are just ahead of schedule from the masses and we have to get a grip quite quickly. To keep to the point, let me refer you to some books that will accelerate your consciousness beyond belief. The books I am going to refer to are not the run-of-the-mill books that you will find in a bookstore.

1. The Arcane Formulas or Mental Alchemy - MUST READ! Read this first and practice it with all your heart until mastered.
2. Vril - Vital Magnetism - MUST READ! Read this second and apply it as if your life depended on it.

These are advanced when you feel you are ready:

1. Secrets of Power, Volume 1 by Ingo Swann
2. Secrets of Power, Volume 2 by Ingo Swann
3. Reality Boxes by Ingo Swann
4. Wisdom Category by Ingo Swann

I hope that you will read at least the first two books recommended and apply what you read whole-heartedly. They will give you keys to unlocking the magnificent potential lying within you. As an Indigo, I not only believe that you will benefit greatly from them, I believe that you have an obligation to the whole human race to understand them thoroughly and apply them with earnest intent. Then, read the last 4 books and apply what you learn and you will be light years beyond even your teachers who think they can teach you something.

As an extra note, you might want to study one of the greatest Masters ever: Apollonius of Tyana. The two best books are called The Life of Apollonius of Tyana books 1 and 2. They were originally written by Philostatus. You can find the dual translation versions with Greek and English by F.C. Conybeare. These are available from Harvard University Press.

There are many pearls in these volumes:
Volume 1 <http://www.hup.harvard.edu/catalog/L016.html>
Volume 2 <http://www.hup.harvard.edu/catalog/L017.html>

I would also highly recommend studying the Technical Remote Viewing courses from Psi Tech. They have the original protocols as well as having proprietary rights to them. All other remote viewing courses are adulterated and bastardized versions, which branched out from this original system. I would study the Gen II kit or take the online course. Then, take the advanced course.

Take care and don't wait around for a better world. Just WILL it into existence. Focus in your mind what you want and experience it as if you are there and know you are. Just BE it and it will BE. We need to stick together and we need to find the Light without all the hype. Keep the faith and keep striving for Truth. You will know the answers. Just remember that the perimeter to the cosmos is nowhere and the center of the Universe is everywhere. No matter where you are, you ARE the LIGHT and you ARE the center of the Universe!

To contact me directly for questions or correspondence visit www.aaronmurakami.com


**Aaron M. (Age 31)**
**Spokane, Washington**

## The Portal

There have been many times (too many to count) where I can see myself (chuckling) as an "X-MAN" in my reality and in my non-reality life. It is hard for me to single out one particular moment, but one that stands out over the rest happened a couple years ago while visiting a supposed haunted mansion. A dear friend of mine, Ronnie Foster (Laura Lee's Ghostbusting partner), who has strong intuitive and empathic abilities took me to the basement. It was as if a switch had been turned on. A switch that seems to have a mind of its own when needed.   I felt as if I was not in charge of the situation at hand, and I had a sense that I was taking a step aside while the ancient practices that I once performed like a theatrical stage play, took hold.   I began seeing an apparition of a young, terrified woman crouched behind a broken down stone wall to my right.   She was hiding as if she could see me, and she knew I was able to see her.   Just ahead of me in the darkness of the basement, amongst some rubble, I could see a man around the age of 30, wearing a green coat with  many buttons down the front.   I asked Ronnie, (AngelGirl), to go right while I went left to corner him.   After I said that out loud, I thought, "How do you corner a spirit who knows what your doing?"   After chuckling to  ourselves, I went left anyway and he countered my action by recessing further into the darkness.   I returned to my friend and began to do something that I would never have thought of doing myself under any circumstances.   I began to open a portal to the other side.   How did I know what to do or even how to do it?   Well it was one of those things where you just do it and stand aside.   Something within me very ancient took over and I began to pump up energy and raise my hands upward to the sky.   My eyes closed with my head slightly bent.   I called forth a whirling cloud of Light with the most beautiful shades of orange and yellow permeating out of the center in the form of rays of piercing Light. Ronnie came up to my side and said, "Perhaps we need to open a portal...wow one seems to be already open."   I heard her say, but was too busy completing my task, so I just acknowledged her presence but not her comment.   About that time two angels came through and held the portal open on both sides with their hands.   While a third came through with his arms held open wide in a gesture of love and welcome.   All three looked directly at me, and the smile they gave me was unlike any smile I have ever seen.   I thought, "Oh my God...they love, acknowledge and know me!   How is this possible?"   But I did not skip a beat.   Ronnie said, "They're holding the portal open, why didn't I think of that?   Laura Lee and I have always held the portal open ourselves!"   I thought to myself chuckling, "Work smarter not harder."

Now if that is not interesting enough for you, what happened next is truly amazing.   The female spirit looked at the portal and then looked at the male spirit.   The feeling of being terrified ran through my being, as I picked up on her thought process like a receiver antenna, when she looked at him while still hiding behind the  dilapidated  wall.   I could hear her planning her escape with such passion.   This is her chance to escape him and the terror he has bestowed upon her for so may unknown years.   I could see her looking at him with a welling up of courage. He looked at her with a stare of, "don't even think about it," as he came out of the shadows and was highlighted by the back light of the portal. I could see him more clearly now. His garments that I saw earlier became more in focus. He was wearing a long green coat draping down past his hips. There must have been 20 or so metal buttons tightly spaced apart down the front of the coat. The coat collar was wide and the base of the opening of the coat was unbuttoned and displayed the front of his brown wool pants. His shoes were brown, and slightly coming apart at the toes. He had a slight scraggly beard and a look in his eye of dominance and hatred. He looked at the angels and stepped back past the dividing line of light and darkness. The woman took the opportunity and bolted to the light. As she ran past my left side in between Ronnie and I, I could not only feel the wind as she sped past, but the intensity of the movement caused Ronnie and I to part like two repelling magnets. The movement actually forced us away from each other to the point that we had to regain our balance. She was finally through, now there was one left. He looked at the angels and they looked back at him as if to say, "Lets go home." He just stood there staring at his options. Finally, something washed over him and he stepped toward the light and slowly began to make his way to the portal opening. He looked back at Ronnie, and then looked at the angels. After that he entered the portal in a stubborn manly fashion as if to say, "This is my decision and not yours. I choose to do this, not you!" As quickly as it began, it was over. The two angels holding the portal open returned to the center light after looking at me directly in the eye with their Godly blue, inhuman eyes. They were so piercing and so spiritual that it is hard to describe them four years later as I am writing you this account. The remainder of the three angels recessed back into the light as the portal closed. But before it was over the angel said to me, "You are well loved, you are to do many great things to come and you have done well today." Then the portal closed from a circle of Light to a small pinpoint, and then nothing.

I was speechless. I mustered all my strength to say something...something at all, something profound and wise to Ronnie standing near me. What came out of my mouth next were the words, "What the hell just happened here? How did I just do that, and what took over in me to be able to do such a heavenly thing?" But as I asked the question I answered, or something within me answered. And the answer brought me comfort still to this day. Some things that are given to you from the spirit world are very profound and should not be mocked or spoken of for fear of losing the lesson that was bestowed upon you in such a way.

I believe this is one of those times. I could share the message I was given for those of you who are reading this now, but I think right now that this would cheapen the experience. What I can say is that I am far from being done with my gifts and they get more and more powerful each time they are called upon. I was not given a prediction of the future, I was just simply informed. Informed that I have been somewhat chosen like many others before me and after, and that is why I remembered how to do these (what some may call miraculous) feats. In a glimpse that must have lasted a split second, I was told that I am very old and that my time here is part of my job within the larger picture. It was an experience like no other I have ever had. There was a sense that I knew them and that I have seen them before, but I am still trying to unlock the recesses of my mind to remember where. More than likely it is not time yet or I am not to remember while I am here.

I have had other such experiences since that time in the mansion, too many to count and they keep coming and teaching me. A First Wave Indigo is only held back by his or her own fear of knowing. By letting go of the fear and trusting in the gifts, there is nothing that we will not be able to do. I truly believe this.

Joel G. (33)
Spokane, Washington
jgreen12@earthlink.net

# *Earth Life According To Adele*

I have discovered so many things since learning of Indigos—what they are, what they do, and quite simply—I AM one. It means so much, yet it means nothing. One of the most important things to remember is...that it doesn't matter if someone is an Indigo or if someone is not. We are all here for the experiential journey of existing as a human being. We are all equally loved, and we are all important.

With that said...I was unusual from the get go. My family tells stories of me being develop-mentally ahead of children my age. I was holding my head up a few days after birth and always aware of what was going on around me. My mother says that I have always had really good "ESP." My siblings and mother were always very protective of me and still are to this day. Though I was well looked after, abuses during my childhood did happen. They ran the gamut of mental, physical, and sexual. I know that some people had it worse then me; others had it not as bad. No matter, it was how I created who I am today.

School was not a place I would have chosen to spend my time. Most of the children my age didn't like or understand me. When I wasn't being ignored, I was being picked on to the point of tears. In their infinite wisdom, my mother and the parents of my peers forced rela-tionships where they weren't welcome. School was boring, and since I didn't understand the importance of education, why do it? To this day, if I don't understand why I am doing some-thing, I have difficulty following through.

One of the trials I faced when starting school was the label of "retard." Doctors diagnosed me as having audio perception, a type of hearing dyslexia. Later, I understood what was really happening. I heard what people thought and felt as opposed to what came out of their mouths. You can understand how this would make things complicated. In first grade, my teacher only taught the "smart" kids, while those of us who had a difficult time in the school setting were put in the back of the classroom and basically ignored. Included in this humilia-tion were the daily trips I made to the special education room. There, I was taught how to listen and tried to work on reading. I flunked the first grade, along with half the kids in my class. Mind you, there were two first grade teachers and all the kids who didn't pass were from my classroom.

The school district was so concerned about children learning to read, they actually had a first and 1/2 grade, which was obviously half way between a first and second grader. I did really well in this class. Mr. Wagner was a wonderful teacher who truly cared about the success of all his students. Halfway through the year, along with my mother pushing me even harder, my grades improved and I went into the second grade. Unfortunately, by this time, I was told one too many times that I was un-teachable... and I chose to believe them. Thereafter, my report cards were mediocre at best (even though, in third grade, some of my poems were published and in my senior year I was being published in national teen magazines).

While I loved to write, and still do, reading had never been my forte...until a baby wizard lived through the attack from You Know Who. Around the age of 25, I was introduced to Harry Potter who showed me that reading doesn't have to be painful. Until then, I had read maybe ten books in my whole life, including two years of college and all those textbooks. That year, I read seven novels from cover to cover. The first four were Harry Potter followed by the Mists of Avalon series by Marion Zimmer Bradley. When I talked with my mom about this, she was absolutely floored and wondered what the heck happened to cause me to read. I guess I finally realized that I could read what interested ME and not what I was expected to read. I've never dealt well with being told what to do.

Even though I have always been unappreciative of authority figures, I was actually one of those kids who did everything I was told and tried not to disobey anyone. I learned that was the best way to not get beaten or yelled at. I handle myself rather differently now. I give everyone a degree of respect from the get go and let their actions dictate how I carry out my relationship with them. Through trial and error, I have learned that everyone deserves the same amount of respect. Whether they keep that respect is their choice, regardless of the level of respect I have for them... I love them.

At this point in my life, I am dealing with feelings of anger, resentment, and indignation. I decided to look up those words. Resentment is to feel aggrieved about something or toward somebody often because of a perceived wrong or injustice. Indignation is anger aroused by something unjust, unworthy, or mean. I think it is safe to say that these are my perceptions of our worldly society. Yes, I would like to heal the injustices and meanness of our world. And yes, that is one of the things I am here for. But first, I must heal the injustices and wrong doings within myself. You will never guess what word follows indignation in the dictionary... "Indigo."

So many times we as Indigos, are seen as these loving creatures—full of compassion, sensitivity, unconditional love, and extremely intuitive. While this picture is accurate to some extent, enter duality. While I am a light of love, I am also the shadow of hate. Duality is a doctrine in which the Universe is under the dominion of two opposing principles, one of which is good and the other evil.  Each of us fully encompasses this duality; we just choose which side we operate from.  I function out of the Light, knowing my shadow defines those boundaries.

There are times that it would be so easy to give in to the shadow, to violate my standing.  We have all had those thoughts, "What would happen if I took a life, be it someone else's or mine?"  I have battled my homicidal tendencies toward myself for years.  Some of those thoughts have faded... the cloud of darkness isn't as prevalent as it once was.  The fog from the drugs and alcohol has dissipated.  Therapy and medication silenced the shadow for a time, but being drugged into submission isn't my idea of a good time either.  I sense the darkness ever with me, it remains on the horizon defining and redefining the boundaries of my Light.

It has been said that Indigos want to know their boundaries:  That we challenge authority, laws, rules, and society in general, to see where our boundaries lay or where theirs lay.  I feel we are here to break the "old" boundaries of thought, society...existence in general.  One of these thoughts that I feel needs to change is the importance we place on labels.  Yes, even the label of Indigo.  In the world as we know it, Indigo types are looked upon as "freaks" and unacceptable.  This helps to perpetuate the feeling of ostracism.  Now, put us in a metaphysical community, and we are looked upon as saviors and put on pedestal.  Again, perpetuating ostracism.  In Truth, the Divine loves us all.  None more or less than the other.  Those who came before us and those that will come after... were all loved equally.  This is how it will continue to be through what we know as time.

**Adele S. (Age 31)**
**Spokane, Washington**
**asteiger13@hotmail.com**

# Rude Awakening

I can remember when I was twenty-six. My life was almost perfect. I thought I had life all figured out: School, work, girlfriend, and friends. Good times and good conversation was what I lived for. What else could I want? What more was there? Then my life changed. It changed into something that I wasn't sure I wanted, wasn't sure I knew how to handle. It was something that I was almost sure was a curse. I wasn't sure if it was a curse from God or the devil. Seeing that I am Catholic, I thought that I was being punished or that Karma was getting back at me for something that I did horribly wrong in my life. It had gotten to the point that I just didn't care. I just knew that I didn't want whatever it was that I had. I didn't feel human anymore.

My friends knew something had changed in me ~ that something was amiss with me and that I might be having nervous breakdown at 26. Most of my friends work in the medical profession and have seen people with delusions and other mental problems. I can remember my best friends, Chris and Pete, talking in the next room during a Bar-B-Q. One of the questions that Chris asked was, "Is Apker going crazy? Should we be worried about this?" Pete responded, "No, he has all his mental faculties and is not a danger to himself or others. If he was trying to hurt himself to get rid of the voices or hurt others because of it, then I would be worried." It was reassuring to know that I wasn't going crazy. But I still wasn't sure what was going on or why this was happening to me. My friends tried to help as much as they could, but I still found myself looking everywhere for something, anything that might help.

I sought answers and reasons for why this was happening to me. I didn't know that this had happened to anybody else and I found myself being taught by one woman who, in a very few words, is evil. Mind you I didn't know that at the time. She is loathingly known now as a spider-woman. I was caught in her web and was having the life sucked out of me and didn't realize it until it was almost too late. She was my friend and I trusted her to show me the path and answer the questions that I had. She said that I was her student and that she turned my powers on. Something, that to this very day, I think is completely nuts and a total lie. She said that I could not go out and seek other peoples' help.....I could not go out and seek the answers to the questions that I had, to seek the truth in life that I was now forced to live with. I was meant to be taught by her and only by her, (or so she said). She is a very dark person and she wanted to have someone that she could turn to be like her. In my own defense I didn't know any better because I wasn't sure of what was happening. She counted on that. She counted on the fact that I was a trusting soul, an honest man and a man of my word. Once she had me, like a pit bull she would not let go easily.

She told me that it was the same for her and that she surpassed her master. He, from what I was told (but now know is false), quit practicing because of it. I didn't know any better, so for three years I was helpless to know anything different than the way I was being trained, for lack of a better word. I had no idea what I could really do, or for that matter what I was meant to do with what I had.

I first found out that I am empathic and I was taught to use it against people. I was taught to use their feelings, their fears, their likes, their hates and even their loves against them. I was being trained in the dark arts: Hate, fear, lies, anger, manipulation, deceit, and mistrust. Everything that Yoda said about the Dark Side in Star Wars, I was being taught. I learned and used it well. I was and still am, to a certain extent, evil. It is an everyday fight not to use what I have against people. It is hard not to fall back into the ways that I was taught. But unlike what Yoda said, "Once you start down the dark path, forever will it dominate your destiny. Control you it will." I did have a choice and could choose my own path and how to use what I have for other purposes. There had come a time where I had enough of everything that was going on. I had gotten tired of being lied to and being controlled and used. I had allowed this out of a pure sense of feeling that I owed her something. So I fought back the only way I knew how. I used some of my capabilities against her, to change the situation that I was in, and to help me get out.

Shortly after, I was reunited with my high school friend Lena. She began to tell me about what she had gone through in the last ten years. I was starting to see the bigger picture and was starting to see that there was more out there than just what I was being taught. She introduced me to a wonderful woman named Laura Lee, (or as I endearingly call her, Rorie from the Gilmore Girls - Loralei, Rorie.)

Rorie showed me that there are many, many, many other people on this planet like me and that everyone who was nice to me didn't always have a hidden agenda. She also said that I DID have the right to my own inspiration about what was best for me instead of listening to the dictates of a deceiving Guru.

231

It has been said to me that everything happens for a reason. I didn't really understand that phrase in full until I had an Indigo reading from Rorie. In the reading she listed some of the things that I have volunteered to do (first rule of the military is don't ever volunteer for anything) in the time that I'm here. And in true Apker style, I have bitten off more than I can chew (19 in total, a lot from what I hear). One of which was to detect evil. I guess there is a reason why I spent three years of my life being taught the dark arts.

Now, after less than three months, I have learned, done, and seen more than I did in three years. I have been guided into so many more things than I could ever have learned before. Rorie has supported me, encouraged me and pointed me in the right direction to find the answers that I seek. She began to show me the right way to use what I have. I did finally realize that there was another way of living my life. My life changed again, but this time in the right way.....in the way that I was looking for during the past three years.

I was thinking about all of this over the last couple of weeks since Rorie mentioned something in passing about an Indigo reading she had done for a young man. He had asked her when he was going to be able to do the things that the X-Men could do. She said, "You do, just in your own way." After that, after all of the things that I have seen, I realize one thing. We ARE the X-Men, the Jedi, and the Knights of old. We are the line in the sand, the last line of defense of this realm, and we are the ones that bump back. No one else can, no one else will, and no one else knows what we do on a daily basis. Our lives are a collection of deeds that are repute with looking out for the humans of this world.

And there are those people that want to rule. They want to rule over all of this. They want to control and destroy and make the world in their own image. Not for the good of the rest of mankind, but for themselves. They are the ones, like the spider woman, that want nothing more than to control and use people and have their way with the world. They think that it is their right and that it is their privilege and that everyone must bow to them. I have no real names for them other than what the movies and T.V. has named them. They are The Sith, The Brotherhood of Mutants, the Gou'auld, The Shadow government, call them what you will. It's the evil that lies just beneath the surface of all that is, and if you just look a little bit deeper you will see it staring back at you.

To Rorie, the only woman that I will ever bow to in my life and one of very few women that I trust and know that she guards my back.   To Ann, my other Tesla half. (Remember the line, "What do I look like, a tour guide?" in the middle of our dream?)   You are one of very few women that I trust and know that you guard my back also.   And last but not least, to Lena, (even though I haven't told you this) thank you for showing me another way to live my life.....

Thank you all for teaching me, and being there when I needed you the most.

(And a Special thanks to Hal & Charlie Reaver.   Life has one too many things not to laugh at on a daily basis..... eh boys?)

**J. Apker (Age 29)**
**Chattaroy, Washington**
**harpermatrix@netzero.net**

**Authors Note:** These last three paragraphs may not make much sense to you, so here is a little background.  In July 2005  J. Apker found himself in the middle of an amazing and intense interdimensional, interstellar adventure that changed reality for many people.....(you may be one of them).   The details of this escapade will appear in upcoming Mistyc House Literature...including the remarkable transformation of "The Reaver" from one of THE most ruthless Gangstas in the Universe, to one of my most trusted comrades .   Perhaps in a future speaking engagement, I will bring some of these magical and heroic epics to the audience.   If fate is on our side, I will even bring some of the X-Men & X-Women who starred in these adventures, to tell it first hand!

# My Little Book of Blasphemies...
## and Other Thoughts From the Shower

The following are excerpts from a wonderful little thought provoking, and soon to be published book by Michael Adams. Michael is a First Wave Indigo I have known now for nearly a decade. He has been in the film industry for years and brings a spiritual element to every project he works on. I love his free-thinking style and never-ending sense of humor, which is evident in his book....(yes, I have a copy of a limited first edition.) Reading these excerpts is a real teaser....I'm hoping he will make this book available soon!

◆ ◆ ◆ ◆ ◆ ◆ ◆ ◆ ◆

"Does it make sense that the most powerful, most creative, most intelligent force that ever was or ever will be, could screw up his creation so bad, that he should have to create a grand junk yard, complete with an incinerator, then hire the ultimate bad guy (who by the way, is also his arch-enemy,) to run the joint? Then have this bad guy slowly burn, torture, and destroy the masterpieces that didn't quite turn out the way the Master Architect had planned? The whole idea says that God is not perfect, and that he/she is pretty pissed off about it. Does that make any sense?"

If God chose to judge us the way that we judge each other, this show would've been over a long time ago.

Okay, figure this one out:

According to Webster's dictionary, the name Lucifer comes from the Latin words luc, meaning light, and fer, meaning bearing. The name literally means light bearing.

Just stick with me and reserve judgment till the end. Now Webster defines Lucifer thusly:

1- used as a name of the devil    2: the planet Venus when appearing as the morning star.

Venus, in astrological terms, is known as the planet of love. So the star that brings the light of love to our planet is called Lucifer. Huh? The devil brings the light of love?

Now here's where it gets really troublesome and confusing. In the last book of the Bible, Revelations, Jesus is quoted as saying:

Rev. 22:16 - I am the root and the offspring of David, and the bright and morning star.

How do you reconcile the fact that the morning star is called Lucifer and Jesus said he is the morning star? People will say that Lucifer was of the light as an archangel, but after his fall he became the devil. Why then would Jesus, after the fall, make this association?

Again, we are not getting the full story.

If God turned a whole race of people's skin black as a punishment, was he only slightly annoyed at the Japanese? Or, is the story perhaps a myth perpetrated by ignorance, fear and a separatist attitude?

"If God really had so many rules, don't you think she would have enforced them by now?"

**Michael Adams (Age 40 ish)**
**L.A. California**
**info@mylittlebookofblasphemies.com**
**www.MyLittleBookOfBlasphemies.com**

# A Final Note from Laura Lee Mistycah

I pay tribute to all the First Wave Indigos in hot pursuit of memories of who they are and what they're committed to do here. We are living on (and in service to) what I consider the most polluted, corrupted planet in the Universe – the very reason you are HERE!

Remember that NOT ALL First Wave Indigos are fully awake, have their Altered Egos in check, or are in full command of their emotions, responses, and Indigo Powers. For this reason, I urge you to use your Indigo Intuition in dealing with anyone who claims to be Indigo. They may truly be a First Wave Indigo, but they may NOT have their armor oiled and shined up. I have encountered many First Wave Indigos so fractured by the hideous experiences they have endured that they cause much chaos and hardship on those around them. It takes a tremendous amount of determination and willpower for these beings to fix their broken pieces. Some of them turn into eternal drama-kings and queens because creating chaos and discord is what they are most comfortable with. Many of them play the part of "Light Distracters" during this period.

There are ways to heal these fractures, but it takes so much focus, effort, and commitment that many of them give up. They invariably take the easy road and avoid looking at the unwanted inventory and broken pieces of themselves.

I must also tell you that there are what I call "partial Indigos" here on Earth. These are beings who went to the Ultraviolet Realm for instruction but were not fully trained when the cry for help came from Earth and this Universe. The situation was so critical here that the Emperor and Empress sent everyone they could spare.....even partial training was better than no training!

When I first encountered beings that were "almost Indigo" I thought that was the craziest thing I had ever heard and doubted my scanning. I'd always assumed that being an Indigo was a zero-sum game: you either were or were not a First Wave Indigo. This reading was as ludicrous to me as saying "she is sort of pregnant."

I came across more and more of these Beings before I got the vision of what really happened ... and then it made perfect sense to me.

I have been to the depths of Hell getting some of the information for this book, and many of the stories and wisdom I gleaned will be revealed in my next book, "Indigo Inc.: Incorporating Earth Life into the Indigo Mind."

As all the insanity of my life unraveled, I wrote down a collection of insights that evolved into my own personal philosophy. I hope it helps you as much as it has me.

## "5 Insights"

1- We never quite know what will happen next...that is why the game is so exciting!

2- Just when we think we've got things figured out, the rules and/or the game changes; Living in the moment is all we know for sure.

3- Change is one of the few things that are permanent and constant.

4- Instant Karma is alive again, and picking up momentum....what a relief to some, terrifying to others.

5- If you don't keep your sense of humor you will lose all your senses!

For those pursuing their wake-up call, here is something taught in Knight's training in another time and place....perhaps you will remember it... (May I remind you of the obvious... there are also many women Knights.)

Knighthood is NOT an easy path...if it were, everyone would be doing it! It is a life-long path of service and commitment. It means living life by a strict code of ethics and conduct that stresses chivalry, truth and honor above all else – and that means at all times, not just when it's convenient. Walking the path of a Knight means placing the life and well-being of those to whom you are in service ahead of your own... always.

The true Knight is a man/woman of deeds, not words. Being a Knight is not something that you merely declare. True Knights have no need to feed their ego by calling themselves this title.

True Knights prefer to be recognized by their deeds – because Knights consistently demonstrate their dedication in thought, word, and deed.

A Knight owns all of the responsibility of his or her position, actions and orders – not just when it is expedient or convenient for him/her.

A Knight's only response when given sacred orders by his Emperor or Empress, is "Yes, Your Highness," because he/she honors them and trusts in their wisdom. (A noble Empress/Emperor in turn, always listens to the input from a knight before giving final orders.)

And here is the rest of the story...

*ON THIS DAY JULY 14, 1998*
*AND FROM THIS DAY FORTH…..*


*A UNIVERSAL CALL IS MADE*
*TO ACTIVATE ALL THE REAL MEN AND WOMEN*
*WHO REMEMBER AND ARE WILLING TO LIVE BY…..*

YOU ARE NOW HEREBY BEING CALLED TO ACTION.
IT IS TIME FOR BATTLE!
(……OR THERE WILL BE NOTHING LEFT TO BATTLE FOR.)

AS YOU DON YOUR ARMOR AND TAKE UP YOUR
SHIELD AND SWORD…..
DO YOU HAVE THE MEMORY AND THE COURAGE
TO ACTIVATE YOURSELF…..
**AND BRING FORTH A LIVING, BREATHING, KNIGHT**
**INTO THIS NEW MILLENNIUM?**

DO YOU HAVE THE WISDOM, THE WILL, THE FEARLESSNESS,
THE STRENGTH AND THE POWER IT TAKES TO BE A KNIGHT.....
AND LIVE BY THE KNIGHT'S CODE FROM THIS DAY FORTH
UNTIL THE MOMENT OF YOUR LAST BREATH?

OH GREAT AND VALIANT KNIGHTS OF THE EARTH
COME FORTH NOW AND BE COUNTED
THE TIME HAS FINALLY COME.
(YOU KNOW WHO YOU ARE)

## *Wake Up... Arise...*
## *Let Your Destiny Begin!*

# "The Knight's Code"

## *(An Old Code For A New Era)*

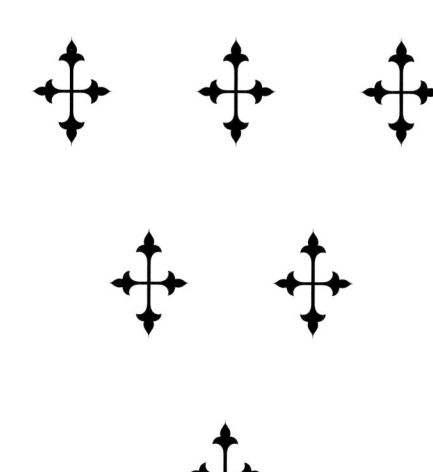

~A KNIGHT IS TRUE "BLUE"...AND IS AT PEACE WITH HIS/HER GOD!
  As A Knight, You Will Be Honest & Just In All Business And Personal Relationships!

~A KNIGHT CAN BE TRUSTED FOR A KNIGHT HONORS HIS/HER WORD!
  As A Knight, You Will Do What You Committed To Do, When You Committed To Do
  It, Or Make Other Arrangements...Or Die In The Process!

~A KNIGHT HAS A PROFOUND SENSE OF SELF RESPECT,
  Paving The Way To Fully Love And Honor His/Her Beloved.

~A KNIGHT OWNS HIMSELF/HERSELF. NO INFLUENCE OR SUBSTANCE
 DICTATES OR RUNS THEIR LIFE AND THE LIVES OF THOSE AROUND THEM.
  As A Knight You Overcome All Your Addictions. The True Armor Of Knighthood Is
  On The Inside, Not The Outside.

~A KNIGHT THINKS BEFORE SPEAKING, FOR ONCE WORDS ARE SPOKEN,
As A Knight, You Are Bound By Your Words!

~A KNIGHT USES WISDOM AND DISCRETION IN WORD AND ACTION,
As A Knight, You Are Considerate And Compassionate In All Things!

~A KNIGHT TAKES DAILY ACTION TO FORTIFY AND STRENGTHEN
Your Body, Your Mind, And Your Spirit!

~A KNIGHT IS CONFIDENT AND ABHORS ARROGANCE.
As A Knight, You Know That The Arrogant **Think** They're Grand...
The Confident **Are** Grand!

~A KNIGHT IS STRONG.....YET GENTLE WITH WOMEN, CHILDREN & ANIMALS.
As A Knight, You Use Your Might To Defend The Weak!

~A KNIGHT ACTIVATES THE BRAIN BEFORE USING BRAWN
When Faced With A Challenge Or An Opponent!

~A KNIGHT HAS A LIGHT HEART AND A SENSE OF HUMOR!
As A Knight, You Make Even The Most Grueling Task Fun And Memorable!

~A KNIGHT KNOWS WHEN A JOKE IS DESTRUCTIVE,
As A Knight, You Are Willing To Take A Stand When A Joke Is Harmful!

~A KNIGHT USES GRACE AND DIGNITY IN WORDS AND ACTIONS
Especially In The Company Of Women And Children!

~A KNIGHT HONORS AND RESPECTS PROCREATIVE POWER,
As A Knight, You Always Take Responsibility When Using These Powers!

~A MALE KNIGHT HONORS AND REVERES WOMEN AND THEIR FEMININE NATURE.
As A Knight, You Know That Proper Interaction With Feminine Power Is A Link Back To
Your Source, Therefore You Are Ready And Willingly Protect And Defend That Power –
Even Unto Death!

~A KNIGHT HAS A PASSIONATE LOVE AND RESPECT FOR NATURE AND
MOTHER EARTH.
As A Knight, You Use Your Strength & Courage To Act When They Are Threatened Or Violated.

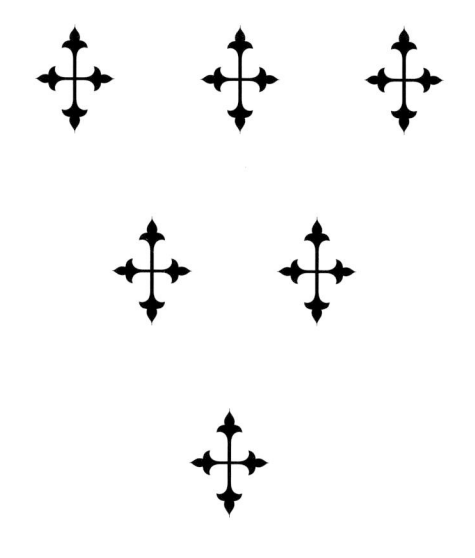

# Oh Great, Honorable, And Noble Knights Of This World.....

STEP OUT OF YOUR HATE, YOUR ANGER,
AND THE PAINS OF YOUR PAST!

STEP OUT OF YOUR CORPORATE WORLDS...
AND THE HUNGER FOR USELESS POWER!

PUT ON YOUR ARMOR OF HONOR,
PICK UP YOUR SHIELD OF LOVE,
AND YOUR MIGHTY SWORD OF TRUTH!

BE LIVING PROOF THAT CHIVALRY AND VALOR
ARE ALIVE AND UNYIELDING!

DO YOU HAVE THE STRENGTH, THE COURAGE,
THE WISDOM, THE ANCIENT ENCODED MEMORIES
AND THE PASSION IT TAKES...

# To Be A Millennial Knight?

*This decree given to Laura Lee Mistycah July 14, 1998 on Mt. Spokane
By "The Lady Of The Lake".....Auraura* ©

# Contact information/ Suggested reading and music list

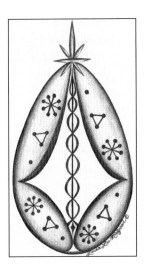

Laura Lee Mistycah
www.mistychouse.com
knights@mistychouse.com
**Mistyc House Publishing**
**816 West Francis #244**
**Spokane WA. 99205**
**(509) 487-0151**
**Knights@MistycHouse.com**

If you would like a Consultation/Psychic Reading with Laura Lee Mistycah to find out if you (or someone you are connected with) is a First Wave Indigo and how best to assist them, send an E-Mail to: *knights@mistychouse.com*
with *"Indigo"* on the subject line,
or call (509) 487-0151

In these readings you can also get information on what some of your Spiritual Contracts/Agreements are, what some of your psychic abilities are, and also what some of your fields of expertise are that you may or may not have been aware of. In addition, Laura Lee also gives guide and guardian readings to help you be aware of who/what you have to personally guide and protect you on your missions here. Know that after this book is released, there may be a large demand for these readings, and you may be put on a waiting list for an appointment. These readings require a tremendous amount of psychic energy and therefore, Laura Lee can only give 2-3 readings per day.

These readings are $50.00 per half hour and can be purchased in 15 minute increments on the Shopping Cart at www.mistychouse.com/treasure/M.H.treasures.htm or by check. As a complimentary gift, the first 15 minutes for an Indigo Consultations are free. (Indigo readings take at least an hour.)

For more information on these readings, and how to prepare for one, go to
**www.mistychouse.com/Psychic/Readings.htm**


Here are some of the books that are highly recommended to help you understand yourselves and how this Universe operates:

*Kryahgenetics, the Simple Secrets of Human Alchemy:  Laura Lee Mistycah
*Holographic Universe:  Michael Talbot.
*Conversations with God:  Neal Donald Walsh
*Celestine Prophecy:  James Redfield
*The Twelfth Planet: (and subsequent books):  Zecharia Sitchen
*The Montauk Project (and subsequent books):  Peter Moon & Preston Nichols
*Bloodline of the Holy Grail:  Sir Laurence Gardner
*Welcome to Planet Earth:  Hannah Beaconsfield
*The Starseed Transmissions:  Ken Carey
*Angels Don't Play this HAARP:  Dr. Nick Begich and Jeane Manning
*Reinventing The Wheel, The Universal Wheel: Tool of Global Unity:  Meria Heller
*Duck Soup for the Soul: The Way of Living Louder and Laughing Longer:  Swami Beyondanan da.

Music is a vital tool for rediscovering your authentic self.  Here is a list of some exceptional music that will help activate your memory codes:

*The Lost Cord:  Jonathan Goldman
*Quest of the Dream Warrior:  David Arkenstone
*Harmonic Concordance:  Steven Pike
*Transcendence:  Robin Miller
*Song of Isis:  Anne Williams
*New Romantics:  Hearts of Space Classical Collection
*Voices of the Wind:  Wayra
*Echoes of the Canyon:  Runa Pacha
*Serpents Egg:  The Dead Can Dance
*Pathways to Surrender:  Chris Spheeris
*Magic Carpet:  David Michael & Randy Mead